Neural Networks
Theory and Applications

Neural Networks
Theory and Applications

Edited by

Richard J. Mammone
CAIP Center and
*   The Department of Electrical & Computer Engineering*
Rutgers University
Piscataway, New Jersey

Yehoshua Y. Zeevi
Department of Electrical Engineering
Technion–Israel Institute of Technology
Haifa, Israel

ACADEMIC PRESS, INC.
Harcourt Brace Jovanovich, Publishers

Boston   San Diego   New York
London   Sydney   Tokyo   Toronto

This book is printed on acid-free paper. ⊚

Cover illustration by John VanCleaf

ACADEMIC PRESS, INC.
1250 Sixth Avenue, San Diego, CA 92101

United Kingdom Edition published by
ACADEMIC PRESS LIMITED
24–28 Oval Road, London NW1 7DX

Neural networks: theory and applications / Richard J. Mammone,
 Yehoshua Y. Zeevi.
 p.   cm.
 In Nov. 1990, the CAIP Center of Rutgers University organized and
hosted a workshop.
 Includes bibliographical references and index.
 ISBN 0-12-467050-4 (alk. paper)
 1. Neural networks (Computer science)   I. Mammone, Richard J.
II. Zeevi, Y. Y. III. Rutgers University. Center for Computer Aids
for Industrial Productivity.
QA76.87.N49   1991
006.3'3 — dc20   91–2688
                                                           CIP

Printed in the United States of America
91 92 93 94   9 8 7 6 5 4 3 2

Contents

Preface

In November 1990, the CAIP Center of Rutgers University organized and hosted a workshop on Neural Networks. The workshop attracted over 120 leaders in the field from the United States and abroad. The goal of the workshop was to assess the current state-of-the-art Neural Network architectures and algorithms and to consider the most promising directions for further research in this rapidly developing field. This book is an outgrowth of the workshop and constitutes a collection of some of the important papers presented and discussed.

The field of Neural Networks has attracted the interest of scientists from a number of diverse disciplines. Engineers are interested in applying Neural Networks to a variety of pattern recognition and optimization problems and in the design of adaptive systems that are trained to cope with complex tasks by learning from examples. Biologists have long been concerned with issues related to our understanding of the brain, and are discovering a fruitful approach to the functional analysis of Neural Networks without physiological access to the function of hidden neurons. Mathematicians and computer scientists are intrigued by the computational capabilities of nonlinear dynamic models of Neural Networks; they are also interested in the uniqueness and convergence of heuristic training methods. Physicists have found that seemingly unrelated phenomena, such as spin glasses, are mathematically similar to neural computing methods. Psychologists are interested in models of learning and cognition, while philosophers have used Neural Network models to question the ability of machines to perform cognitive functions.

Interest in Neural Networks has waxed and waned since its origins in the 1940s. The current resurgence in interest is largely due to the powerful new methods that are emerging, as well as to the availability of computational power suitable for simulation of the behavior of massively interconnected Neural Networks. The field is particularly exciting today in that Neural Network algorithms and architectures can be implemented in VLSI technology.

The goal of this book is to review the salient features of Neural Network systems and to present the most promising approaches of addressing the issues involved in designing a neural system. The first chapter, by Igor Aleksander, describes how the concept of General Neural Unit (GNU) can be used to design Neural Networks. It is shown that the storage capacity of the resulting network is dependent primarily on the fan-in of the nodes, and the stability of the network is dependent on the starting state. Aleksander shows strong analogies of these characteristics with biological Neural Networks.

The second chapter, by Roger Brockett, introduces a gradient flow approach to neural system design that can be used to solve combinatorial problems. Problems that are generally the domain of discrete mathematic methods such as linear programming, sorting, and quantization can be solved by implementing the analog flow equations. The gradient flow method is shown to degenerate to conditional probability estimation techniques under certain conditions. This new approach offers a useful analog tool for solving a very diverse set of discrete combinatorial problems.

The third chapter, by Gail Carpenter, Stephen Grossberg, and John Reynolds, describes a self-organizing expert system called ARTMAP. Elaborating on the well-known ART Neural Network, ARTMAP can distinguish rare but important ambiguous events. It is shown to perform with an extremely high correct classification rate as demonstrated by the difficult example which uses poisonous and benign mushroom data. This new neural system uses the concept of focusing its attention on the small but important data points. This idea appears in several other new approaches as well.

The fourth chapter, by Leon Cooper, the 1972 Nobel laureate for Physics, gives an overview of hybrid Neural Networks, which show properties of relaxation and exhibit selective attention characteristics. Cooper describes the GENSEP concept, which is designed to resolve the ambiguous situations that may arise infrequently yet that greatly affect performance. Here too, a type of attention mechanism is suggested.

The fifth chapter, by Rolf Eckmiller, Nils Goerke and Jürgen Hakala, describes the use of Neural Networks for robot motor control. The most recent models of the primate occulomotor system are reviewed and compared with an artificial Neural Network solution of the robotic problems. The use of Neural Networks for coordinate transformations, inverse kinematics, and position modeling are discussed. The future of neural-based robotic systems is shown to be quite optimistic.

The sixth chapter, by Kunihiko Fukushima and Taro Imagawa, discusses the use of Neural Networks in recognition of handwritten characters. They use a selective attention model. Once again, as is the case in the chapters by Carpenter et al, and by Cooper, a focus of attention mechanism is introduced to hand-off difficult parts of the problem to specialized networks. The system presented is a hierarchical multilayered network. The system is demonstrated to work quite well on handwritten characters even when the characters are highly distorted relative to the prototypical exemplars.

The seventh chapter, by Allen Gorin, Steven Levinson, A. Gertner, and E. Goldman, describes how Neural Networks can be used to acquire language understanding. The concept of "learning by doing" is introduced. This approach requires the neural system to learn without being given a desired response but rather only one bit of information is fed back, i.e., whether the response is right or wrong. The system is free to select symbols and, in effect, its own language to accomplish the desired task. The system is demonstrated on an example where it acts as the telephone operator for a department store. The system learns by trial and error how to route arbitrary inquiries to the correct department.

In the eighth chapter, Stephen Josè Hanson and David Burr describe learning and representation in connectionist networks. Their chapter provides background information regarding the connectionist approach to computing. A taxonomy of the various models is presented. The basic principles underlying neuron unit operation and learning, and representation of information are described. This chapter and its references offer an overview of Neural Networks.

The ninth chapter is by Bela Julesz, one of the most eminent scientists in the field of Vision Research, who has contributed significantly to our modern understanding of the human visual system. In this chapter the idea of visual attention is discussed. The point is made that visual attention is frequently confused with foveation. In other words, a subject may be looking at a small region of an image but not paying attention to it. It is argued that many "foveating" neural approaches for solving Machine Vision problems are missing this important point. Many other important features of the human visual system as it applies to neural systems are given in the references of this chapter.

Chapter 10, by Robert Hecht-Nielsen, describes a hierarchical matched filter neural system. The new system is particularly well-suited for applications such as speech where the input might occur on a warped scale relative to the exemplars. A self-organizing spatio-temporal feature detector layer is introduced which compensates the input signal for such warping.

Chapter 11, by Gary Kuhn and Norman Herzberg, describes various modifications to the recurrent network training algorithm that eliminate the need for a target function, avoid backpropagation of error derivatives, increase learning rate, and provide better generalization. The method is demonstrated on the very difficult problem of discriminating between the sounds corresponding to "b", "d", "e" and "v". The performance demonstrates the superior performance of the neural system presented.

In Chapter 12, S.Y. Kung, K. Diamantaras, W. Mao, and J. Taur describe the use of generalized nonlinear elements in Neural Networks. A general training rule is derived and the optimum step size rule is given. Projection and conjugate gradient methods of training are presented, and the performance of the training approaches is demonstrated. A competition based approach is also described.

In Chapter 13, Ananth Sankar and Richard Mammone present a new method of implementing Neural Networks. A new architecture called the Neural Tree Network is given and a learning rule is described. The new method is shown to provide comparable generalization to other Neural Network techniques. However, the training time is much less and the network grows to the correct size as it is trained. In addition, the new architecture can be implemented very economically by using only one physical neural node. The new method is demonstrated to yield favorable performance on various benchmark problems.

In Chapter 14, Eduardo Sontag presents some new results on the capabilities and training of feedforward Neural Networks. It is shown that Neural Networks using sigmoidal nonlinear elements have at least twice the classification capacity of the networks using linear threshold elements. However, it is also shown that for approximation of implicit functions, linear threshold units are more useful.

In Chapter 15, Shu-jen Yeh and Henry Stark describe a new learning algorithm for multilayer Neural Networks based on projection methods. A new training algorithm based on the method of projection onto convex sets (POCS) as well as generalized projections is introduced. The method is suggested as a means to estimate quickly a good starting point for the more conventional descent methods. Computer simulations show a significant increase in the initial learning rate for the new method.

The chapters by Steve Hanson and Eduardo Sontag deal with the basic principles of Neural Networks. Hanson's chapter addresses the basic concepts underlying Neural Networks, whereas Sontag gives a detailed mathematical analysis and comparisons of the nonlinear elements that are commonly used. The remaining chapters all deal with enhancements, refinements, and substitutions of various components of the basic Neural Network systems in order to improve performance, i.e., training rate, generalization, and complexity. These improvements are generally demonstrated by specific numerical examples.

As Leon Cooper states, Neural Networks were originally seen as a panacea but are now more realistically perceived as a "solution to certain classes of problems". In this book, we hope to show how, with some modifications of the basic concept, Neural Networks can be customized to fit particular applications. The required modifications are, of course, very much domain-dependent.

The wealth of new information on Neural Networks, and the distribution of articles over many diverse journals, make it difficult to master and assimilate . The primary purpose of this book is to make available in one publication the important features of the methodologies that are currently being investigated. Principles of promising approaches and the demonstration of their utility in various domains of applications are emphasized throughout the text. We hope that this text helps to illustrate how Neural Networks can be integrated into various learning systems.

We would like to take this opportunity to thank all of the contributing authors. In addition, we gratefully acknowledge the partial support of the workshop by the Air Force Office of Scientific Research (AFOSR), the Army Research Office (ARO), the Strategic Defense Initiative Organization, Innovative Science & Technology Office (SDIO/ISTO), the Intel corporation, and the NEC Research Institute. We also thank the past and present directors of the CAIP center, Prof. Herbert Freeman and Prof. James L. Flanagan, as well as the entire CAIP staff, its member companies, and the New Jersey Commission on Science and Technology for their support and encouragement. A special debt of gratitude goes to Ananth Sankar whose help made it possible to generate the text in a uniform format.

Richard Mammone
New Jersey, U.S.A.

Yehoshua Y. Zeevi
Haifa, Israel

Contributors

Numbers in parenthesis indicate the pages on which authors' contributions begin.

Igor Aleksander (1), *Imperial College of Science, Technology and Medicine, London, UK*

R.W. Brockett (23), *Harvard University, Cambridge, Massachussets*

David J. Burr (169), *Bellcore, Morristown, NJ*

Gail A. Carpenter (43), *Center for Adaptive Systems, Boston University, Massachussets*

Leon N. Cooper (81), *Physics Department, Brown University, Providence, Rhode Island*

K. Diamantaras (245), *Princeton University, Princeton, NJ 08544*

Rolf Eckmiller (97), *Division of Biocybernetics, Heinrich-Heine-Universtät, Düsseldorf, Germany*

Kunihiko Fukushima (113), *Faculty of Engineering Science, Osaka University, Japan*

A.N. Gertner (125), *AT&T Bell Laboratories, Murray Hill, NJ*

Nils Goerke (97), *Division of Biocybernetics, Heinrich-Heine-Universtät, Düsseldorf, Germany*

E. Goldman (125), *AT&T Bell Laboratories, Murray Hill, NJ*

A.L. Gorin (125), *AT&T Bell Laboratories, Murray Hill, NJ*

Stephen Grossberg (43), *Center for Adaptive Systems, Boston University, Massachussets*

Jürgen Hakala (97), *Division of Biocybernetics, Heinrich-Heine-Universtät, Düsseldorf, Germany*

Stephen José Hanson (169), *Siemens Corporate Research, Inc., Princeton, NJ*

Robert Hecht-Nielsen (217), *HNC, Inc., San Diego, CA and University of California, San Diego, CA*

Norman Herzberg (233), *Center for Communications Research–IDA, Princeton, NJ*

Taro Imagawa (113), *Faculty of Engineering Science, Osaka University, Japan*

Bela Julesz (209), *Laboratory of Vision Research, Psychology Dept., Rutgers University, New Brunswick, NJ 08903*
and
Division of Biology, California Institute of Technology, Pasadena, CA 91125

Gary M. Kuhn (233), *Center for Communications Research–IDA, Princeton, NJ*

S.Y. Kung (245), *Department of Electrical Engineering, Princeton University, Princeton, NJ*

S.E. Levinson (125), *AT&T Bell Laboratories, Murray Hill, NJ*

Richard J. Mammone (281), *CAIP Center and Department of Electrical Engineering, Rutgers University, Piscataway, NJ 08855-1390*

W.D. Mao (245), *Princeton University, Princeton, NJ*

John H. Reynolds (43), *Center for Adaptive Systems, Boston University, Massachussets*

Ananth Sankar (281), *CAIP Center and Department of Electrical Engineering, Rutgers University, Piscataway, NJ 08855-1390*

Eduardo D. Sontag (303), *Mathematics Department, Rutgers University, Piscataway, NJ 08855*

Henry Stark (323), *Illinois Institute of Technology, Chicago, IL*

J.S. Taur (245), *Princeton University, Princeton, NJ*

Shu-jen Yeh (323), *Rensselaer Polytechnic Institute, Troy, NY*

Weightless Neural Tools: Towards Cognitive Macrostructures

Igor Aleksander
Imperial College of Science, Technology and Medicine
London, UK

1 Introduction

The word "weightless" is used to stress our belief that the future of neural nets lies in understanding the properties of nets with variable function nodes for which the function is loaded by a local algorithm, but not necessarily one constrained by weight variations. The approach dates back to 1965.[2] In 1981, with the advent of inexpensive silicon RAM, it led to the design of an adaptive pattern recognition system called the WISARD (after its designers: Bruce WIlkie, John Stonham, Igor Aleksander, [Recognition Device]).[3] With the current revival of interest in neural computing, it has been possible to show that the RAM approach fully covers the achievements of standard weighted approaches, with the added properties of direct implementability with conventional VLSI techniques and sufficient generality to represent the increasingly complex descriptions of real neurons .[4][5]

A full overview of weightless neural devices is presented in a companion paper.[1] Here we present a brief description of these systems and concentrate on a fundamental tool we call the General Neural Unit (GNU). This is a flexible associator that can be used as a building brick for advanced neural systems. Specifically, we address interest in neural networks stimulated by Hopfield [12], Aleksander [11][13] and Hinton et al. [14] which comes from the discovery that a cluster of interconnected neurons has, as an emergent property, the

1

ability to enter stable firing patterns, stimulated by the presentation of parts of these patterns.

2 Weightless RAM Nodes

2.1 Functional Description

The atomic unit of weighless sytems is the RAM node storing B-bit words. The symbol for a RAM node is shown in fig 1and 1s fully described by Aleksander[1] and Aleksander & Morton[4][5]. Recently , the B bits have been considered to store a number in the interval from 0 to 1 which represents the "firing probability", $P(1)$, of the neuron in a way that can be achieved in hardware [6] . Gorse and Taylor [7] have indeed assumed that B is so large as to allow them to analyse their node (which they called a p-RAM) as storing continuous values of firing probability. Myers [8] has investigated RAM systems with $M = 2^{\{B\}}$ well-defined probabilistic states calling them M-PLNs: M-valued Probabilistic Logic Nodes .

2.2 Training

It is assumed that a RAM node (the discourse is restricted here to M-PLNs) receives global training signls of a "reinforcement" kind. That is, a reward or punish signal is distributed globally to a prescribed section of the system, and every node in that section receives the same signal. In this paper it is assumed that the set of M values has at least three elements:

$$P(1) = 0, P(1) = 1 \text{and} P(1) = 0.5$$

At the commencement of training all nodes for all inputs store $P(1) = 0.5$. As a final assumption, a clocked timing system is required. At the arrival of every clock signal each node will either fire or not fire (i.e. output a 1 or a 0 respectively). Over a stretch of many clock periods the node will have fired with a frequency approaching $P(1)$. At the arrival of a reinforcement signal, each node "knows" whether at the last clock point it fired or not. If the reinforcement is

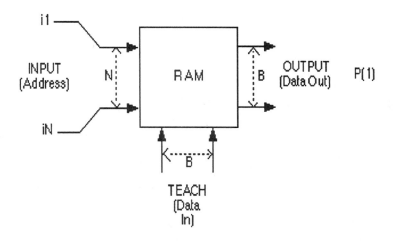

Figure 1: A RAM node

positive (i.e. a reward) the last firing value (0 or 1) is stored. If the reinforcement is negative and the stored value is 0 or 1 the value is returned to 0.5.

2.3   The Generalising RAM

A modified RAM - the G-RAM - which generalizes internally has been suggested by Aleksander [10]. This (to date, hypothetical) device operates in three phases. Two of them are the usual learning phase and operating phase during which the device records the addresses with their required response and uses the stored information, respectively. The third phase is unusual: it is called the "spreading" phase.

Spreading refers to a process of affecting the content of storage locations, not addressed during training, by the use of a suitable algorithm which may be implemented on-chip or through appropriate actions in the control machinery. Whatever the implementation, spreading is something that can be done "off line", that is, between the time that training information has been captured (which may have to be done in some kind of "real time") and the time that the nodes have to use what has to be learnt (which, too, may have to be done at speed).

2.4   Characterizing the Generalization

In this paper we assume that spreading has taken place and use a simple model of its effect. The training set sets some of the addresses to 0 and others to 1. Full generalization means that any other address will be set to 0 if it is closest in Hamming distance to one of 0 training patterns or 1 if it is closest to one of the 1 training patterns. So if the training patterns were 00000000 set to 0 and 11110000 set to 1, only addresses that are equidistant from these two patterns (such as 00110011) would be left with $P(1)=0.5$, while others such as 00001110 and 10000000 would both be set to 0 as they are distinctly nearer to the 00000000 pattern. The simple model is this:

If a node is sampling N points of a pattern, given an unknown pattern u and that a majority of N is in a pattern area that distinguishes between a required 0 output and a required 1 output, the appropriate pattern will be generated for u.

3   The General Neural Unit

The structure of a General Neural Unit is shown in fig. 2.The circuit parameters of the GNU are: K the number of neurons in the unit; W the width of a binary input interface; N the number of connections that each neuron receives from the input; Q the proportion of K that each neuron receives as input. So the number of inputs to each neuron is $N+QK$. We generally let $F = QK$ as this is the number of inputs that a node receives from other nodes in the GNU. A further parameter that needs specification is the degree of generalization G of each neuron. It is of some interest that the properties of the unit can be discussed without detailed reference to the function or structure of the node. In fact, the most direct thing that can be done is to assume that the node is a G-RAM with maximum generalization as specified in section 2.4.

With this set of parameters, particularly, with the variation of Q

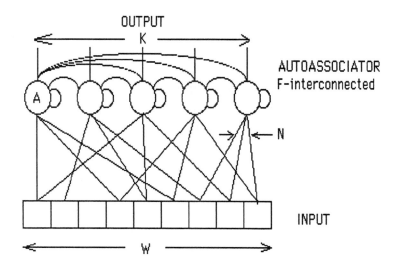

Figure 2: A General Neural Unit

the GNU can be varied from a single layer of a feed-forward structure ($Q = 0$) to a Hopfield-like autoassociator ($N = 0, Q = 1$). But what is more interesting are the modes of behaviour that can be obtained between these extremes. Some examples now follow.

4 Weakly Interconnected Autoassociators

The Hopfield model provides an explanation for useful autoassociation properties in systems which by our formulation have $Q = 1, N = 0$ and the node generalization of linearly separable functions associated with weighted neurons. Additionally much of the analysis depends on the existence of reciprocal conections between neurons. From the point of view of biological modelling this seems wrong, because, as far as the writer is aware, neural clusters with $Q = 1$ have not been found in living brains. More typical are areas such as CA3 in the hippocampus where Q is of the order of 5% . These have been highlighted by Rolls and have led others to use statistical mechanics methods to analyse low connectivity auto associators [15]. From a technological standpoint too, it is important to understand the effect that low Q has on the memory properties of the GNU, as Q determines the cost growth of the unit with K. Here, systems with $N = 0$ are analysed and it is shown that constant number of inputs per neuron leads to constant performance independently of K. Technologically this is good news because cost increases linearly with size of GNU, the performance being set by the number of feedback inputs F per neuron. So Q becomes a dependent parameter of the system with $Q = F/K$.

The training of a GNU with $N = 0$ consists of assuming that, one by one, the patterns of a training set $T = \{t1, t2, ..., tn\}$ are forced on to the output terminals of the neurons so determining their inputs as well as their target outputs. The adaptation in the neurons is such as to cause the inputs to generate the target outputs, keeping each of tj "stable" in the net with time. Given an unknown pattern u it is expected that, after a number of transient states, the GNU will stabilize in the element of T which, in some way (say, in Hamming distance) is most similar to u. The primary performance parameters, therefore, are, first, this retrieval ability and second, the storage capacity (i.e. the number of pattens S that T can contain and that are absorbed by the GNU without interference). A secondary performance parameter is the speed (i.e. number of transient steps) within which the retrieval is achieved. It will first be shown that storage capacity is independent of K and heavily dependent on F.

Consider a binary pattern u currently present at the K binary state variables of what, after all, is an autonomous finite-state machine. The next value (assuming the presence of a clock) of a particular state variable will be solely determined by the computation that can be achieved on the basis of its F input terminals. Assuming that they are randomly connected to the K state variables, and that the computation is related to some measure of similarity with the F-tuples seen during training, the statistical distribution of the next value of the K state variables can only be related to the amount of information contained in K independent F-tuples. This depends on the relative similarities of the patterns in T and pattern u, which can be specified in terms of proportional pattern areas rather than being a function of K. To be clearer about this we shall look at some specific performance parameters in simplified circuit conditions.

4.1 Storage Capacity

This needs to be defined probabilistically, to which end the concept of a contradiction is used. A contradiction occurs if, after training on tj, training on tk causes tj no longer to be a stable pattern in the GNU. For two patterns tj and tk that are the same for ajk of the area of the entire pattern, a contradiction occurs if for any one of the K neurons different targets are required for the same input. The storage capacity of the GNU is then determined by the number of training patterns (and assumptions about their similarity) that yeild some tolerable level of contradiction probability. More precisely, consider two patterns tj and tk that have a proportional overlap area ajk. The probability that any neuron will have the same input for the two patterns is $(ajk)F$ while the probability that such neurons require different outputs is $(1 - ajk)$. So the probability of a contradiction for patterns tj and tk, $P(Cjk)$ is

$$P(Cjk) = (1 - ajk)(ajk)^F \tag{1}$$

It can easily be shown that if S patterns are to be stored in such a system, and if there is choice over the coding of the patterns, such that the overlap between any two of them is the same and minimal, this minimal overlap $ajk(min)$ is:

$$ajk(min) = 1 - 2/S \tag{2}$$

This gives a lowest bound on the probability of contradiction for any two training patterns:

$$P(Cjk)min = (2/S)(1 - 2/S)^F \tag{3}$$

This needs to be extended to take into account the cumulative effect of $S - 1$ patterns on the disruption of any one pattern. The principle involved in doing this is to account for new disruptions threatened as new training patterns are added to the GNU. As seen, the disruptive effect of $t2$ on $t1$ is $(2/S)((S-2)/S)F$. If one now considers the additional effect of $t3$ on $t1$, a new group of $1/S$ differing neuron outputs becomes threatened again by an area of $((S-2)/S)F$ equal inputs. Also $1/S$ differing neuron outputs that have already been accounted for in $t2$, now are threatened by a new group of inputs that is identified by the expression

$$((S-2)/S)^F - ((S-3)/S)^F \tag{4}$$

Repeating this to account for all the S-1 patterns, leads to the overall probability of disrupting a trained pattern $Pd(S)$:

$$Pd(S) = \{2(S-1)[(S-2)/S]^F - (S-2)[(S-3)/S]^F\}/S \tag{5}$$

Result 4-1: There are several characteristics of this somewhat bizarre expression that are worth noting:

- It confirms that which is obvious: any GNU can store two orthogonal patterns as $Pd(S)$ evaluates to 0 for $S = 2$.

- It also confirms that for large S the probability of disruption tends to 1.

- More interestingly, it provides a relationship between F and S for a given limit of acceptability for the value of $Pd(S)$. For example, the following list of values has been computed empirically for Pd(S) between 10% and 15%:
  F= 2 4 8 16 32 ——— Large F
  S= 3 4 7 14 27 ———-0.8(Large F)

- Also, it shows that if S is held to the same value as F, the probability of disruption tends to 22.08%.

- The last observation can be generalised as one would expect the limiting value of $Pd(S)$ for large S to fall logarithmically with F/S. An empirical relationship is:

$$Log10[Pd(S)] = 0.3 - 0.85F/S \qquad (6)$$

Result 4-2: A major conclusion can be drawn from this analysis. The storage capacity depends primarily on the "fan-in" F of each node as a result of being able to model the K-node output pattern as a field of signals which the node inputs sample. This has implications not only for the design of artificial perceptual systems but also for the analysis of biological systems as F is a measurable parameter.

We shall return to the biological theme later.

Result 4-3: Expressions such as (6) can be used for design purposes, as the accuracy of retrieval can be related to cost through parameter F. It is also useful for inferring the likely accuracy of storing patterns in areas of the brain where F is known (e.g. the hippocampus).

It is noted that storage capacity calculated as a count of potentially stable patterns in a GNU is not a sufficient indicator of whether the patterns are stable or metastable. These points will be considered in the sections that follow. We note that Wong and Sherrington have obtained similar results [17] for RAM nets trained with reducing amounts of noise.

4.2 A Biological Application

Result 4-4: As mentioned earlier, it is well known (e.g.Rolls, 1989) that in area CA3 of the human hippocampus, a cell may have a 5% probability of being reached by the collateral (output) of another cell . As it is also known that that the number of cells in the same area is 2.5x106, this gives us a figure for F of 1.25x105. It has also been suggested that the hippocampus could have values of S as large as one million. Our formulation shows (according to (5)) that the probability of contradiction for $S = 1,000,000$ and $F = 1.25x105$ leads to a contradiction probability $Pd(1,000,000)$ of 87%. This suggests that the storage capacity may be lower. For example $S = 100,000$ gives a more reasonable contradiction probability of 14%. This means that, on average, 86% of any memorised pattern can potentially be retrieved.

4.3   Retrieval of Two Orthogonal Patterns

Just for the sake of seeing how F affects the retrievability of patterns stored, training on two orthogonal patterns is considered. This removes the masking effect that could be brought about by contradictions. It may be easily shown that for neurons with no generalisation the trained patterns themselves are metastable That is, if a training pattern is disturbed by a minimum amount of noise, it will drift into a sequence of arbitrary patterns (noise). We shall therefore assume, in the first instance, that the neural node has maximum generalisation (i.e. it is a "fully spread G-RAM " as described in section 2-4 of this report. This means that if a proportional area "a" of an input pattern is the same as that of a training pattern and the majority of terminals of the RAM is in "a" then the node will respond in the same way as it was required to do for the training pattern. Failing that, it will respond with $P(1) = 0.5$.

Say that at any point in time the GNU is in a state that has a proportional overlap of area a1 $(0 >= a1 >= 1)$ with training pattern t1 (t1 and t2 being the two orthogonal training patterns). The probability of a node firing as in t1 is then given by the probability of connecting the majority of F inputs to area a1. We call this $fm(a1, F)$ where

$$fm(a1, F) = \sum_{j=[N/2]}^{F} \binom{F}{j} (a1)^j (1 - a1)^{F-j} \qquad (7)$$

where [x] is the nearest integer above X.

Using the law of large numbers it is possible to say that if a1(t) is the overlap as above at time t then at the next instant of time the a1$(t + 1)$ is given by:

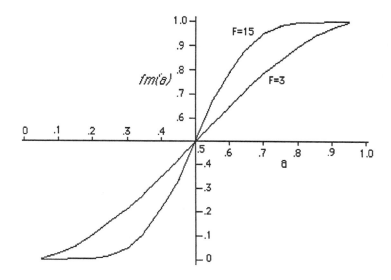

Figure 3: The shape of (8)

$$a1(t+1) = fm(a1) \qquad (8)$$

The shape of this expression is shown in figure 3 and shows that if a1 is greater than 0.5 then $a1(t+1)$ is greater than a1, meaning that, in time, the system will enter the trained state which has the greater overlap with u.The shape of (8) suggests that the effect of N is such that the larger is N the more rapidly will the system converge. This is confirmed by fig. 4.

Result 4-5: Expression (7) is a fundamental and general model of the behaviour of a generalising neuron.

4.4 General Retrieval

Extending the argument to training with more non-orthogonal patterns follows similar lines. At the heart of the analysis is the fact that for t training patterns in set T, the physical output

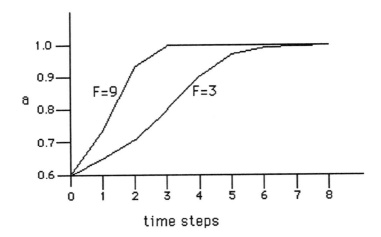

Figure 4: The effect of N on retrieval speed for a=0.6

space of the GNU is partitioned into 2t areas. These are shown for the example in fig. 5 where there are three training patterns T1, T2, T3 and, consequently , eight areas labelled p,q, ... w, in the physical output space.

Each of these areas is trained in a different way. For example, q is trained to output a 1 for T1 only and a 0 for T2 and T3. So these areas represent all the possible logical combinations of training and this may be used to predict the response of the net to the all-1 test pattern. The technique for doing this is to consider the probability of producing correct and incorrect responses in these areas. Imagine that the test pattern is the all-1 image and ask the question of how much like T1 will be the response to this all-1 pattern. The correct responses for T1 are 1s in q,r u and t, and 0s in p,s,v and w. To obtain a 1 in area q the majority of the input of a fully generalising node must be in the common area between the all -1 pattern and T1 , but not in "ambiguous" areas such as r where an output in q would have been trained to output both a 0 and a 1. In fact this kind of accounting leads to the conclusion that nodes with

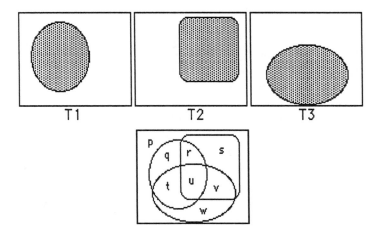

Figure 5: Partition of the output area as a result of training on three patterns.

the majority of inputs only in area q will lead to the correct output in area q. This probability is precisely mf(q).. Similarly, a node with an output in area r has a probability of giving the correct response of mf(q)+mf(s). The total contribution of nodes in some area such as r, say, to the correct or incorrect firing is, at most r, making the correct contribution of this area , r(mf(q)+mf(s).). At the end of this accounting process, we obtain a total proportion of correctly firing nodes Q1 (the 1 belonging to T1, there being a different, but eqally derived Q2 for T2 and Q3 for T3).

$$Q1 = mf(q) + mf(s)(r + u + w + p) + mf(w)(t + u + s + p) \quad (9)$$

But this is not the only contribution to correctly firing nodes, there are nodes that are in the $P(1) = 0.5$ state, half of which at any one time fire correctly. In fact their total number is

$$R1 = (1 - mf(q) - mf(s) - mf(w)) \quad (10)$$

So , remembering that 1/2 of R1 fire correctly at any one time
and given the pattern u (t) (all-1) at time t, which has the
similarity $a1(t)$ to T1 at time t, at time t+1 this similarity is :

$$a1(t + 1) = Q1 + 0.5R1 \tag{11}$$

While this expression (applied simputaneously to all training
patterns to obtain a2(t+1) and a3(t+1) as well) needs to be
studied in greater detail, it may be used to show that the training patterns are stable against small differences. It also predicts
a chaotic region of state space with all the nodes firing at random and also predicts whether an unknown pattern will lead
towards the retrieval of a training pattern or to the chaotic
behaviour.

To determine the stability of the system we define a performance function E based on measuring a "distance" of u from
the assumed target and the chaotic region. Without loss of generalization, we assume that it is expected that T1 will become
stable in the net a1target =1. Referring to figure 5, it is implied
that a2target= r+u+w+p, and a3target=t+u+v+s+p. So the
initial distance of the state from the target is:

$$D_{target}(t) = \sqrt{\{(1-a1(t))^2+(a2_{target}-a2(t))^2+(a3_{target}-a3(t))^2\}} \tag{12}$$

Similarly, we have a distance from the target at time t+1 which
is the same as the above, but with t+1 replacing t. Further,
distances from the chaotic region (where aj becomes 0.5) may
be defined:

$$D_{chaos}(t) = \sqrt{\{(0.5 - a1(t))^2 + (0.5 - a2(t))^2 + (0.5 - a3(t))^2\}} \tag{13}$$

This, again, can be defined for t+1.

A performance paremeter E may be defined as follows:

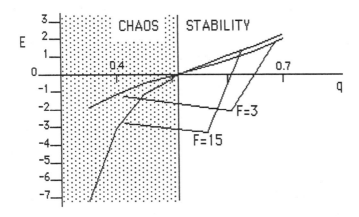

Figure 6: Pattern Retrieval

$$E(t+1) = (D_{chaos}(t)/D_{target}(t)) - (D_{chaos}(t+1)/D_{target}(t+1)) \tag{14}$$

This is negative if the a(t) state changes towards chaos at a(t+1) or positive if it changes towards the target. As an example, consider a set of patterns for which , initially, p=.37, q=.35, r=.02, s=.1, t=.02, u=.02, v=.02, w=.1 . Increasing q at the expense of p. That is, T1 is changed to be more and more similar to the all-1 starting pattern, without changing the overlap with the other training patterns. It is shown in fig. 6 that as this similarity is increased, the GNU switches from instability to retrieval leading to some empirically stated results.

Result 4-4: The change from chaos to retrievability is predictable from equations (9) to (13).

Result 4-5: Large F effectively decreases the retrieval time (gain of the system) without affecting the changeover point between chaos and retrievability (synonimous with stability).

This somewhat empirical approach has again shown that the behaviour of weakly connected autoassociators is dependent on network topology and the nature of the training patterns. Other forms of GNU topologies are considered in an internal report [16]. Here we go on to consider the synthesis of systems using such devices as building bricks.

5   System Design With GNUS

In summary, the characteristics of a GNU are: association, which has been discussed in this paper and shown to be heavily dependent on Q, and temporal properties, which clearly exist but have not been analysed in this paper (theywill be considered in future publications). There are two types of temporal action input ,which refers to the fact that the net can be sensitive to the order in which input messages are applied and output, which refers to the possibility of the net stepping through a sequence of states while the input is held constant. Clearly, which of these properties is in force depends on the way that the net is trained.

5.1   Design Specification

This design example is included for the purpose of illustrating a methodological framework only: it is completely fictional in all other respects. The target is to develop a system that investigates a visual buffer containing circles, squares and triangles, finding one such object by under a describing its position with a voice synthesizer or describing the scene in terms of the position of all the objects as required by a linguistic command. So the input is constrained to the following two sentence types:

- FIND ¡CIRCLE/SQUARE/TRIANGLE¿
- DESCRIBE

Figure 7 indicates an attempt at a solution. The emphasized oblongs are the GNUs. The process of reasoning that leads to this scheme will now be described.

5.2 General operation

The user issues a command (either by speaking , in which case a speech-to-phoneme net is required, or by typing the words on a keyboard). This is detected by the Word Recognition (WR) GNU which has a unique state for each word. The grammar of the input words is very simple:

s:= Find x/Describe
x:= Circle/Square/Triangle

s is the starting symbol, x is the only other non-terminal symbol, and the rest of the words are all terminal symbols. So there are only four possible sentences in the grammar.

The Phrase Recognition (PR) GNU translates the state of the WR into firing patterns on five terminals, one for each word. Note that a phrase such as "Find Circle" should cause firing at two of the PR outputs. This is passed on to the Speech/Vision Association (SVA) GNU, which also receives an input from a window generated by a buffer that holds an image of the scene. The buffering arrangements are executed by conventional means. However, a foveal window is made to move from object to object through the action of the Position Control (PC) GNU which is trained to output the window position increment coordinates to move to another object in the foveal input to the PC itself. Note that the window which provides input to the SVA is not foveal, but presents single objects in its field.

The SVA, by association, finds the code that is appropriate to the window-centered image and passes this on to Speech Sequencing (SS) GNU. This also receives position signals from the vision buffer, and outputs a sequence of signals received

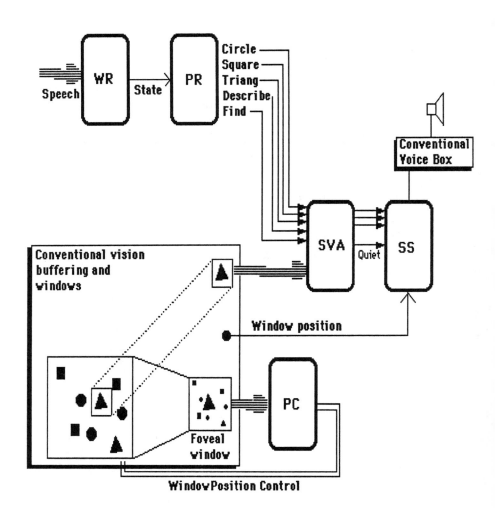

Figure 7: A scene describer

by a conventional "stored speech" box which might be preprogrammed to output synthesized speech such as "Circle at X 5 and Y 10". During a FIND x operation the SVA is trained to operate slightly differently, in the sense that it does not issue an output until the image matches x. This very rough description leads us to appreciate some of the parameters of the GNUs.

5.3 GNU Characteristics

<u>WR, Word Recognition</u>: Input temporal sensitivity is required, as a sequence has to be transformed into a state. This means that a non-zero Q is required.

<u>PR, Phrase Recognition</u>: Short input temporal sensitivity is required so as to be able to pair words such as "FIND CIRCLE". Hence, non-zero Q is required. Also the length of time that the output persists, controls the point at which the whole operation stops.

<u>PC, Position Controller</u>: This requres no temporal sensitivity. However it needs to be probabilistic in the sense that the choice of which should be the next centered object should be arbitrary. This would prevent the system from getting into a two-state cycle between two objects and would ensure that most objects would be visitied (perhaps more than once) during a DESCRIBE operation. A zero Q could be used in this case.

<u>SVA, Speech/Vision Associator</u>: There are no temporal requirements, but a non-zero Q is required to perform the necessary associations. SS, Speech Sequencer: This GNU requires output temporal capacity, in the sense that it needs to produce a sequence of signals to drive the voice box. Again non-zero Q is required.

6 Summary

The detailed results of this paper relate to storage capacity and pattern retrievability in the GNU, while the major overall results are the following.

- The capacity of GNU autoassociators in general is largely independent of size of the net, but heavily dependent on the fan-in of the nodes.

- The stability of the net is largely independent of the fan-in of the nodes and the size of the net, but heavily dependent on the relationship of the training patterns to the starting state of the net .

- These findings have considerable biological significance.

In the final parts of the paper we presented a way in which an engineer might use these tools in the creation of macrostructures which perform cognitive tasks.

Bibliography

[1] Aleksander, I.(1991)."WISARD and Other Weightless Neurons", To be published.

[2] Aleksander, I.(1965) "Fused Adaptive Circuit which Learns by Example," Electronics Letters 1(6).

[3] Aleksander, I., Thomas, W.V. and Bowden, P.A.(1984). "WISARD, a Radical Step Forward in Image Recognition," Sensor Review 4(3), 120-124.

[4] Aleksander I. and Morton H.B.(1990a). An Introduction to Neural Computing London: Chapman and Hall.

[5] Aleksander, I. and Morton H B (1990b). "An Overview of Weightless Neural Systems", International Joint Neural Networks Conference, Washington .

[6] Aleksander, I.(1989a). "Are special chips necessary for neural computing?" In Delgado-Frias and Moore (Eds), VLSI for Artificial Intelligence, Norwell, Mass.: Kluwer.

[7] Gorse, D. and Taylor, J. G.(1989). "An analysis of noisy RAM and neural nets," Physica D, 34, 90-114.

[8] Myers, C.(1990). Learning with Delayed Reinforcement in an Exploratory, Probabilistic Logic Neural Network. PhD thesis, University of London (Imperial College).

[9] Wilkie, B.(1983) A Stand-Alone, High Resolution Adaptive Pattern Recognition System, PhD Thesis, Brunel University, Uxbridge, UK.

[10] Aleksander,I.(1990c). "Ideal neurons for neural computers", Proceedings ICNC Dusseldorf, , Springer Verlag.

[11] Aleksander, I.(1989b). "The Logic of Connectionist Systems", in Aleksander, I. (Ed.) Neural Computing Architectures , London: Chapman and Hall, Boston MIT Press.

[12] Hopfield, J.J.(1982). "Neural networks and physical systems with emergent collective properties", Proc. Nat. Acad. Sci. USA, 79, 2554-2558.

[13] Aleksander, I.(1983). "Emergent Intelligent Properties of Progressively Structured Pattern Recognition Nets," Pattern Recognition Letters 1, 375-384

[14] Hinton, G. E., Sejnowski , T. J., and Ackley, D.(1984),"Boltzmann Machines: Constraint Satisfaction Networks that Learn," (Tech. Rep. CMU CS 84, 111. Carnegie-Mellon Univ.)

[15] Rolls, E.T.(1989).In The Computing Neuron, eds. R Durbin, C Miall and G Mitchison, Addison Wesley pp. 125-159.

[16] Aleksander, I. (1990). Weightless Neural Technology: A Report For 1990. Imperial College Neural systems Engineering Group, Dept. of Electrical Engineering.

[17] Wong K.Y.M. and Sherrington D.(1988). "Storage Properties of Boolean Neural Nets", Proc NEuro88, Paris.

An Estimation Theoretic Basis for The Design of Sorting and Classification Networks [1]

R. W. Brockett
Harvard University
Cambridge, Massachussets

1 Introduction

The large and growing literature related to the idea of defining systems of differential equations which, on the basis of incoming stimuli, define categories and assign successive temporal segments to these categories attests to the intrinsic appeal of such an idea. Systems of this type could be used as building blocks in more complex intelligent machines, especially in the lower level "unsupervised" learning portion of such structures. However, because the differential equations which accomplish these tasks are not unique; the choice of a particular system may be difficult to justify. In this paper we show that, in a significant set of cases, algorithms based on the gradient flow equation $\dot{H} = [H, [H, N(u)]]$ can be interpreted as providing a mechanism for computing conditional probabilities. This probabilistic interpretation not only shows that $H(t)$ contains the complete statistical summary of the past stimuli but also provides an interpretation for the undetermined constants which appear.

In [1] we investigated signal processing systems of the form

$$\dot{H} = [H, [H, N_0 + uN_1]]$$

[1] This work was supported in part by the U.S. Army Research Office under grant DAAL03-86-K-0171, the National Science Foundation under grant CDR-85-00108, and DARPA grant AFOSR-89-0506.

with a view toward using the results previously established for the autonomous system $\dot{H} = [H, [H, N]]$ in this more general setting. Signal processing problems, such as that of generating a quantized version of a signal or that of processing a quantized version of the input with automata-like transformations, were considered explicitly. In order to establish circumstances under which one can interpret equations of this form as being conditional probability propagators, we consider the problem of estimating the state of a finite state stochastic process which is observed with additive white noise. The main new results are to be found in sections [3] and [4] where it is asserted that, under suitable assumptions, this equation does admit such an interpretation and that by suitably choosing the eigenvalues of $H(0)$ we can use this equation as a means for generating a type of associative memory in which the learning and operational aspects are merged.

2   The Double Bracket Equation

The constraint sets which are encountered in linear programming are described by combinations of equalities and inequalities. Likewise the set of probability vectors in R^n i.e. $\{x | \sum x_i = 1; x_i \geq 0\}$ is described by equalities and inequalities. Although the simplex method works directly with such descriptions of the constraint set, the so called interior methods usually rely on transforming the variables so that no explicit inequalities appear. Out of one such line of work there has emerged a methodology for analog (or neural network) optimization/signal processing organized along the following principles. (See [2] for more details.)

i) A theorem of A. Horn asserts that the diagonal entries of a symmetric n by n matrix H with eigenvalues $\{\lambda_1, \lambda_2, \cdots \lambda_n\}$ can lie anywhere in the $(n-1)$-dimensional convex polytope in R^n whose $n!$ extreme points have coordinates $(\lambda_{\pi(1)}, \lambda_{\pi(2)}, \cdots, \lambda_{\pi(n)})$ for π an arbitrary permutation. I. Schur had previously shown that the diagonal entries were necessarily confined to this polytope. This Schur-Horn polytope $P(\lambda_1, \lambda_2, \cdots, \lambda_n)$ is thus describable by smooth functions.

ii) An arbitrary linear functional on the Schur-Horn polytope can be expressed as $\phi(H) = \text{tr}(HN)$ with N being a diagonal matrix.

iii) Relative to a certain natural Riemannian metric on the set of symmetric n by n matrices with fixed eigenvalues, the gradient assent equation for tr HN is

$$\dot{H} = [H, [H, N]]$$

where $[A, B] \overset{\text{def}}{=} AB - BA$. If the eigenvalues of H are unrepeated and the eigenvalues of N are unrepeated then there is a unique local maximum for tr HN which is, therefore, the global maximum.

According to this point of view the given data from a linear programming problem is mapped into a pair of self adjoint operators, $H(0)$, and N; $H(0)$ codes the constraints through its eigenvalues and N codes the linear functional that is to be optimized. The gradient assent equation steers the diagonal of H to the optimal point as measured by $\text{tr}(HN)$. It is possible to use this point of view to generate solutions to a variety of interesting problems involving linear inequalities. In these solutions, only smooth constraints appear. However, because not every constraint set of possible interest takes the form $P(\lambda_1, \lambda_2, \cdots, \lambda_n)$, this procedure is not completely general. In [2] we show how it can be modified so as to deal with the general compact polytope in R^n.

This work rests on a number of properties associated with the equation for symmetric n by n matrices

$$\begin{aligned} \dot{H} &= [H, [H, N]] \\ &= [H, HN - NH] \\ &= H^2 N - 2HNH + NH^2 \end{aligned}$$

Included among these are the fact that the flow is isospectral, i.e. $\det(Is - H(t)) = \det(Is - H(0))$ for all t and the fact that

$$\frac{d}{dt} tr(HN) = ||HN - NH||^2$$

Because $H = H^T$ and the eigenvalues of H do not change over time it is clear that H remains bounded; because tr HN is monotone increasing as long as $HN \neq NH$ we see that as t increases to infinity $H(t)$ approaches a matrix which commutes with N. Thus, if N is a diagonal matrix with unrepeated entries $H(t)$ approaches a diagonal matrix whose diagonal entries are the eigenvalues of $H(0)$. It is also established in [2] that (except for highly unusual initial conditions) if N is diagonal the order in which the eigenvalues of $H(0)$ appear on the diagonal of $H(\infty)$ is determined by the relative sizes of the diagonal entries of N. For example, if $n_{11} > n_{22} > ... > n_{nn}$ then h_{11} approaches the largest eigenvalue of H, h_{22} the next largest, etc. In general, the diagonal entries of $H(\infty)$ and the diagonal entries of N (assuming it is diagonal) will be similarly ordered in the sense that at $t = \infty$ for any permutation π

$$\sum h_{ii} \, n_{ii} \geq \sum h_{\pi(i)\pi(i)} n_{ii}$$

This sorting property which has also been studied in several related contexts [2,12], plays a crucial role in what follows.

As noted above, by replacing $\dot{H} = [H, [H, N]]$ with $\dot{H} = [H, [H, N_0 + uN_1]]$ with u being a time dependent input, one can use this equation to solve a number of common signal processing tasks. Perhaps the simplest example is the use the equation

$$\dot{H} = [H, [H, \, N_0 + uN_1]] \; ; \; y = \text{tr}(HN_1)$$

as a quantizer. In [1] the following scheme was discussed. Suppose that one wants to map signal u into the set of levels $\{q_1, q_2, \cdots q_n\}$. Suppose that the the levels are ordered $q_1 \leq q_2 \leq \cdots \leq q_n$. Let the eigenvalues of $H(0)$ be $\{q_1, q_2, \cdots q_n\}$; let N_0 be a diagonal matrix $N_0 = \text{diag}\,(a_1, a_2, \cdots a_{n-1}, 0)$ and let $N_1 = \text{diag}\,(0, 0, \cdots, 0, 1)$. If u is a constant such that $a_1 \geq a_2 \geq \cdots a_r > u > a_{r-1} \cdots a_n$

then as t goes to infinity $y(t)$ will approach q_r. In fact, if $u(\ )$ is piecewise constant then, except at the points of discontinuity of u, $y(t)$ is approaching q_r and in that sense the solution will track the quantized version, provided that the jumps are not too frequent. In this case $y(t)$ spends most of the time near one of the q_i, the particular q_i being determined by the size of $u(t)$ relative to $a_1, a_2, \cdots, a_{n-1}$.

As an alternative to this approach we may consider the problem of finding a system which will, for a given set $\{a_1, a_2, \cdots a_n\}$, identify the index i which minimizes $(u - a_i)^2$. For example, we could ask for a system such that in steady state the h_{ii} take on the value zero or one with h_{ii} being one if $(u - a_i)^2 < (u - a_j)^2$ for all $j \neq i$. To accomplish this we can take $H(0)$ to have eigenvalues $(1, 0, 0, \cdots 0)$ and let $N(u)$ be of the form $N_0 + uN_1 + u^2 I$. Specifically, we let $N(u)$ be

$$N(u) = \begin{bmatrix} -(u - a_1)^2 & 0 & \cdots & 0 \\ 0 & -(u - a_2)^2 & \cdots & 0 \\ \cdots & \cdots & \cdots & \cdots \\ 0 & 0 & \cdots & -(u - a_n)^2 \end{bmatrix}$$

In this case, if u is a slowly changing function of time then H will be nearly piecewise constant, being approximated by diagonal matrices of the form $H(t) \approx \mathrm{diag}(0, 0 \cdots 0, 1, 0, \cdots, 0)$ with the nonzero entry being in the ii^{th} location where i is the index which minimizes $(a_i - u(t))^2$. We can think of this equation as being an equation for the pointer that designates which of the a_i's is closest to $u(t)$. Of course any positive multiple of $N(u)$ could be substituted for $N(u)$ without changing this argument.

It may be observed that in the expression $N(u) = N_0 + u\, N_1 + u^2 I$ the u^2 term has no effect because $\dot{H} = [H, [H, N_0 + uN_1 + u^2 I]]$ and $[H, I]$ vanishes. Thus, although it is easier to motivate the form of this equation using the full form of $N(u)$ as given, only the N_0 and N_1 terms

$$N_0 = \begin{bmatrix} -a_1^2 & 0 & \cdots & 0 \\ 0 & -a_2^2 & \cdots & 0 \\ \cdots & \cdots & \cdots & \cdots \\ 0 & 0 & \cdots & -a_n^2 \end{bmatrix} ; \ N_1 = \begin{bmatrix} 2a_1 & 0 & \cdots & 0 \\ 0 & 2a_2 & \cdots & 0 \\ \cdots & \cdots & \cdots & \cdots \\ 0 & 0 & \cdots & 2a_n \end{bmatrix}$$

actually matter.

It may happen that a problem involves more than one incoming stimulus. Suppose we have a vector input $u_1, u_2, \cdots, u_k$ and suppose we want to associate with u the point in the sample space which is closest, with closest now being interpreted in the euclidean sense. One solution is to take $H(0)$ to be of rank 1 and trace 1 and let $\dot{H} = [H[H, N(u)]]$ with

$$N(u) = -\mathrm{diag}\left(\sum_{i=1}^{k}(u_i - d_{i1})^2 \ , \ \sum_{i=1}^{k}(u_i - d_{i2})^2, \cdots \sum_{i=1}^{k}(u_i - d_{in}) \right)$$

In this case $H(0)$, which is necessarily of the form pp^T with p being a vector such that the sum of the squares of its components is one, will evolve in such a way as to track the entry on the diagonal of $N(u)$ which has the smallest square error distance to the vector u.

The remainder of this section is devoted to several more technical points which go beyond what we have said above about the qualitative properties of $\dot{H} = [H, [H, N]]$. The reader may wish to examine related material in the work of Bloch, Faybusovich and Helmke cited in the references.

It will simplify matters to have a special symbol for the set of symmetric matrices whose eigenvalues have a particular pattern of repetition. We let $M(\nu_1, \nu_2, \cdots \nu_k)$ denote the space of $\sum \nu_i$ by $\sum \nu_i$ symmetric matrices which have eigenvalues of multiplicity $\nu_1, \nu_2, \cdots \nu_k$. For example, $M(\nu_1, n - \nu_1)$ is the set of all n by n symmetric matricies with two distinct eigenvalues, one of which is of multiplicity ν and one of which is of multiplicity $n - \nu$. We denote the set of n by

n orthogonal matricies with positive determinant by $SO(n)$.

Lemma 1: Let $\lambda_1 > \lambda_2 > \cdots > \lambda_k$ be given. The set of all $H \in M(\nu_1, \nu_2, \cdots \nu_k)$ such that λ_1 is an eigenvalue of multiplicity ν_1, λ_2 an eigenvalue of multiplicity ν_2, etc. can be identified with the homogeneous space

$$SO(n)/(SO(\nu_1) \times SO(\nu_2) \times \cdots SO(\nu_k))$$

and thus admits the structure of a differentiable manifold of dimension

$$d = \frac{1}{2}(n(n-1) - \sum \nu_i(\nu_i - 1))$$

Sketch of Proof: As is well known, any n by n symmetric matrix with eigenvalues $(\alpha_1, \alpha_2, \cdots, \alpha_n)$ can be transformed into any other with the same eigenvalues by a congruence transformation $H \to \Theta H \Theta^T$ with $\Theta \in SO(n)$. On the other hand, if H is diagonal and if it belongs to $M(\nu_1, \nu_2, \cdots \nu_k)$ then for a suitable ordering of the diagonal elements we see that $\Theta H \Theta^T = H$ if and only if Θ is block diagonal with the blocks being of size ν_1 by ν_1, ν_2 by $\nu_2, \cdots \nu_k$ by ν_k. Using the fact that $SO(\nu)$ is a $\nu(\nu - 1)/2$ parameter group we see that the dimension formula follows.

In the special case of $M(1, n-1)$ this manifold is diffeomorphic to the $(n-1)$-dimensional spherical shell; i.e. the set of all unit vectors in R^n.

We also collect here a few basic facts about the solutions of $\dot{H} = [H, [H, N]]$ when $H(0)$ belongs to $M(\nu_1, \nu_2, \cdots \nu_k)$.

Lemma 2: Suppose that $\dot{H}(t) = [H(t), [H(t), N(t)]]$. Then

i) if $H(0) \in M(\nu_1, \nu_2, \cdots, \nu_k)$ it follows that $H(t) \in M(\nu_1, \nu_2, \cdots \nu_k)$ for all time.

ii) if $H(0) \in M(\nu, n - \nu)$ and if its eigenvalues are zero and one, it follows that $H(t) = H^2(t)$ for all time and hence $\dot{H} =$

$[H, [H, N]]$ is equivalent to the Riccati equation $\dot{H}(t) = H(t)N(t) - 2H(t)N(t)H(t) + N(t)H(t)$.

iii) if $H(0) \in M(1, n-1)$ and if $\dot{\Phi}(t) = \alpha N(t)\Phi(t)$ with $\Phi(0) = I$ and $\alpha = \mathrm{tr}\,H(0)$ it follows that $H(0)$ is of the form $H(0) = bb^T$ and

$$H(t) = (b^T b)\, \Phi(t)\, bb^T\, \Phi^T(t) \cdot (b^T\, \Phi^T(t)\, \Phi(t)b)^{-1}$$

Proof: i) This is an immediate consequence of the isospectral property. ii) If we write $H(0)$ as $H(0) = \Theta \Lambda \Theta^T$ with Λ diagonal then, because the eigenvalues are zero and one, $\Lambda^2 = \Lambda$: thus $H^2(0) = \Theta \Lambda \Theta^T \Theta \Lambda \Theta^T = \Theta \Lambda^2 \Theta^T = \Theta \Lambda \Theta = H(0)$. The rest follows from i). iii) Since $H(t) \in M(1, n-1)$ it can be written as $\eta(t)\eta^T(t)$. Substituting this into $\dot{H} = H^2 N - 2HNN + NH^2$ we get

$$\dot{\eta}(t)\eta^T(t) + \eta(t)\dot{\eta}^T(t) = (\eta(t)\eta^T(t)N(t) + N(t)\eta(t)\eta^T(t))\eta^T(t)\eta(t) \\ -2\eta(t)\eta^T(t) \cdot \eta^T(t)N(t)\eta(t)$$

From isospectrality we see that $\eta^T(t)\eta(t) = \eta^T(0)\eta(0)$. Say $\eta^T(0)\eta(0) = \alpha$. Then we see that

$$\dot{H} = \alpha(HN + NH) - \beta(t)H$$

the effect of the β-term is just to scale the solution so that we see that

$$H(t) = \gamma(t)\Phi(t)H(0)\Phi^T(t)$$

Solve for γ using $\mathrm{tr}\,H(t) = \mathrm{tr}\,H(0)$ to get the expression given.

There is one final important point. As noted in [1], if N_0 and N_1 are both diagonal and if $H(t)$ is diagonal then $[H, [H, N_0 + uN_1]]$ vanishes, regardless of the value of u. Thus the linearization of $\dot{H} = [H, [H, N(u)]]$ at an equilibrium contains no contribution from u. It may happen that for some values of u the equilibrium point is unstable, but even then $H(t)$ will remain unchanged until some unmodeled effect disturbs H. Anticipating the results of the next section we point out that altering N_0 so as to make it nondiagonal changes matters completely.

Lemma 3: Suppose that D and H_e are diagonal n by n matrices with D having unrepeated eigenvalues and suppose that E is an arbitrary symmetric n by n matrix. Then for ϵ sufficiently small there exists $H_e(\epsilon)$ such that $[H_e(\epsilon), D + \epsilon E] = 0, H_e(\epsilon) = H_e^T(\epsilon), H_e(\epsilon)$ has the same spectrum as H_e and

$$\frac{d\, h_{ij}(\epsilon)}{d\, \epsilon}\Big|_{\epsilon=0} = \frac{h_{jj}(0) - h_{ii}(0)}{d_{jj}(0) - d_{ii}(0)} e_{ij}$$

Proof: Let $\Theta(\epsilon)$ be such that $\Theta(\epsilon)(D + \epsilon E)\Theta^T(\epsilon)$ is diagonal. Then to first order we have $\Theta(\epsilon) = I + \epsilon\, \Omega$ for $\Omega = -\Omega^T$ and

$$(I + \epsilon\Omega)\, (D + \epsilon E)\, (I - \epsilon\Omega) = \text{diagonal}.$$

From this we see that

$$\Omega D - D\Omega + E = 0$$

and so

$$\omega_{ij} = e_{ij}(d_{jj} - d_{ii})^{-1}$$

Of course $\Theta[H, N]\Theta^T = [\Theta H \Theta^T, \Theta N \Theta^T]$ so that if $\Theta N \Theta^T$ is diagonal with distinct eigenvalues and if $[H, N] = 0$ it follows that $\Theta H \Theta^T$ is diagonal as well. Thus expanding $\Theta(\epsilon) H_e(\epsilon)\Theta^T(\epsilon)$ as above we see that

$$\begin{aligned} h_{ij}(\epsilon) &= h_{ij}(0) + \omega_{ij}(h_{jj} - h_{ii}) \\ &= h_{ij}(0) + \frac{(h_{jj}-h_{ii})}{(d_{jj}-d_{ii})} e_{ij} \end{aligned}$$

The effect of linearizing the $\dot{H}$ equation about an equilibrium point of $\dot{H} = [H, [H, N_0 + uN]]$ when N_0 is not diagonal can now be described in some detail. As might be anticipated, a great deal depends on how much repetition there is in the eigenvalues of $H(0)$.

Lemma 4: Suppose that $N_0 = D + \epsilon E$ with D diagonal and $E = E^T$. Let N be diagonal and let $H(0)\epsilon M(\nu_1, \nu_2, \cdots \nu_k)$. Then for ϵ positive but sufficiently small the linearization of

$$\dot{H}(t) = [H(t), [H(t), N_0 + uN]]$$

at the equilibrium point $H_e(\epsilon)$ in the neighborhood of diag $(\lambda_1, \lambda_2, \cdots, \lambda_n)$ has dim $M(\nu_1, \nu_2, \cdots \nu_k)$ controllable modes provided that the set real numbers $(\lambda_{ii} - \lambda_{jj})(d_{ii} - d_{jj})$ contains dim $M(\nu_1, \nu_2, \cdots, \nu_k)$ distinct entries and

$$\frac{n_{ii} - n_{jj}}{d_{ii} - d_{jj}} e_{ij} \neq 0$$

for all i and j such that $\lambda_i \neq \lambda_j$.

Sketch of Proof: As suggested by the proof of lemma 3, we want to find $\Theta(\epsilon)$ so that $\Theta(\epsilon)(D + \epsilon E)\Theta^T(\epsilon)$ is diagonal and then apply Θ in the same way to H and N. Using the fact that $\Theta(\epsilon)H_e\Theta^T(\epsilon)$ is diagonal and the fact that the ij^{th} entry of $\Theta(\epsilon)N\Theta^T(\epsilon)$ is to first order

$$\tilde{n}_{ij} = n_{ij} + \omega_{ij}(n_{jj} - n_{ii})$$

we see that if we let $\hat{H} = \Theta(\epsilon)H\Theta^T(\epsilon)$ then in terms of these variables the linearized system is decoupled

$$\frac{d}{dt}\hat{h}_{ij} = (\lambda_{ii} - \lambda_{jj})(\hat{d}_{ii} - \hat{d}_{jj})\hat{h}_{ij} + e_{ij}\left(\frac{n_{ii} - n_{jj}}{d_{ii} - d_{jj}}\right) u$$

with $\hat{d}_{ii}$ being the eigenvalues of $D + \epsilon E$. Since $\hat{d}_{ii}$ agrees with d_{ii} to within a correction that vanishes at $\epsilon = 0$, for ϵ small the hypothesis insures that the eigenvalues of this system are distinct in the sense of the hypothesis. Appealing to standard results in control theory we see that if the coefficients of u are nonzero and if the eigenvalues are distinct the system is controllable on a space of dim $M(\nu_1, \nu_2, \cdots \nu_k)$.

3   The Conditional Density

There are, of course, many ways to model the process whereby one uses observations about the world to estimate some aspect of its true state. One of the simplest of these is the following. Let x be a Markov process which takes on values in the set $\{x_1, x_2, ... x_n\}$. Denote the aprori probability that $x(t) = x_i$ by $\tilde{p}_i(t)$ and suppose that $d\tilde{p}_i/dt = \sum a_{ij}\tilde{p}_j$. Assume that the observations consist of a noisy version of x modeled as $y(t) = x(t) + \dot{w}(t)$ where $\dot{w}(t)$ is white noise. (In this paper we express all stochastic differential equations using the Stratonovic calculus as opposed to the Îto calculus. This is done for purely notational convenence as discussed in [11].) It is a well known result that the conditional probability p_i for $x(t) = x_i$, given the observation y on $[0, t]$, satisfies a differential equation involving y which takes the form, (see [10])

$$\dot{p} = (A - 1/2D^2)p + y\,D\,p - p\,\alpha(p)$$

with D being the diagonal matrix $D = \text{diag}\,(x_1, x_2, ..., x_n)$ and α being a normalization term

$$\alpha(p) = \sum_i \left(\sum_j a_{ij}\,p_j - x_j^2 p_j \right) - x_i\,y\,p_i$$

In this case $p_i(t)$ is the probability that $x(t) = x_i$, conditioned on the observation of y over the internal $[0, t]$.

It has been noted (See [9] for various references) that the solution of this system can be obtained from the solution of the simpler equation

$$\frac{d}{dt}\hat{p} = (A - 1/2D^2)\hat{p} + y\,D\,\hat{p}$$

via the relationship $p = \hat{p}/\sum \hat{p}_i$. In the estimation theory literature the simpler equation is sometimes called the unnormalized conditional density equation. This equation and its infinite dimensional versions have been studied extensively in the nonlinear filtering literature. In its original form, with the α term present, p evolves in such a way as to keep $\sum p_i = 1$, as is appropriate for a probability vector.

For our present purposes we point out that one can also use an alternative normalization based on $\sum p_i^2 = 1$. This leads to an equation in which the conditionial probability vector is scaled so that it lies on the unit sphere in Euclidean $n-$ space. In this case one easily sees that the appropriate conditional probability equation is

$$\frac{d}{dt}\tilde{p} = (A - 1/2D^2)\tilde{p} + y\ D\ \tilde{p} - \tilde{p} < \tilde{p}, (A - 1/2D^2 + yD)\tilde{p} >$$

where $< a, b > = \sum a_i b_i$. Our reason for introducing this alternative normalization is that, in the important case where $A = A^T$, it allows us to make contact with the results of the previous section, even though at first sight they seem to be quite unrelated. First of all, notice that D is diagonal and therefore symmetric. The infinitesimal generator A may or may not be symmetric but if it is then $H = \tilde{p}\tilde{p}^t$ satisfies the equation $\dot{H} = [H, [H, N]]$ provided that we take N to be $A - 1/2D^2 + yD$. Note that the actual conditional probability p is related to H by

$$\sqrt{h_{ii}} = \tilde{p}_i = p_i / \sqrt{\sum p_i^2}$$

and so

$$p_i = \sqrt{h_{ii}} / \sum \sqrt{h_{ii}}$$

We may also point out that an equation of the form $\dot{p} = Mp - p < p, Mp >$ in the work of Oja. (See the recent paper [3] for references). Oja arrives at such an equation through a principal component analysis much as we arrive at its "square" in our paper [8] through a study of principal component analysis. Despite the superficial similarity, however, the principal component approach is quite different in that u enters only through its sample covariance, i.e. quadratically, not linearly as it does here.

Theorem 1: Let x be a finite state, continuous time, real valued Markov process taking on values in the set $\{x_1, x_2, \cdots, x_n\}$ and let

$p_i(t)$ be the probability that $x(t) = x_i$. Suppose $\dot{p} = Ap$ with $A = A^T$ and let $D = \text{diag}(x_1, x_2, \cdots, x_n)$. If one observes $y(t) = x(t) + \dot{w}(t)$ with $\dot{w}$ being the standard white noise model and if H satisfied the equation

$$\dot{H}(t) = [H(t), [H(t), A - \frac{1}{2}D^2 + y(t)\,D]]$$

then the conditional probabilities for the x_i are

$$\hat{p}_i = \sqrt{h_{ii}} / \sum \sqrt{h_{ii}}$$

provided that $H(0) = \hat{p}(0)\hat{p}^T(0)$.

In this sense, then, we can think of $\dot{H} = [H, [H, N_0 + uN_1]]$ as being the conditional density propagator for a continuous time jump process provided that N_1 is diagonal and $N_0 + 1/2 N_1^2$ is the infinitesimal generator of a continuous time jump process. (That is to say, the off-diagonal entries of the matrix $N_0 + 1/2 N_1^2$ should be nonnegative and its columns should sum to zero.) In this case the rank one initial condition on $H(0)$ admits a conditional density interpretation.

Remark: If it happens that one is able to observe more than one attribute of the state x_i then one arrives at a vector input version of this equation which can be written in the form

$$\dot{H}(t) = [H(t), [H(t), A - 1/2 \sum (D_i - y_i I)^2]]$$

In this case the values in the diagonal matricies D_i can be thought of as reflecting the possible values of the particular property that y_i is measuring.

4   Category Generation

Insofar as one restricts $H(0)$ to be rank one and asks that $N_0 + 1/2\ N_1^2$ be the infinitesimal generator of a continuous time jump process, the algorithms provided by $\dot{H} = [H, [H, N_0 + uN_1]]$ are not fundamentally different from the conditional probability equation of Wonham [10]. However, when the initial value of H is not of rank one the algorithim does not admit such a clean probabilistic interpretation. This is, of course, a reflection of the fact that $(p_1 + p_2)(p_1 + p_2)^T$ is not equal to $p_1 p_1^T + p_2 p_2^T$ and so one can not view the rank $H(t) > 1$ situation as a superposition of two or more independant rank 1 situations. In spite of this we intend to show that the rank $H(0) > 1$ is of great interest when considered in the context of associative memories. These results rest on an extension of the results of section 2. We are mainly interested in the case where N_0 is suitably small; this assumption on N_0 is equivalent to the assumption that the measurements are a much more reliable source of information than the aprori facts about the state transitions.

In order to develop this idea we need some basic results about the stability properties of the solutions of ordinary differential equations in R^n. Consider

$$\dot{x}(t) = f(x(t), t)$$

If x_0 is such that $f(x_0, t) \equiv 0$ then x_0 is said to be an equilibrium point. The solution $x(t) \equiv x_0$ is said to be asymptotically stable if there exists some neighborhood of x_0 such that any solution of this equation starting in this neighborhood stays in some (possibly larger) neighborhood of x_0 and converges to x_0. The linearization of f at x_0 yields a linearized equation

$$\dot{\delta}(t) = \left[\frac{\partial f}{\partial x} \right]_{x_0} \delta(t) \stackrel{\text{def}}{=} A(t)\,\delta(t)$$

There is a classical theorem which states that if f is twice differentiable with respect to x and if all solutions of the linearized equation converges to zero at an exponential rate then the solution $x(t) \equiv x_0$ of the original nonlinear system is asymptotically stable. This may be proven by constructing a suitable Liapunov function based on the linearized system or by an application of the Gronwall-Bellman inequality. We may apply these ideas to our present situation in the following way.

Theorem 2: Let $N(\ )$ be a diagonal matrix whose entries are periodic functions of time with period T. Then $\dot{H} = [H, [H, N]]$, considered as a system on $M(\nu, n - \nu)$ with eigenvalues zero and one, is such that the equilibrium solution $H_e = \text{diag}(1, 1, \cdots 1, 0, 0, \cdots, 0)$ is asymptotically stable provided that for $1 \leq i \leq \nu$ and $\nu + 1 \leq j \leq n$ we have

$$\int_0^T n_{ii}(t) - n_{jj}(t) \, dt \; > 0$$

Proof: As in section 2 we see that the linearized equation at the equilibrium point $H_e = \text{diag}(\hat{h}_{11}, \hat{h}_{22}, \cdots \hat{h}_{nn}$ is

$$\dot{h}_{ij} = (\hat{h}_{ii} - \hat{h}_{jj}) (n_{ii} - n_{jj}) h_{ij}$$

However, since dim $M(\nu, n - \nu) = \nu(n - \nu)$ only $\nu(n - \nu)$ of these equations are independent. For the range of indices indicated $\hat{h}_{ii} - \hat{h}_{jj} = -1$ and so for $1 \leq i \leq \nu < j \leq n$ we see that the linearized equations are

$$\dot{h}_{ij} = (n_{jj} - n_{ii})h_{ij} \; ; \; 1 \leq i \leq \nu; \; \nu + 1 \leq j \leq n$$

These have the solution

$$h_{ij}(t) = e^{\int_0^t n_{jj}(\tau) - n_{ii}(\tau)d\tau} h_{ij}(0)$$

and so they are stable under the conditions indicated.

We now show how these ideas can be used to construct a system that defines catagories. In the process we will point out the way in which this system is resistant to the problem associated with many of the growing memory filters, namely the tendency of frequently occurring events to push less frequently occurring events out of the memory.

Suppose that we index the columns and rows of a symmetric matrix H by binary k-tuples $(\alpha_1, \alpha_2, \cdots \alpha_k)$ and define a set of diagonal matrices $D_1, D_2, \cdots D_k$ by specifying that the jj^{th} entry of D_i is one if the binary representations of j has a one in the ith position from the left and is otherwise zero. If $(u_1(t)u_2(t)\cdots u_k(t))$ is a binary k-tuple then the equation

$$\dot{H}(t) = [H(t), [H(t), \sum_{i=1}^{k}(D_i - u_i(t)I)^2]]$$

sorts in the following sense. If $H(0)\epsilon M(\nu, n-\nu)$ and if $H^2(0) = H(0)$ then $H_e = \text{diag}(\beta_1, \beta_2, \cdots, \beta_n)$ is an asymptotically stable equilibrium point if $\beta_l = 1$ implies that the average Hamming distance between $u(\cdot)$ and the binary k-tuple which corresponds to l is one of the ν smallest such averages and $\beta_l = 0$ implies that the average Hamming distance between the binary k-tuple corresponding to l is one of the $n - \nu$ largest such averages. (The Hamming distance between two binary k-tuples is equal to the number of digits for which they fail to agree.) Thus this system, operating over a period of time, will identify those temporal segments of $u( )$ which appear most frequently in this average sense.

Although this algorithim has attractive features there are two aspects which require further work. The first problem is that of determining a suitable way to adjust ν since one may not know in advance how many significant events there will be. The second relates to the fact that in averaging over time, one penalizes a state in proportion to its distance from the state that is then occurring. This is not necessarily appropriate; one would like to simply reward states for a good fit and ignore the quality of fit when the input is a good fit to some other state.

We can put this into an associative memory which for suitably distributed associations will perform in the following way. Let the eigenvalues of $H(0)$ be ordered $\lambda_1 \geq \lambda_2 \cdots \geq \lambda_n$. And suppose that $\lambda_1 > \lambda_2 = \lambda_3 \cdots = \lambda_r$ with $\lambda_{r+1} = \lambda_{r+2} = \cdots = \lambda_n = 0$. Suppose that $\tilde{N}_0$ is small and that $u(t)$, the vector of inputs, takes on only r values, $u_1, u_2, \cdots u_r$. Then the corresponding trajectory of

$$\dot{H} = [H, [H_1 \ N_0 + \frac{1}{2}(u_i I - D_i)^2]$$

will align λ_1 with the current state, and align $\lambda_2, \lambda_3, \cdots \lambda_r$ with the next most popular states leaving $0's$ for the others.

5 Conclusions

The problem of finding a simple analog mechanisms for realizing associative memories has a natural solution via principal component analysis when the problem is such that it can be characterized as learning a subspace. In a more general context it seems that additional research is required. In this paper we have suggested that a modified version of a basic conditional density equation has a number of attractive properties when used as an associative memory. It also fits into a larger context consisting of a family of equations which accomplish a variety of other signal processing tasks.

Bibliography

[1] R.W. Brockett,"Smooth Dynamical Systems Which Realize Arithmetical and Logical Operations," in *Lecture Notes in Control and Information Sciences. Three Decades of Mathematical Systems Theory.* (H. Nijmeijer and J. M. Schumacher, eds.) Springer-Verlag, Berlin, 1989, pp. 19-30.

[2] R.W. Brockett, "Dynamical Systems That Sort Lists, Diagonalize Matrices and Solve Linear Programming Problems", to appear in *Linear Algebra and its applications*, (Preliminary version in *Proceedings of the 1988 IEEE Conference on Decision and Control*), (1988).

[3] E. Oja, Neural Networks, Principal Components and Subspaces, *International Journal of Neural Systems*, Vol. I, (1989) pp. 61-68

[4] T. Sanger, "Optimal Unsupervised Learning in a Single-layer Linear Feedforward Neural Network", *Neural Networks*, Vol. 2, (1989), pp. 459- 473.

[5] A. M. Bloch, "The Kähler Structure of the Total Least Squares Problem, Brockett's Steepest Descent Equations, and Constrained Flows", *Proceedings of the International Symposium MTNS 1989*. M. A. Kaasheck et.al. Eds. Birkhauwser, Boston, MA, 1990.

[6] Leonid Faybusovich, "Hamilton Structure of Dynamical Systems which Solve Linear Programming Problems", (submitted for publication).

[7] U. Helmke, "Isospectral Flows on Symmetric Matrices and The Riccati Equation", (to appear).

[8] R.W. Brockett, "Dynamical Systems That Learn Subspaces", in *Mathematical System Theory: The Influence of R. E. Kalman*, Springer Verlag, Berlin, 1990 (to appear).

[9] R.W. Brockett, "Nonlinear Systems and Nonlinear Estimation Theory," in *Stochastic Systems* (M. Hazewinkel and J. C.

Willems, eds.). Dordrecht, The Netherlands: Reidel Publishing Co., 1981, pp. 441-477.

[10] M. W. Wonham, "Some Applications of Stochastic Differential Equations to Optimal Nonlinear Filtering", *SIAM J. on Control*, Vol. 2, (1965)

[11] R. W. Brockett and J. M. Clark, "The Geometry of the Conditional Density Equations," in *Analysis and Optimization of Stochastic Systems* (O. L. R. Jacobs *et al.*, eds.). New York: Academic Press, 1980, pp. 299-309.

[12] A. M. Bloch, R. W. Brockett and T. S. Ratiu, "A New Foundation of the Generalized Toda Lattice equation and their fixed paint analysis via the momentum map", *Bulletin of the American Math. Soc.*, Vol. 23, No. 2 (1990) pp. 477-485.

A Self-Organizing ARTMAP Neural Architecture for Supervised Learning and Pattern Recognition

Gail A. Carpenter†
Stephen Grossberg‡
John H. Reynolds§
Center for Adaptive Systems
and
Graduate Program in Cognitive
and Neural Systems
Boston University

1 Introduction: A Self-Organizing Neural Architecture for Supervised Learning

This chapter describes a new neural network architecture, called ARTMAP, that autonomously learns to classify arbitrarily many, arbitrarily ordered vectors into recognition categories based on predictive success. This supervised learning system is built up from a pair of Adaptive Resonance Theory modules (ART_a and ART_b) that are capable of self-organizing stable recognition categories in response to arbitrary sequences of input patterns. During training trials, the ART_a module receives a stream $\{a^{(p)}\}$ of input patterns, and ART_b receives a stream $\{b^{(p)}\}$ of input patterns, where $b^{(p)}$ is the correct prediction given $a^{(p)}$. These ART modules are linked by an associative learning network and an internal controller that ensures autonomous system operation in real time. During test trials, the remaining patterns $a^{(p)}$ are presented without $b^{(p)}$, and their predictions at ART_b are compared with $b^{(p)}$.

Tested on a benchmark machine learning database in both

on-line and off-line simulations, the ARTMAP system learns orders of magnitude more quickly, efficiently, and accurately than alternative algorithms, and achieves 100% accuracy after training on less than half the input patterns in the database.

ARTMAP achieves these properties by using an internal controller that conjointly maximizes predictive generalization and minimizes predictive error by linking predictive success to category size on a trial-by-trial basis, using only local operations. This computation increases the vigilance parameter ρ_a of ART_a by the minimal amount needed to correct a predictive error at ART_b. Parameter ρ_a calibrates the minimum confidence that ART_a must have in a category, or hypothesis, activated by an input $\mathbf{a}^{(p)}$ in order for ART_a to accept that category, rather than search for a better one through an automatically controlled process of hypothesis testing. Parameter ρ_a is compared with the degree of match between $\mathbf{a}^{(p)}$ and the top-down learned expectation, or prototype, that is read-out subsequent to activation of an ART_a category. Search occurs if the degree of match is less than ρ_a.

ARTMAP is thus a type of self-organizing expert system that calibrates the selectivity of its hypotheses based upon predictive success. As a result, rare but important events can be quickly and sharply distinguished even if they are similar to frequent events with different consequences.

Between input trials, ρ_a relaxes to a baseline vigilance $\overline{\rho_a}$. When $\overline{\rho_a}$ is large, the system runs in a conservative mode, wherein predictions are made only if the system is confident of the outcome. Very few false-alarm errors then occur at any stage of learning, yet the system reaches asymptote with no loss of speed. Because ARTMAP learning is self-stabilizing, it can continue learning one or more databases, without degrading its corpus of memories, until its full memory capacity is utilized.

2 Predictive ART Architectures

The architecture described herein forms part of Adaptive Resonance Theory, or ART, which was introduced in 1976 in order to analyse how brain networks can autonomously learn in real time about a changing world in a rapid but stable fashion.[7,8] Since that time, ART has steadily developed as a physical theory to explain and predict ever larger data bases about cognitive information processing and its neural substrates.[9-11,13] A parallel development has described a series of rigorously characterized neural architectures—called ART 1, ART 2, and ART 3—with increasingly powerful learning, pattern recognition, and hypothesis testing capabilities.[2-5]

ARTMAP illustrates a class of architectures that are called Predictive ART architectures because they incorporate ART modules into systems that can learn to predict a prescribed m-dimensional output vector $\mathbf{b}$ given a prescribed n-dimensional input vector $\mathbf{a}$ (Figure 1). The present example of Predictive ART is called ARTMAP because its transformation from vectors in $\Re^n$ to vectors in $\Re^m$ defines a *map* that is learned by example from the correlated pairs $\{\mathbf{a}^{(p)}, \mathbf{b}^{(p)}\}$ of sequentially presented vectors, $p = 1, 2, \ldots$.[1,9]

Figure 1 compares properties of the ARTMAP network with those of the Back Propagation network.[17,18,21,22] Both ARTMAP and Back Propagation are supervised learning systems. With supervised learning, an input vector $\mathbf{a}^{(p)}$ is associated with another input vector $\mathbf{b}^{(p)}$ on each training trial. On a test trial, a new input $\mathbf{a}$ is presented that has never been experienced before. This input predicts an output vector $\mathbf{b}$. System performance is evaluated by comparing $\mathbf{b}$ with the correct answer. This property of *generalization* is the system's ability to correctly predict correct answers to a test set of novel inputs $\mathbf{a}$.

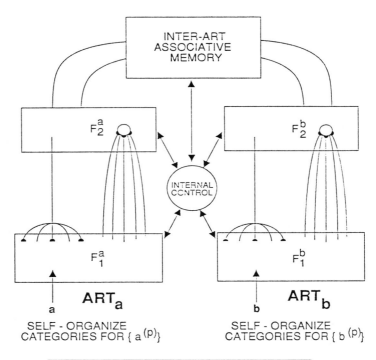

	Predictive ART	Back Propagation
supervised	yes	yes
self-organizing	yes	no
real-time	yes	no
self-stabilizing	yes	no
learning:	fast or slow match	slow mismatch

Figure 1. A Predictive ART, or ARTMAP, system includes two ART modules linked by an inter-ART associative memory. Internal control structures actively regulate learning and information flow. Back Propagation and Predictive ART both carry out supervised learning, but the two systems differ in many respects, as indicated.

3 Conjointly Maximizing Generalization and Minimizing Predictive Error

The ARTMAP system is designed to conjointly *maximize* generalization and *minimize* predictive error under *fast learning* conditions in *real time* in response to an *arbitrary ordering* of input patterns. Using this property, the network can achieve 100% test set accuracy on the machine learning benchmark database described below. The system learns to make accurate predictions quickly, in the sense of using relatively little computer time; efficiently, in the sense of using relatively few training trials; and flexibly, in the sense that its stable learning permits continuous new learning, on one or more databases, without eroding prior knowledge, until the full memory capacity of the network is exhausted. In an ARTMAP network, memory capacity can be chosen arbitrarily large without sacrificing stability of fast learning or accurate generalization.

4 Match Tracking of Predictive Confidence by Attentive Vigilance

An essential feature of the ARTMAP design is its ability to conjointly maximize generalization and minimize predictive error on a *trial-by-trial* basis using *only local operations*. It is this property which enables the system to learn rapidly about rare events that have important consequences even if they are very similar to frequent events with different consequences. This property builds upon a key design feature of all ART systems; namely, the existence of an *orienting subsystem* that responds to the unexpectedness, or novelty, of an input exemplar a by driving a hypothesis testing cycle, or parallel memory search, for a better, or totally new, recognition category for a. Hypothesis testing is triggered by the orienting subsystem if a activates a recognition category that reads out a learned expectation, or prototype, which does not match a well enough. The degree of match provides an analog measure of the predictive *confidence* that the chosen recognition category represents

a, or of the *novelty* of **a** with respect to the hypothesis that
is symbolically represented by the recognition category. This
analog match value is computed at the orienting subsystem
where it is compared with a dimensionless parameter that is
called *vigilance*.[2,3] A cycle of hypothesis testing is triggered
if the degree of match is less than the vigilance. Conjoint
maximization of generalization and minimization of predictive
error is achieved on a trial-by-trial basis by increasing the vigilance parameter in response to a predictive error on a training
trial.[2] The minimum change is made that is consistent with
correction of the error. In fact, the predictive error causes the
vigilance to increase rapidly until it just exceeds the analog
match value, in a process called *match tracking*.

Before each new input arrives, vigilance relaxes to a baseline vigilance value. Setting baseline vigilance to 0 maximizes
code compression. The system accomplishes this by allowing
an "educated guess" on every trial, even if the match between
input and learned code is poor. Search ensues, and a new category is established, only if the prediction made in this forced-
choice situation proves wrong. When predictive error carries
a cost, however, baseline vigilance can be set at some higher
value, thereby decreasing the "false alarm" rate. With positive
baseline vigilance, the system responds "I don't know" to an
input that fails to meet the minimum matching criterion. Predictive error rate can hereby be made very small, but with a
reduction in code compression. Search, or hypothesis testing,
ends when the internal control system (Figure 1) determines
that a global consensus has been reached.

Hypothesis testing terminates in a sustained state of resonance that persists as long as an input remains approximately
constant. The resonance generates a focus of attention that
selects the bundle of critical features common to the bottom-
up input and the top-down expectation, or prototype, that is
read-out by the resonating recognition category. Learning of
the critical feature pattern occurs in this resonant and atten-
tive state, hence the term *adaptive resonance*.

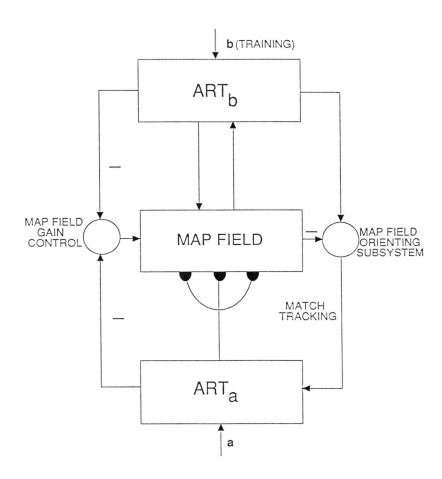

Figure 2. Block diagram of an ARTMAP system. Modules ART_a and ART_b self-organize categories for vector sets **a** and **b**. ART_a and ART_b are connected by an inter-ART module that consists of the Map Field and the control nodes called Map Field gain control and Map Field orienting subsystem. Inhibitory paths are denoted by a minus sign; other paths are excitatory.

5   The ARTMAP System

The main elements of an ARTMAP system are shown in Figure 2. Two modules, ART_a and ART_b, read vector inputs **a** and **b**. If ART_a and ART_b were disconnected, each module would self-organize category groupings for the separate input sets. In the application described below, ART_a and ART_b are fast-learn ART 1 modules coding binary input vectors. ART_a and ART_b are here connected by an inter-ART module that in many ways resembles ART 1. This inter-ART module includes a *Map Field* that controls the learning of an associative map from ART_a recognition categories to ART_b recognition categories. This map does not directly associate exemplars **a** and **b**, but rather associates the compressed and symbolic representations of families of exemplars **a** and **b**. The Map Field also controls match tracking of the ART_a vigilance parameter. A mismatch at the Map Field between the ART_a category activated by an input **a** and the ART_b category activated by the input **b** increases ART_a vigilance by the minimum amount needed for the system to search for and, if necessary, learn a new ART_a category whose prediction matches the ART_b category.

The following sections describe ARTMAP simulations using a machine learning benchmark database. The ARTMAP system is then described mathematically. Further details are found in [6].

6   ARTMAP Simulations that Distinguish Edible and Poisonous Mushrooms

The ARTMAP system was tested on a benchmark machine learning database that partitions a set of vectors **a** into two classes. Each vector **a** characterizes observable features of a mushroom as a binary vector, and each mushroom is classified as edible or poisonous.[19] The database represents the 11 species of genus *Agaricus* and the 12 species of the genus *Lepiota* described in **The Audubon Society Field Guide to**

North American Mushrooms.[16] These two genera constitute most of the mushrooms described in the **Field Guide** from the familiy *Agaricaceae* (order *Agaricales*, class *Hymenomycetes*, subdivision *Basidiomycetes*, division *Eumycota*). All the mushrooms represented in the database are similar to one another: "These mushrooms are placed in a single family on the basis of a correlation of characteristics that include microscopic and and chemical features..." (p. 500).[16] The **Field Guide** warns that poisonous and edible species can be difficult to distinguish on the basis of their observable features. For example, the poisonous species *Agaricus californicus* is described as a "dead ringer" (p. 504) for the Meadow Mushroom, *Agaricus campestris*, that "may be known better and gathered more than any other wild mushroom in North America" (p. 505). This database thus provides a test of how ARTMAP and other machine learning systems distinguish rare but important events from frequently occurring collections of similar events that lead to different consequences.

The database of 8124 exemplars describes each of 22 observable features of a mushroom, along with its classification as poisonous (48.2%) or edible (51.8%). The 8124 "hypothetical examples" represent ranges of characteristics within each species; for example, both *Agaricus californicus* and *Agaricus campestris* are described as having a "white to brownish cap," so in the database each species has corresponding sets of exemplar vectors representing their range of cap colors. There are 126 different values of the 22 different observable features. A list of the observable features and their possible values is given in Table 1. For example, the observable feature of "cap-shape" has six possible values. Consequently, the vector inputs to ART_a are 126-element binary vectors, each vector having 22 1's and 104 0's, to denote the values of an exemplar's 22 observable features. The ART_b input vectors are (1,0) for poisonous exemplars and (0,1) for edible exemplars.

The ARTMAP system learned to classify test vectors rapidly and accurately, and system performance compares favorably with results of other machine learning algorithms applied

TABLE 1: 22 Observable Features and their 126 Values

No.	Feature	Possible Values
1	cap-shape	bell, conical, convex, flat, knobbed, sunken
2	cap-surface	fibrous, grooves, scaly, smooth
3	cap-color	brown, buff, gray, green, pink, purple, red, white, yellow, cinnamon
4	bruises	bruises, no bruises
5	odor	none, almond, anise, creosote, fishy, foul, musty, pungent, spicy
6	gill-attachment	attached, descending, free, notched
7	gill-spacing	close, crowded, distant
8	gill-size	broad, narrow
9	gill-color	brown, buff, orange, gray, green, pink, purple, red, white, yellow, chocolate, black
10	stalk-shape	enlarging, tapering
11	stalk-root	bulbous, club, cup, equal, rhizomorphs, rooted, missing
12	stalk-surface-above-ring	fibrous, silky, scaly, smooth
13	stalk-surface-below-ring	fibrous, silky, scaly, smooth
14	stalk-color-above-ring	brown, buff, orange, gray, pink, red, white, yellow, cinnamon
15	stalk-color-below-ring	brown, buff, orange, gray, pink, red, white, yellow, cinnamon
16	veil-type	partial, universal
17	veil-color	brown, orange, white, yellow
18	ring-number	none, one, two
19	ring-type	none, cobwebby, evanescent, flaring, large, pendant, sheathing, zone
20	spore-print-color	brown, buff, orange, green, purple, white, yellow, chocolate, black
21	population	abundant, clustered, numerous, scattered, several, solitary
22	habitat	grasses, leaves, meadows, paths, urban, waste, woods

Table 1: 126 values of 22 observable features represented in ART_a input vectors.

to the same database. The STAGGER algorithm reached its maximum performance level of 95% accuracy after exposure to 1000 training inputs.[20] The HILLARY algorithm achieved similar results.[14] The ARTMAP system consistently achieved over 99% accuracy with 1000 exemplars, even counting "I don't know" responses as errors. Accuracy of 95% was usually achieved with on-line training on 300–400 exemplars and with off-line training on 100–200 exemplars. In this sense, ARTMAP was an order of magnitude more efficient than the alternative systems. In addition, with continued training, ARTMAP predictive accuracy always improved to 100%. These results are elaborated below.

Almost every ARTMAP simulation was completed in under 2 minutes on an IRIS 4D computer, with total time ranging from about 1 minute for small training sets to 2 minutes for large training sets. This is comparable to 2–5 minutes on a SUN 4 computer. Each timed simulation included a total of 8124 training and test samples, run on a time-sharing system with non-optimized code. Each 1–2 minute computation included data read-in and read-out, training, testing, and calculation of multiple simulation indices.

7 On-line Learning

On-line learning imitates the conditions of a human or machine operating in a natural environment. An input **a** arrives, possibly leading to a prediction. If made, the prediction may or may not be confirmed. Learning ensues, depending on the accuracy of the prediction. Information about past inputs is available only through the present state of the system. Simulations of on-line learning by the ARTMAP system use each sample pair (**a**, **b**) as both a test item and a training item. Input **a** first makes a prediction that is compared with **b**. Learning follows as dictated by the internal rules of the ARTMAP architecture.

Four types of on-line simulations were carried out, using

TABLE 2: On-Line Learning

Average number of correct predictions on previous 100 trials

Trial	$\overline{\rho_a} = 0$ no replace	$\overline{\rho_a} = 0$ replace	$\overline{\rho_a} = 0.7$ no replace	$\overline{\rho_a} = 0.7$ replace
100	82.9	81.9	66.4	67.3
200	89.8	89.6	87.8	87.4
300	94.9	92.6	94.1	93.2
400	95.7	95.9	96.8	95.8
500	97.8	97.1	97.5	97.8
600	98.4	98.2	98.1	98.2
700	97.7	97.9	98.1	99.0
800	98.1	97.7	99.0	99.0
900	98.3	98.6	99.2	99.0
1000	98.9	98.5	99.4	99.0
1100	98.7	98.9	99.2	99.7
1200	99.6	99.1	99.5	99.5
1300	99.3	98.8	99.8	99.8
1400	99.7	99.4	99.5	99.8
1500	99.5	99.0	99.7	99.6
1600	99.4	99.6	99.7	99.8
1700	98.9	99.3	99.8	99.8
1800	99.5	99.2	99.8	99.9
1900	99.8	99.9	99.9	99.9
2000	99.8	99.8	99.8	99.8

Table 2: On-line learning and performance in forced choice ($\overline{\rho_a} = 0$) or conservative ($\overline{\rho_a} = 0.7$) cases, with replacement or no replacement of samples after training.

two different baseline settings of the ART_a vigilance parameter ρ_a: $\overline{\rho_a} = 0$ (forced choice condition) and $\overline{\rho_a} = 0.7$ (conservative condition); and using sample replacement or no sample replacement. With sample replacement, any one of the 8124 input samples was selected at random for each input presentation. A given sample might thus be repeatedly encountered while others were still unused. With no sample replacement, a sample was removed from the input pool after it was first encountered. The replacement condition had the advantage that repeated encounters tended to boost predictive accuracy. The no-replacement condition had the advantage of having learned from a somewhat larger set of inputs at each point in the simulation. The replacement and no-replacement conditions had similar performance indices, all other things being equal. Each of the 4 conditions was run on 10 independent simulations. With $\overline{\rho_a} = 0$, the system made a prediction in response to every input. Setting $\overline{\rho_a} = 0.7$ increased the number of "I don't know" responses, increased the number of ART_a categories, and decreased the rate of incorrect predictions to nearly 0%, even early in training. The $\overline{\rho_a} = 0.7$ condition generally outperformed the $\overline{\rho_a} = 0$ condition, even when incorrect predictions and "I don't know" responses were both counted as errors. The primary exception occurred very early in training, when a conservative system gives the large majority of its no-prediction responses.

Results are summarized in Table 2. Each entry gives the number of correct predictions over the previous 100 trials (input presentations), averaged over 10 simulations. For example, with $\overline{\rho_a} = 0$ in the no-replacement condition, the system made, on the average, 94.9 correct predictions and 5.1 incorrect predictions on trials 201–300. In all cases a 95% correct-prediction rate was achieved before trial 400. With $\overline{\rho_a} = 0$, a consistent correct-prediction rate of over 99% was achieved by trial 1400, while with $\overline{\rho_a} = 0.7$ the 99% consistent correct-prediction rate was achieved earlier, by trial 800. Each simulation was continued for 8100 trials. In all four cases, the minimum correct-prediction rate always exceeeded 99.5% by trial 1800 and always exceeded 99.8% by trial 2800. In all cases, across the total of 40 simulations summarized in Table 2, 100% correct prediction was achieved on the last 1300 trials of each run.

Note the relatively low correct-prediction rate for $\overline{\rho_a} = 0.7$ on the first 100 trials. In the conservative mode, a large number of inputs initially make no prediction. With $\overline{\rho_a} = 0.7$ an average total of only 2 *incorrect* predictions were made on each run of 8100 trials. Note too that Table 2 underestimates prediction accuracy at any given time, since performance almost always improves during the 100 trials over which errors are tabulated.

8　Off-line Learning

In off-line learning, a fixed training set is repeatedly presented to the system until 100% accuracy is achieved on that set. For training sets ranging in size from 1 to 4000 samples, 100% accuracy was almost always achieved after one or two presentations of each training set. System performance was then measured on the test set, which consisted of all 8124 samples not included in the training set. During testing no further learning occurred.

The role of repeated training set presentations was examined by comparing simulations that used the 100% training set accuracy criterion with simulations that used only a single presentation of each input during training. With only a few exceptions, performance was similar. In fact for $\overline{\rho_a} = 0.7$, and for small training sets with $\overline{\rho_a} = 0$, 100% training-set accuracy was achieved with single input presentations, so results were identical. Performance differences were greatest for $\overline{\rho_a} = 0$ simulations with mid-sized training sets (60–500 samples), when 2–3 training set presentations tended to add a few more ART_a learned category nodes. Thus, even a single presentation of training-then-testing inputs, carried out on-line, can be made to work almost as well as off-line training that uses repeated presentations of the training set. This is an important benefit of fast learning controlled by a match tracked search.

Under all training conditions, each of the 8124 ART_a input vectors is a 126-dimensional binary vector with 22 positive entries. Simulation dynamics are illustrated by projecting these vectors onto the first two principal components of the data set.[15] These two components represent 31% of the total variance of the data set.

Figure 3a shows the projections of all 3916 exemplars representing poisonous mushrooms, and Figure 3b shows the 4208 exemplars representing edible mushrooms. These figures show that, in these two dimensions, certain clusters are readily distinguishable, such as the clusters of poisonous samples on the top and left portions of Figure 3a. However, poisonous and edible samples are densely mixed near the positive x-axis.

9   Off-line Forced-Choice Learning

The simulations summarized in Figure 4 and Table 3 illustrate off-line learning with $\overline{\rho_a} = 0$. In this forced choice case, each ART_a input led to a prediction of poisonous or edible. The number of test set errors with small training sets was relatively large, due to the forced choice.

Figure 4 shows the evolution of test set errors as the training set is increased in size from 5 to 500. In Figure 4a, a set of 5 randomly chosen exemplars (3 poisonous, 2 edible) established 2 ART_a categories (1 poisonous, 1 edible) during training. For each of the 8119 test set exemplars, the system was forced to choose between poisonous and edible, even if no category representation was a close match. The system made 73.0% correct predictions. Many of the errors were in the dense cluster of poisonous exemplars in the upper quarter of the graph (Figure 3a). By chance, this cluster was not represented in the 5-sample training set.

Table 3 summarizes the average results over 10 simulations at each size training set. For example, with very small, 5-sample training sets, the system established between 1 and

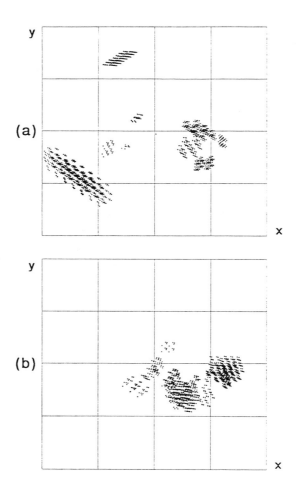

Figure 3. Mushroom observable feature data projected onto first 2 principal components. Each point represents a 126-dimensional ART_a input vector. Axes are scaled to run from -1 to $+1$. (a) 3916 exemplars representing poisonous mushrooms (48.2%). (b) 4208 exemplars representing edible mushrooms (51.8%).

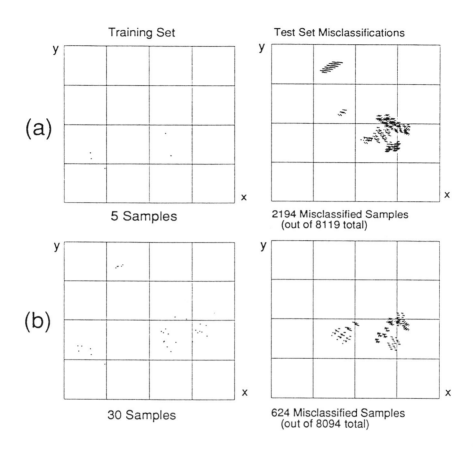

Figure 4. Training sets of increasing size (left column) and test set exemplars that were incorrectly classified (right column), projected onto first two principal components. Baseline vigilance $\overline{\rho_a}$ equals 0. (a) With a 5-sample training set that established 2 ART_a categories, the test set of 8119 inputs made 2194 errors (27.0%). On 10 other 5-sample runs, the number of ART_a categories ranged from 1 to 5 and the error rate ranged from 5.8% to 48.2%, averaging 26.9%. (b) With a 30-sample training set that established 3 ART_a categories, the test set of 8094 inputs made 624 errors (7.7%). On 10 other 30-training sample runs, the number of ART_a categories ranged from 4 to 6; and the error rate ranged from 6.7% to 25.1%, averaging 12.4%.

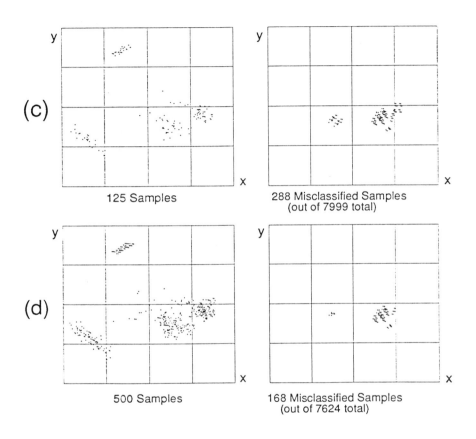

Figure 4 (continued). (c) With a 125-sample training set that established 9 ART_a categories, the test set of 7999 inputs made 288 errors (3.6%). On 10 other 125-training sample runs, the number of ART_a categories ranged from 5 to 14, and the error rate ranged from 1.2% to 8.5%, averaging 4.4%. (d) With a 500-sample training set that established 15 ART_a categories, the test set of 7624 inputs made 168 errors (2.2%). On 10 other 500-training sample runs, the number of ART_a categories ranged from 9 to 22; and the error rate ranged from 0.7% to 3.1%, averaging 1.6%.

TABLE 3: Off-Line Forced-Choice Learning

Training Set Size	Average % Correct (Test Set)	Average % Incorrect (Test Set)	Number of ART_a Categories
3	65.8	34.2	1–3
5	73.1	26.9	1–5
15	81.6	18.4	2–4
30	87.6	12.4	4–6
60	89.4	10.6	4–10
125	95.6	4.4	5–14
250	97.8	2.2	8–14
500	98.4	1.6	9–22
1000	99.8	0.2	7–18
2000	99.96	0.04	10–16
4000	100	0	11–22

Table 3: Off-line forced choice ($\overline{\rho_a} = 0$) ARTMAP system performance after training on input sets ranging in size from 3 to 4000 exemplars. Each line shows average correct and incorrect test set predictions over 10 independent simulations, plus the range of learned ART_a category numbers.

5 ART_a categories, and averaged 73.1% correct responses on the remaining 8119 test patterns. Success rates ranged from chance (51.8%, 1 category) in one instance where all 5 training set exemplars happened to be edible, to surprisingly good (94.2%, 2 categories). The range of success rates for fast-learn training on very small training sets illustrates the statistical nature of the learning process. Intelligent sampling of the training set or, as here, good luck in the selection of representative samples, can dramatically alter early success rates. In addition, the evolution of internal category memory structure, represented by a set of ART_a category nodes and their top-down learned expectations, is influenced by the selection of early exemplars. Nevertheless, despite the individual nature of learning rates and internal representations, all the systems eventually converge to 100% accuracy on test set exemplars using only (approximately) 1/600 as many ART_a categories as there are inputs to classify.

Figure 4 and Table 3 summarize the rate at which learning converges to 100% accuracy. In Figure 4b, 25 exemplars were added to the 5 used for Figure 4a, and the resulting 30-sample training set was presented to a new ARTMAP system. The 25 additional training exemplars increased the number of ART_a categories to 3 and improved the test set correct-prediction rate to 92.3%. The addition of poisonous training exemplars in the upper quarter of the graph eliminated all errors there. However, errors persisted for exemplars near the positive x-axis. On 10 other simulations with 30-sample training sets, the correct prediction rate averaged 87.6% and ranged from 74.9% (4 categories) to 93.3% (6 categories).

The simulation that generated Figure 4c added 95 training samples to the 30 used for Figure 4b. The number of ART_a categories increased to 9 and the correct prediction rate increased to 96.4%. On 10 other simulations with 125 randomly chosen training exemplars, the correct-prediction rate averaged 95.6%, ranging from 91.5% (10 categories) to 98.8% (9 categories).

The simulation of Figure 4d added 375 samples to the set used in Figure 4c. This 500-sample training set increased the correct prediction rate to 97.8% on the test set, establishing 15 categories. On 10 other runs, each with 500 randomly chosen training exemplars, the correct-prediction rate averaged 98.4%, ranging from 96.9% (14 categories) to 99.3% (9 categories). The low error rate of this latter 9-category simulation appears to reflect success of early sampling. On other runs, additional categories were added as errors in early category structures were detected.

With 1000-sample training sets, 3 out of 10 simulations achieved 100% prediction accuracy on the 7124-sample test set. With 2000-sample training sets, 8 out of 10 simulations achieved 100% accuracy on the 6124-sample test sets. With 4000-sample training sets, all simulations achieved 100% accuracy on the 4124-sample test sets. In all, 21 of the 30 simulations with training sets of 1000, 2000, and 4000 samples achieved 100% accuracy on test sets. The number of categories established during these 21 simulations ranged from 10 to 22, again indicating the variety of paths leading to 100% correct prediction rate.

10 Off-line Conservative Learning

As in the case of poisonous mushroom identification, it may be important for a system to be able to respond "I don't know" to a novel input, even if the total number of correct classifications thereby decreases early in learning. For higher values of the baseline vigilance $\overline{\rho_a}$, the ARTMAP system creates more ART_a categories during learning and becomes less able to generalize from prior experience than when $\overline{\rho_a}$ equals 0. During testing, a conservative coding system with $\overline{\rho_a} = 0.7$ makes no prediction in response to inputs that are too novel, and thus initially has a lower proportion of correct responses. However, the number of incorrect responses is always low with $\overline{\rho_a} = 0.7$, even with very few training samples, and the 99% correct-response rate is achieved for both forced choice ($\overline{\rho_a} = 0$) and conservative ($\overline{\rho_a} = 0.7$) systems with training sets smaller than 1000 exemplars.

TABLE 4: Off-Line Conservative Learning

Training Set Size	Average % Correct (Test Set)	Average % Incorrect (Test Set)	Average % No-Response (Test Set)	Number of ART_a Categories
3	25.6	0.6	73.8	2–3
5	41.1	0.4	58.5	3–5
15	57.6	1.1	41.3	8–10
30	62.3	0.9	36.8	14–18
60	78.5	0.8	20.8	21–27
125	83.1	0.7	16.1	33–37
250	92.7	0.3	7.0	42–51
500	97.7	0.1	2.1	48–64
1000	99.4	0.04	0.5	53–66
2000	100.0	0.00	0.05	54–69
4000	100.0	0.00	0.02	61–73

Table 4: Off-line conservative $(\overline{\rho_a} = 0.7)$ ARTMAP system performance after training on input sets ranging in size from 3 to 4000 exemplars. Each line shows average correct, incorrect, and no-response test set predictions over 10 independent simulations, plus the range of learned ART_a category numbers.

Table 4 summarizes simulation results that repeat the conditions of Table 3 except that $\overline{\rho_a} = 0.7$. Here, a test input that does not make a 70% match with any learned expectation makes an "I don't know" prediction. Compared with the $\overline{\rho_a} = 0$ case of Table 3, Table 4 shows that larger training sets are required to achieve a correct prediction rate of over 95%. However, because of the option to make no prediction, the average test set error rate is almost always less than 1%, even when the training set is very small, and is less than .1% after only 500 training trials. Moreover, 100% accuracy is achieved using only (approximately) 1/130 as many ART_a categories as there are inputs to classify.

11 ARTMAP Category Structure

Each ARTMAP category code can be described as a set of ART_a feature values on 1 to 22 observable features, chosen from 126 feature values, that are associated with the ART_b identification as poisonous or edible. During learning, the number of feature values that characterize a given category is monotone decreasing, so that generalization within a given category tends to increase. The total number of classes can, however, also increase, which tends to decrease generalization. Increasing the number of training patterns hereby tends to increase the number of categories and decrease the number of critical feature values of each established category. The balance between these opposing tendencies leads to the final net level of generalization.

Table 5 illustrates the long term memory structure underlying the 125-sample forced-choice simulation shown in Figure 4c. Of the 9 categories established at the end of the training phase, 4 are identified as poisonous (P) and 5 are identified as edible (E). Each ART_a category assigns a feature value to a subset of the 22 observable features. For example, Category 1 (poisonous) specifies values for 5 features, and leaves the remaining 17 features unspecified. The corresponding ART_a weight vector has 5 ones and 121 zeros. Note that the fea-

TABLE 5

#	Feature	1=P	2=E	3=E	4=E
1	cap-shape				
2	cap-surface				
3	cap-color				
4	bruises?				
5	odor		none		
6	gill-attachment	free	free		free
7	gill-spacing	close			close
8	gill-size		broad		
9	gill-color				
10	stalk-shape				
11	stalk-root				
12	stalk-surface-above-ring			smooth	smooth
13	stalk-surface-below-ring			smooth	
14	stalk-color-above-ring				
15	stalk-color-below-ring				
16	veil-type	partial	partial	partial	partial
17	veil-color	white	white		white
18	ring-number	one		one	one
19	ring-type			pendant	
20	spore-print-color				
21	population				
22	habitat				
	# coded/category:	2367	1257	387	1889

Table 5a: Critical feature values of the first 4 out of 9 category prototypes learned in the 125-sample simulation illustrated in Figure 4c $(\overline{\rho_a} = 0)$. Categories 1, 5, 7 and 8 are identified as poisonous (P) and categories 2, 3, 4, 6, and 9 are identified as edible (E). These prototypes yield 96.4% accuracy on test set inputs.

#	5=P	6=E	7=P	8=P	9=E
1					
2					
3					
4			yes	no	yes
5		none			
6	free	free	free	free	free
7	close	close	close	close	close
8				narrow	broad
9				buff	
10				tapering	enlarged
11				missing	club
12	smooth	smooth	smooth	smooth	smooth
13					smooth
14	white	white	white	pink	white
15			white		white
16	partial	partial	partial	partial	partial
17	white	white	white	white	white
18		one	one	one	one
19			pendant	evanescent	pendant
20				white	
21	several	several	scattered	several	scattered
22					
# coded/ category:	756	373	292	427	251

Table 5b: Critical feature values of the last 5 out of 9 category prototypes.

TABLE 6

#	Feature	1=E	2=P	3=P	4=E
1	cap-shape				
2	cap-surface				
3	cap-color				
4	bruises?			no	
5	odor	none			
6	gill-attachment	free	free		
7	gill-spacing			close	close
8	gill-size	broad			broad
9	gill-color				
10	stalk-shape				enlarging
11	stalk-root				
12	stalk-surface-above-ring				smooth
13	stalk-surface-below-ring				
14	stalk-color-above-ring				
15	stalk-color-below-ring		white		
16	veil-type	partial	partial	partial	partial
17	veil-color	white	white	white	
18	ring-number		one		one
19	ring-type				pendant
20	spore-print-color				
21	population				
22	habitat				
	# coded/ category:	3099	1820	2197	883

Table 6: Critical feature values of the 4 prototypes learned in a 125-sample simulation with a training set different from the one in Table 6. Prediction accuracy is similar (96.0%), but the ART_a category boundaries are different.

tures that characterize category 5 (poisonous) form a subset of the features that characterize category 6 (edible). Recall that this category structure gave 96.4% correct responses on the 7999 test set samples, which are partitioned as shown in the last line of Table 5. When 100% accuracy is achieved, a few categories with a small number of specified features typically code large clusters, while a few categories with many specified features code small clusters of rare samples.

Table 6 illustrates the statistical nature of the coding process, which leads to a variety of category structures when fast learning is used. Test set prediction accuracy of the simulation that generated Table 6 was similar to that of Table 5, and each simulation had a 125-sample training set. However, the simulation of Table 6 produced only 4 ART_a categories, only one of which (category 1) has the same long term memory representation as category 2 in Table 5. Note that, at this stage of coding, certain features are uninformative. For example, no values are specified for features 1, 2, 3, or 22 in Table 5 or Table 6; and feature 16 (veil-type) always has the value "partial." However, performance is still only around 96%. As rare instances form small categories later in the coding process, some of these features may become critical in identifying exemplars of small categories.

We will now turn to a description of the components of the ARTMAP system.

12 ART Modules ART_a and ART_b

Each ART module in Figures 1 and 2 establishes compressed recognition codes in response to sequences of input patterns **a** and **b**. Associative learning at the Map Field links pairs of pattern classes via these compressed codes. One type of generalization follows immediately from this learning strategy: If one vector **a** is associated with a vector **b**, then any other input that activates **a**'s category node will predict the category of pattern **b**. Any ART module can be used to self-organize the ART_a and ART_b categories. In the application above, **a** and

b are binary vectors, so ART_a and ART_b can be ART 1 modules. The main computations of an ART 1 module will here be outlined. A full definition of ART 1 modules, as systems of differential equations, along with an analysis of their network dynamics, can be found in Carpenter and Grossberg.[2]

In an ART 1 module, an input pattern **I** is represented in field F_1 and the recognition category for **I** is represented in field F_2. We consider the case where the competitive field F_2 makes a choice and where the system is operating in a fast-learn mode.

Fast-learn ART 1 with binary $F_0 \rightarrow F_1$ input vector **I** and choice at F_2 can be simulated by following the rules below. Fields F_0 and F_1 have M nodes and field F_2 has N nodes.

Initial values—Initially all F_2 nodes are said to be *uncommitted*. Weights Z_{ij} in $F_1 \rightarrow F_2$ paths initially satisfy

$$Z_{ij}(0) = \alpha_j, \tag{1}$$

where $\mathbf{Z}_j \equiv (Z_{1j}, \ldots, Z_{Mj})$ denotes the bottom-up $F_1 \rightarrow F_2$ weight vector. Parameters α_j are ordered according to

$$\alpha_1 > \alpha_2 > \ldots > \alpha_N, \tag{2}$$

where

$$0 < \alpha_j < \frac{1}{(\beta + |\mathbf{I}|)} \tag{3}$$

for $\beta > 0$ and for any admissible $F_0 \rightarrow F_1$ input **I**. In the simulations in this article, α_j and β are small.

Weights z_{ji} in $F_2 \rightarrow F_1$ paths initially satisfy

$$z_{ji}(0) = 1. \tag{4}$$

The top-down, $F_2 \rightarrow F_1$ weight vector $(z_{j1}, \ldots, z_{jM})$ is denoted $\mathbf{z}_j$.

F_1 **activation**—The binary F_1 output vector $\mathbf{x} \equiv (x_1, \ldots, x_M)$ is given by

$$\mathbf{x} = \begin{cases} \mathbf{I} & \text{if } F_2 \text{ is inactive} \\ \mathbf{I} \cap \mathbf{z}_J & \text{if the } Jth \ F_2 \text{ node is active.} \end{cases} \tag{5}$$

$F_1 \rightarrow F_2$ **input**—The input T_j from F_1 to the jth F_2 node obeys

$$
T_j = \begin{cases}
|\mathbf{I}|\alpha_j & \text{if } j \text{ is an uncommitted} \\
& \text{node index} \\
|\mathbf{I} \cap \mathbf{z}_j|/(\beta + |\mathbf{z}_j|) & \text{if } j \text{ is a committed} \\
& \text{node index.}
\end{cases} \tag{6}
$$

The set of committed F_2 nodes and update rules for vectors $\mathbf{z}_j$ and $\mathbf{Z}_j$ are defined iteratively below.

F_2 **choice**—If F_0 is active ($|\mathbf{I}| > 0$), the initial choice at F_2 is one node with index J satisfying

$$
T_J = \max_j (T_j). \tag{7}
$$

If more than one node is maximal, one of these is chosen at random. After an input presentation on which node J is chosen, J becomes *committed*. The F_2 output vector is denoted by $\mathbf{y} \equiv (y_1, \ldots, y_N)$.

Search and resonance—ART 1 search ends upon activation of an F_2 category with index $j = J$ that has the largest T_j value and that also satisfies the inequality

$$
|\mathbf{I} \cap \mathbf{z}_J| \geq \rho|\mathbf{I}| \tag{8}
$$

where ρ is the ART 1 vigilance parameter. If such a node J exists, that node remains active, or in *resonance*, for the remainder of the input presentation. If no node satisfies (8), F_2 remains inactive after search, until $\mathbf{I}$ shuts off.

Fast learning—At the end of an input presentation the $F_2 \rightarrow F_1$ weight vector $\mathbf{Z}_J$ satisfies

$$
\mathbf{Z}_J = \mathbf{I} \cap \mathbf{z}_J^{(\text{old})} \tag{9}
$$

where $\mathbf{z}_J^{(\text{old})}$ denotes $\mathbf{z}_J$ at the start of the current input presentation. The $F_1 \rightarrow F_2$ weight vector $\mathbf{Z}_J$ satifies

$$
\mathbf{Z}_J = \frac{\mathbf{I} \cap \mathbf{z}_J^{(\text{old})}}{\beta + |\mathbf{I} \cap \mathbf{z}_J^{(\text{old})}|}. \tag{10}
$$

13 ARTMAP Architecture

The ARTMAP system incorporates two ART modules and an inter-ART module linked by the following rules. ART_a and ART_b are fast-learn ART 1 modules. Inputs to ART_a may, optionally, be in the complement code form. Embedded in an ARTMAP system, these modules operate as outlined above, with the following additions. First, the ART_a vigilance parameter ρ_a can increase during inter-ART reset according to the *match tracking* rule. Second, the Map Field F^{ab} can *prime* ART_b. That is, if F^{ab} sends nonuniform input to F_2^b in the absence of an $F_0^b \rightarrow F_1^b$ input **b**, then F_2^b remains inactive. However, as soon as an input **b** arrives, F_2^b chooses the node K receiving the largest $F^{ab} \rightarrow F_2^b$ input. Node K, in turn, sends to F_1^b the top-down input z_K^b. Rules for match tracking and complement coding are specified below.

Let $\mathbf{x}^a \equiv (x_1^a \ldots x_{Ma}^a)$ denote the F_1^a output vector; let $\mathbf{y}^a \equiv (y_1^a \ldots y_{Na}^a)$ denote the F_2^a output vector; let $\mathbf{x}^b \equiv (x_1^b \ldots x_{Mb}^b)$ denote the F_1^b output vector; and let $\mathbf{y}^b \equiv (y_1^b \ldots y_{Nb}^b)$ denote the F_2^b output vector. The Map Field F^{ab} has N_b nodes and binary output vector $\mathbf{x}$. Vectors $\mathbf{x}^a, \mathbf{y}^a, \mathbf{x}^b, \mathbf{y}^b$, and $\mathbf{x}$ are set to **0** between input presentations.

Map Field learning—Weights w_{jk}, where $j = 1 \ldots N_a$ and $k = 1 \ldots N_b$, in $F_2^a \rightarrow F^{ab}$ paths initially satisfy

$$w_{jk}(0) = 1. \tag{11}$$

Each vector $(w_{j1}, \ldots, w_{jNb})$ is denoted $\mathbf{w}_j$. During resonance with the ART_a category J active, $\mathbf{w}_J \rightarrow \mathbf{x}$. In fast learning, once J learns to predict the ART_b category K, that association is permanent; i.e., $w_{JK} = 1$ for all times.

Map Field activation—The F^{ab} output vector $\mathbf{x}$ obeys

$$\mathbf{x} = \begin{cases} \mathbf{y}^b \cap \mathbf{w}_J & \text{if the Jth } F_2^a \text{ node is active \& } F_2^b \text{ is active} \\ \mathbf{w}_J & \text{if the Jth } F_2^a \text{ node is active \& } F_2^b \text{ is inactive} \\ \mathbf{y}^b & \text{if } F_2^a \text{ is inactive \& } F_2^b \text{ is active} \\ \mathbf{0} & \text{if } F_2^a \text{ is inactive \& } F_2^b \text{]is inactive.} \end{cases} \tag{12}$$

Match tracking—At the start of each input presentation the ART_a vigilance parameter ρ_a equals a baseline vigilance $\overline{\rho_a}$. The Map Field vigilance parameter is ρ. If

$$|\mathbf{x}| < \rho |\mathbf{y}^b|, \tag{13}$$

then ρ_a is increased until it is slightly larger than $|\mathbf{a} \cap \mathbf{z}_J^a| |\mathbf{a}|^{-1}$. Then

$$|\mathbf{x}^a| = |\mathbf{a} \cap \mathbf{z}_J^a| < \rho_a |\mathbf{a}|, \tag{14}$$

where $\mathbf{a}$ is the current ART_a input vector and J is the index of the active F_2^a node. When this occurs, ART_a search leads either to activation of a new F_2^a node J with

$$|\mathbf{x}^a| = |\mathbf{a} \cap \mathbf{z}_J^a| \geq \rho_a |\mathbf{a}| \tag{15}$$

and

$$|\mathbf{x}| = |\mathbf{y}^b \cap \mathbf{w}_J| \geq \rho |\mathbf{y}^b|; \tag{16}$$

or, if no such node exists, to the shut-down of F_2^a for the remainder of the input presentation.

Complement coding—This optional feature arranges ART_a inputs as vectors

$$(\mathbf{a}, \mathbf{a}^c) \equiv (a_1 \ldots a_{Ma}, a_1^c \ldots a_{Ma}^c), \tag{17}$$

where

$$a_i^c \equiv 1 - a_i. \tag{18}$$

Complement coding may be useful if the following set of circumstances could arise: an ART_a input vector $\mathbf{a}$ activates an F_2^a node J previously associated with an F_2^b node K; the current ART_b input $\mathbf{b}$ mismatches $\mathbf{z}_K^b$; and $\mathbf{a}$ is a subset of $\mathbf{z}_J^a$. These circumstances never arise if all $|\mathbf{a}| \equiv$ constant. For the simulations in this article, $|\mathbf{a}| \equiv 22$. With complement coding, $|(\mathbf{a}, \mathbf{a}^c)| \equiv M_a$.

14 ARTMAP Processing

The following nine cases summarize fast-learn ARTMAP system processing with choice at F_2^a and F_2^b and with Map Field vigilance $\rho > 0$. Inputs $\mathbf{a}$ and $\mathbf{b}$ could appear alone, or one before the other. Input $\mathbf{a}$ could make a prediction based on prior learning or make no prediction. If $\mathbf{a}$ does make a prediction, that prediction may be confirmed or disconfirmed by $\mathbf{b}$. The system follows the rules outlined in the previous section assuming, as in the simulations, that all $|\mathbf{a}| \equiv$ constant and that complement coding is not used. For each case, changing weight vectors $\mathbf{z}_J^a, \mathbf{z}_K^b$, and $\mathbf{w}_K$ are listed. Weight vectors $\mathbf{Z}_J^a$ and $\mathbf{Z}_K^b$ change accordingly, by (11). All other weights remain constant.

Case 1: a only, no prediction. Input $\mathbf{a}$ activates a matching F_2^a node J, possibly following ART_a search. All $F_2^a \rightarrow F^{ab}$ weights $w_{Jk} = 1$, so all $x_k = 1$. ART_b remains inactive. With learning $\mathbf{z}_J^a \rightarrow \mathbf{z}_J^{a(\text{old})} \cap \mathbf{a}$.

Case 2: a only, with prediction. Input $\mathbf{a}$ activates a matching F_2^a node J. Weight $w_{JK} = 1$ while all other $w_{Jk} = 0$, and $\mathbf{x} = \mathbf{w}_J$. F_2^b is primed, but remains inactive. With learning, $\mathbf{z}_J^a \rightarrow \mathbf{z}_J^{a(\text{old})} \cap \mathbf{a}$.

Case 3: b only. Input $\mathbf{b}$ activates a matching F_2^b node K, possibly following ART_b search. At the Map Field, $\mathbf{x} = \mathbf{y}^b$. ART_a remains inactive. With learning, $\mathbf{z}_K^b \rightarrow \mathbf{z}_K^{b(\text{old})} \cap \mathbf{b}$.

Case 4: a then b, no prediction. Input $\mathbf{a}$ activates a matching F_2^a node J. All x_k become 1 and ART_b is inactive, as in Case 1. Input $\mathbf{b}$ then activates a matching F_2^b node K, as in Case 3. At the Map Field $\mathbf{x} \rightarrow \mathbf{y}^b$; that is, $x_K = 1$ and other $x_k = 0$. With learning $\mathbf{z}_J^a \rightarrow \mathbf{z}_J^{a(\text{old})} \cap \mathbf{a}$, $\mathbf{z}_K^b \rightarrow \mathbf{z}_K^{b(\text{old})} \cap \mathbf{b}$, and $\mathbf{w}_J \rightarrow \mathbf{y}^b$; i.e., J learns to predict K.

Case 5: a then b, with prediction confirmed. Input $\mathbf{a}$ activates a matching F_2^a node J, which in turn activates a single Map Field node K and primes F_2^b, as in Case 2. When input $\mathbf{b}$ arrives, the Kth F_2^b node becomes active and the prediction is confirmed; that is,

$$|\mathbf{b} \cap \mathbf{z}_K^b| \geq \rho_b |\mathbf{b}|. \tag{19}$$

Note that K may not be the F_2^b node $\mathbf{b}$ would have selected without the $F^{ab} \to F_2^b$ prime. With learning, $\mathbf{z}_J^a \to \mathbf{z}_J^{a(\text{old})} \cap \mathbf{a}$ and $\mathbf{z}_K^b \to \mathbf{z}_K^{b(\text{old})} \cap \mathbf{b}$.

Case 6: a then b, prediction not confirmed. Input $\mathbf{a}$ activates a matching F_2^a node, which in turn activates a single Map Field node and primes F_2^b, as in Case 5. When input $\mathbf{b}$ arrives, (19) fails, leading to reset of the F_2^b node via ART_b reset. A new F_2^b node K that matches $\mathbf{b}$ becomes active. The mismatch between the $F_2^a \to F^{ab}$ weight vector and the new F_2^b vector $\mathbf{y}^b$ sends Map Field activity $\mathbf{x}$ to $\mathbf{0}$, by (12), leading to Map Field reset, by (13). By match tracking, ρ_a grows until (14) holds. This triggers an ART_a search that will continue until, for an active F_2^a node J, $w_{JK} = 1$, and (15) holds. If such an F_2^a node does become active, learning will follow, setting $\mathbf{z}_J^a \to \mathbf{z}_J^{a(\text{old})} \cap \mathbf{a}$ and $\mathbf{z}_K^b \to \mathbf{z}_K^{b(\text{old})} \cap \mathbf{b}$. If the F_2^a node J is uncommitted, learning sets $\mathbf{w}_J \to \mathbf{y}^b$. If no F_2^a node J that becomes active satisfies (15) and (16), F_2^a shuts down until the inputs go off. In that case, with learning, $\mathbf{z}_K^b \to \mathbf{z}_K^{b(\text{old})} \cap \mathbf{b}$.

Case 7: b then a, no prediction. Input $\mathbf{b}$ activates a matching F_2^b node K, then $\mathbf{x} = \mathbf{y}^b$, as in Case 3. Input $\mathbf{a}$ then activates a matching F_2^a node J with all $w_{Jk} = 1$. At the Map Field, $\mathbf{x}$ remains equal to $\mathbf{y}^b$. With learning, $\mathbf{z}_J^a \to \mathbf{z}_J^{a(\text{old})} \cap \mathbf{a}$, $\mathbf{w}_J \to \mathbf{y}^b$, and $\mathbf{z}_K^b \to \mathbf{z}_K^{b(\text{old})} \cap \mathbf{b}$.

Case 8: b then a, with prediction confirmed. Input $\mathbf{b}$ activates a matching F_2^b node K, then $\mathbf{x} = \mathbf{y}^b$, as in Case 7. Input $\mathbf{a}$ then activates a matching F_2^a node J with $w_{JK} = 1$ and all other $w_{Jk} = 0$. With learning $\mathbf{z}_J^a \to \mathbf{z}_J^{a(\text{old})} \cap \mathbf{a}$ and $\mathbf{z}_K^b \to \mathbf{z}_K^{b(\text{old})} \cap \mathbf{b}$.

Case 9: b then a, prediction not confirmed. Input $\mathbf{b}$ activates a matching F_2^b node K, then $\mathbf{x} = \mathbf{y}^b$ and input $\mathbf{a}$ activates a matching F_2^a node, as in Case 8. However (16) fails and $\mathbf{x} \to \mathbf{0}$, leading to a Map Field reset. Match tracking resets ρ_a as in Case 6, ART_a search leads to activation of an F_2^a node (J) that either predicts K or makes no prediction, or F_2^a shuts down. With learning $z_K^b \to z_K^{b(\mathrm{old})} \cap \mathbf{b}$. If J exists, $z_J^a \to z_J^{a(\mathrm{old})} \cap \mathbf{a}$; and if J initially makes no prediction, $\mathbf{w}_J \to \mathbf{y}^b$, i.e., J learns to predict K.

15 ARTMAP as a Self-Organizing Expert System

The ARTMAP architecture helps to explain how, as we move freely through the world, we can attend to both familiar and novel objects, and can rapidly learn to recognize, test hypotheses about, and learn to name novel objects without unselectively disrupting our memories of familiar objects. ARTMAP provides a rigorous example of fast, yet stable, online recognition learning, hypothesis testing, and adaptive naming in response to an arbitrary stream of input patterns.

A successful autonomous agent must be able to learn about rare events that have important consequences, even if these rare events are similar to frequent events with very different consequences. Survival may hereby depend on fast learning in a *nonstationary* environment. Many learning schemes are, in contrast, slow learning models that average over individual event occurrences and are degraded by learning instabilities in a nonstationary environment.[4,12] ARTMAP is capable of recognizing such rare events, as Table 5 illustrates.

An efficient recognition system also needs to be capable of many-to-one learning. For example, each of the different exemplars of the font for a prescribed letter may generate a single compressed representation that serves as a visual recognition category, say at level F_2^a of ART_a. This exemplar-to-category transformation is a case of many-to-one learning. In addition, many different fonts—including lower case and upper case printed fonts and scripts of various kinds—can all lead to the same verbal name for the letter, say at level F_1^b of ART_b. This is a second sense in which learning may be many-to-one.

Learning may also be one-to-many, so that a single object can generate many different predictions or names. For example, upon looking at a banana, one may classify it as an oblong object, a fruit, a banana, a yellow banana, and so on. A flexible knowledge system may thus need to represent in its memory many predictions for each object, and to make the best prediction for each different context in which the object is embedded. Figure 4 and Table 5 illustrate how ARTMAP incorporates these properties.

Why does not an autonomous recognition system get trapped into learning only that interpretation of an object which is most salient given the system's initial biases? One factor is the ability of that system to reorganize its recognition, hypothesis testing, and naming operations based upon its predictive success or failure. For example, a person may learn a visual recognition category based upon seeing bananas of various colors (or mushrooms with various observable features!) and associate that category with a certain taste (or poisonous/edible consequences). Due to the variability of color features compared with those of visual form, this learned recognition category may incorporate form features more strongly than color features. However, the color green may suddenly, and unexpectedly, become an important differential predictor of a banana's taste.

The different taste of a green banana triggers hypothesis testing that shifts the focus of visual attention to give greater weight, or salience, to the banana's color features without negating the importance of the other features that define a banana's form. A new visual recognition category can hereby form for green bananas, and this category can be used to accurately predict the different taste of green bananas. The new, finer category can form, moreover, without recoding either the previously learned generic representation of bananas or their taste association. Future representations may also form that incorporate new knowledge about bananas, without disrupting the representations that are used to predict their different tastes.

Predictive feedback hereby provides one means whereby many-to-one and one-to-many recognition and prediction codes can form through time, by using hypothesis testing and attention shifts that support new recognition learning without forcing unselective forgetting of previous knowledge. In this sense, ARTMAP and more generally, Predictive ART architectures, provide examples of a new class of self-organizing expert systems that can learn to predict their environment without learning explicit rules.

Bibliography

[1] Carpenter, G.A. (1989). Neural network models for pattern recognition and associative memory. *Neural Networks*, **2**, 243-257.

[2] Carpenter, G.A. and Grossberg, S. (1987a). A massively parallel architecture for a self-organizing neural pattern recognition machine. *Computer Vision, Graphics, and Image Processing*, **37**, 54-115.

[3] Carpenter, G.A. and Grossberg, S. (1987b). ART 2: Stable self-organization of pattern recognition codes for analog input patterns. *Applied Optics*, **26**, 4919-4930.

[4] Carpenter, G.A. and Grossberg, S. (1988). The ART of adaptive pattern recognition by a self-organizing neural network. *Computer*, **21**, 77-88.

[5] Carpenter, G.A., and Grossberg, S. (1990). ART 3: Hierarchical search using chemical transmitters in self-organizing pattern recognition architectures. *Neural Networks*, **3**, 129-152.

[6] Carpenter, G.A., Grossberg, S. and Reynolds, J. (1991). ARTMAP: Supervised real-time learning and classification of nonstationary data by a self-organizing neural network. *IEEE Expert*, **6**, in press.

[7] Grossberg, S. (1976a). Adaptive pattern classification and universal recoding, I: Parallel development and coding of

neural feature detectors. *Biological Cybernetics*, **23**, 121-134.

[8] Grossberg, S. (1976b). Adaptive pattern classification and universal recoding, II: Feedback, expectation, olfaction, and illusions. *Biological Cybernetics*, **23**, 187-202.

[9] Grossberg, S. (1982). **Studies of mind and brain: Neural principles of learning, perception, development, cognition, and motor control.** Boston: Reidel Press.

[10] Grossberg, S. (Ed.) (1987a). **The adaptive brain, I: Cognition, learning, reinforcement, and rhythm.** Amsterdam: Elsevier/North-Holland.

[11] Grossberg, S. (Ed.) (1987b). **The adaptive brain, II: Vision, speech, language, and motor control.** Amsterdam: Elsevier/North-Holland.

[12] Grossberg, S. (1988a). Nonlinear neural networks: Principles, mechanisms, and architectures. *Neural Networks*, **1**, 17-61.

[13] Grossberg, S. (Ed.) (1988b). **Neural networks and natural intelligence.** Cambridge, MA: MIT Press.

[14] Iba, W., Wogulis, J., and Langley, P. (1988). Trading off simplicity and coverage in incremental concept learning. In **Proceedings of the 5th international conference on machine learning.** Ann Arbor, MI: Morgan Kaufmann, 73-79.

[15] Kendall, M.G. and Stuart, A. (1966). **The advanced theory of statistics, Volume 3.** New York: Haffner, Chapter 43.

[16] Lincoff, G.H. (1981). **The Audubon Society field guide to North American mushrooms.** New York: Alfred A. Knopf.

[17] Parker. D.B. (1982). Learning-logic. Invention Report S81-64, File 1, Office of Technology Licensing, Stanford University.

[18] Rumelhart, D.E. and McClelland, J.L. (Eds.), (1986). **Parallel distributed processing, Volume 1.** Cam-

bridge, MA: MIT Press.

[19] Schlimmer, J.S. (1987a). Mushroom database. UCI Repository of Machine Learning Databases. (aha@ics.uci.edu)

[20] Schlimmer, J.S. (1987b). Concept acquisition through representational adjustment (Technical Report 87-19). Doctoral dissertation, Department of Information and Computer Science, University of California at Irvine.

[21] Werbos, P. (1974). Beyond regression: New tools for prediction and analysis in the behavioral sciences. Cambridge, MA: Harvard University.

[22] Werbos, P. (1982). Applications of advances in nonlinear sensitivity analysis. In A.V. Balakrishnan, M. Thoma, R.F. Drenick, and F. Kozin (Eds.), **Lecture notes in control and information sciences, Volume 38: System modeling and optimization.** New York: Springer-Verlag.

†Supported in part by BP (98-A-1204), DARPA (AFOSR 90-0083), and the National Science Foundation (NSF IRI-90-00539).

‡Supported in part by the Air Force Office of Scientific Research (AFOSR 90-0175 and AFOSR 90-0128), the Army Research Office (ARO DAAL-03-88-K0088), and DARPA (AFOSR 90-0083).

§Supported in part by DARPA (AFOSR 90-0083).

Acknowledgements: The authors wish to thank Carol Y. Jefferson for her valuable assistance in the preparation of the manuscript.

Hybrid Neural Network Architectures: Equilibrium Systems That Pay Attention [1]

Leon N Cooper
Brown University

Attitudes toward Neural Networks have, in the short span of my memory, progressed from skepticism through romanticism to what we have at present: general realistic acceptance of neural networks as the preferred - most efficient, most economic - solution to certain classes of problems.

In this brief paper I would like to present an outline of what seem to me to be the major issues and some of the outstanding problems that confront us. In addition, I would like to present a brief account of how our own thinking has progressed

Neural Networks come in several broad categories:

1. Relaxation neural networks that can be regarded as methods of approximating non-linear dynamics.

2. Equilibrium neural networks that classify or assign probabilities

3. Equilibrium hybrid neural networks that via feed-forward and/or feed-back show some properties of relaxation of dynamic networks and display such phenomena as selective attention.

In what follows, we present hybrid equilibrium neural networks that are designed for high efficiency in classification and/or prob-

[1] The work on which this article is based was supported in part by the National Science Foundation, the Army Research Office, the Office of Naval Research and Nestor Incorporated.

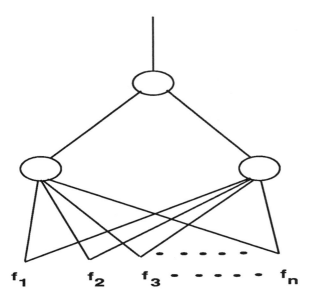

Figure 1

ability ranking and which further have some of the properties of relaxation networks and display selective attention.

Neural networks, in general, do not give optimal solutions. We may regard them in many ways as giving sometimes adequate solutions, sometimes very rapidly. Even training a 3-neuron network as has been shown by Blum and Rivest (Blum 89) is NP-complete. Training a general network is NP-complete, even with only three examples and with two-bit inputs and in some cases they can't even approximate well (Judd 87).

Suppose we attempt to train a general neural network made of the usual individual elements (Fig. 1), let us say one with m levels k_m hidden or internal units per level as in Figure 2, using the generalized gradient descent method (Back Propagation) (Werbos, 74; Rumelhart 86).

The network can be characterized as a non-linear mapping of an input, f, into an output

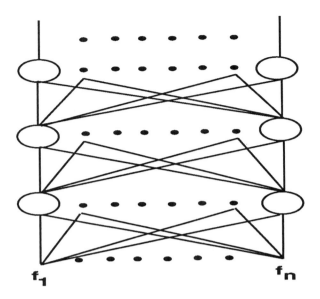

Figure 2

$$M[f] \tag{1}$$

We can construct an energy function as follows:

$$E = \frac{1}{2} \sum_A (t^A - M[f^A])^2 \tag{2}$$

Where t^A is the desired (or target) response to the input f^A.

A general picture of the energy as a function of the neural network weights and thresholds is shown in figure 3. It displays many local minima that are far from the desired solution.

The object of the search is to find a solution, if one exists, of zero energy (all of the outputs precisely as desired). The gradient descent method guarantees that at each modification, the energy remains unchanged or decreases. But finding an adequate solution to this problem can be harder than finding the proverbial needle in an actual haystack.

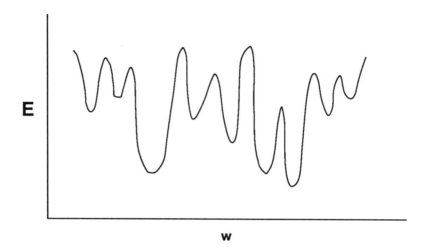

E

W

Figure 3

If, for example, the best solution is a network of 'weakly coupled' sub-networks as in figure 4. It is highly unlikely, that by a method of gradient descent, we can find this solution among all the other possibilities.

Referring to Figure 3, as anyone who has used back propagation knows, the starting point is often as important as the method of descent; one starts over and over to try to find an adequate solution. Since the starting point is determined by the data presented and the choice of initial weights, the problem is one of choosing these in an appropriate fashion that will allow one to descend to an appropriate solution.

As most workers in the field have concluded, the general black learning box is a romantic illusion, and what we are now doing is constructing specific architectures for classes of problems. We have recognized for many years is that different types of neural networks work best in different situations. For example, back propagation or charge clustering networks (Scofield 88 a, b) enable us to generate new representations and work extremely well in some situations (such as, for example, the parity problem). They have proved very useful in dimension reduction reducing an original high dimensional

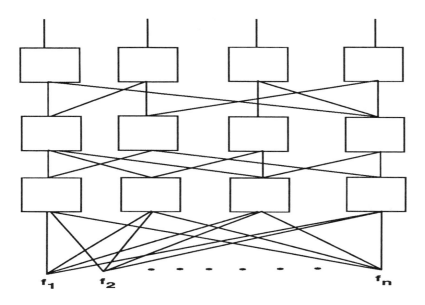

Figure 4

input space, thus helping to overcome what is known as the curse of dimensionality. RCE networks (Reilly 82) are best for classification. They work very well when the feature set is reasonable.

In what follows, we outline procedures we have employed for the past few years in putting together what we have called multi-neural network or hybrid neural network system that consist of different types of neural networks functioning together in a single overall network or system using each to its best advantage. (Reilly 87, 88).

We begin by discussing the problem of classification. To classify a decision space, we must choose an appropriate feature set so that the decision space is reasonably divided. In addition, one has the problem of resolution in each of the features. Classification is possible when the classes are separable, at least in principle, and the appropriate features have been chosen. The RCE solution for classification (newly fashionable as radial basis functions or radius limited perceptron) was introduced to map non-linear boundaries. This method

1. always can do this (produces a Borel covering of the space)

2. always converges

3. learns very rapidly

4. spends most of its learning time at complex boundaries

5. can add classes without retraining since learning is local

6. does not have to specify size of network beforehand

Thus the RCE solution achieves the goal of rapid learning and concentration of effort on difficult regions. Among the problems of RCE, it does not work well if

1. classification is not possible

2. features are badly chosen

Also, the RCE solution is not economical in number of prototypes; it is not efficient for serial computation

If classification is not possible, the RCE neural network has been generalized to assign probabilities. [Scofield 1987]

Dealing with the question of economy, we note that in spaces higher than two dimensions, no computationally efficient method exists to delineate geographies. However, the brain, inspiration for networks, very likely performs this function using many neurons in parallel. Further the problem of computational efficiency, important for simulations on Von-Neuman computers, would likely become much less significant as parallel hardware (neural network chips) become available.

In many cases, features are chosen initially in a manner that allows some classification and results in confusion regions. This problem is attacked using hybrid architectures. In one situation for a given set of features, the decision space appears as in figure 5.

For another set of features, the space might be divided as shown in Figure 6.

To the extent that the feature space is well divided, a method such as that of RCE that has been described in detail elsewhere does

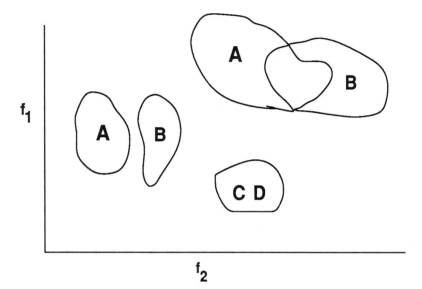

Figure 5

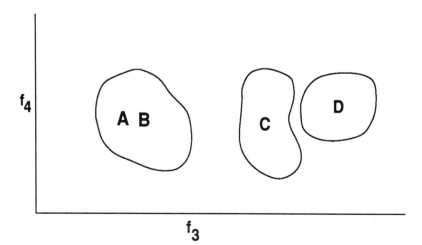

Figure 6

excellent and very rapid classification. (e.g. Reilly 82) Referring to Figure 5, there will be no problem to separate and A and B regions for the feature space for f_1, f_2 . Referring to Figure 6, there will be no problem in classifying the C and D regions for the feature space f_3, f_4. However, the classification of A and B is not possible using the features of f_3 and f_4 whereas the classification of C and D will not be possible using features f_l and f_2. In Figure 5 we see also another domain in which A and B are partially separated and partially ov⁻⁻lap.

Of course, it happens very often that no set of features can completely separate the classes. In such a situation one would need probablistic estimaᵗ⁻s (Scofield, 87).

To resolve sucn problems, we constructed what we call multi-neural network/coupled learning systems. The behavior of such systems has been described in detail elsewhere. [Reilly 1987] Such coupled learning systems automatically assign the classification task to the appropriate network as indicated in Figures 7and 8. The input A is assigned to the sub-network one where it is classified, while the input C is automatically assigned to sub-network 2 where it is classified. An extremely important point is that one does not have to know in advance which network will classify which inputs. Coupled learning assigns the appropriate network as part of the learning procedure.

Why not, we might ask, put the four features f_1, f_2, f_3, f_4 , into a single network. The simplest way to understand the advantage of the multi-neural network system is to consider the problem of resolution.

Suppose that one has n features, with N bit total input capacity. Divided equally, one has N/n bits for each feature. But it might be necessary in order to make some distinctions to have more than N/n bits for certain features. Consider, for example, the problem of distinguishing a U from a V. Some of the early multi-neural network units might properly classify A's and B's, but deliver a confusion for U's and V's; that is to say, deliver the judgement that the incoming entry is either a U or V. Now this is regarded as valuable information, because this confusion region can be directed to a network that can separate the confusion. In effect, this network is constructed as a

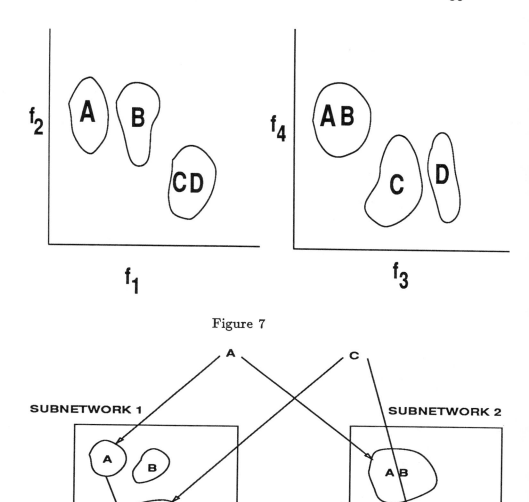

Figure 7

Figure 8

specialist where all of the resolution might be concentrated at the lower part of the figure. This is useful for separating U's and V's, but is not necessarily useful for separating other characters.

What we see here then, is that if one can automatically train a system of networks to perform functions such as this U, V separation, we are, in fact, using equilibrium networks in a manner that is reminicent of relaxation networks. Instead of feeding the output back to the same network, one is, in effect, feeding the output of one network into another. Another way of looking at this is to regard this as building selective attention into an equilibrium network. What the network is doing, is making a preliminary classification, saying that the class is either U or V; then as we do ourselves, it focuses attention on the element that will distinguish U's from V's. What the network does is to pass the provisional classification to a network which is a specialist at separating U's from V's.

It is clear, that in functioning this way, the network can perform much more efficiently than it could if it attempted to make the distinction between U's and V's as part of its overall classification. It can concentrate its entire attention for maximum resolution.on those features that are best at distinguishing U's from V's. In early systems, the network had to choose between the initial feature sets to decide which to emphasize. [Reilly 1988] In later more automated systems, we expect that the networks themselves, as part of the process, will construct the appropriate feature sets: these are what we call hybrid networks. My students as well as my colleagues at Nestor have been working with me on such systems for some time. Some examples are given in the following references. [Zemany 1989, Scofield 1990, Intrator 1990, Scofield 1991].

An early solution to this problem is to

- first construct the multi-neural network architecture, as was done for example in the Nestor system (NDS)

- then to find proper features and their distribution by trial and error

Thus the diagnostics of NDS enabled the user to see which classifications were not being made properly, and to construct a new

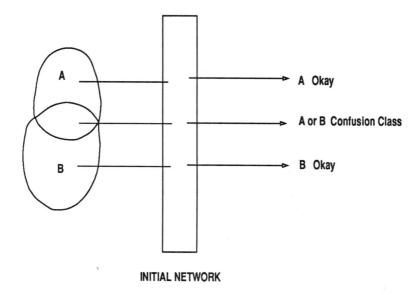

INITIAL NETWORK

Figure 9

network with the appropriate features–this enabled a highly efficient interaction between the user and the system and enabled the users to construct efficient neural networks quickly.

In some cases, such as the ECG analysis system (Carroll 89) the user discovered that the initial features were not sufficient to make the distinctions he desired; he had to add new features. The discovery process is made simpler by a system such as NDS that has diagnostics that allows one to focus quickly on the specific problem.

It is typical of classification problems that a good deal of the input data can be classified easily. What often happens is that it is very difficult to go beyond the initial easy classifications. The systems described above enable one to concentrate on those regions of the classification space that are particularly difficult to separate.

A more sophisticated solution to the problem of constructing a multi-neural network system is to design a system in which the initial multi-neural network system yields some classification and some confusion.

In an architecture we developed called GENSEP [Reilly 1988], the system constructs a separating network specialized to separate the $A - B$ confusion of figure 9 in a very simple way : by taking those features for which $f^A - f^B$ is the largest.

We note that the construction of these separaters is done automatically by the multi-network system and does not have to be put in by hand. A number of networks independently compete to accomplish the required class distinction. The multi-network system learns from experience which networks have the most effective separaters and those determine the final classification.

Hybrid multi-neural network architectures may be regarded as descendents of GENSEP.

- multi-network RCE does initial classification

- confusion regions are fed into sub-networks that can generate non-linear mappings of the original feature set specialized to separate the confusion regions. Back propagation or charge clustering are examples of learning procedures that can perform this function.

- this makes an enormous improvement in training time and accuracy because the time consuming gradient descent learning algorithms need function on very small but critical subsets of the entire data set.

- such a method is related to the advantage of training near boundaries (Ahmad 88).

This last point is illustrated for the perceptron in figure 10.

For Backpropagation using the energy function (2), there is no change in weights and/or thresholds if $t^A = M[f^A]$.

We must select patterns close to the decision region for faster action (figure 11).

Hybrid networks can be thought of as doing this automatically.

- multi - RCE does rapid classification of regions far from boundary

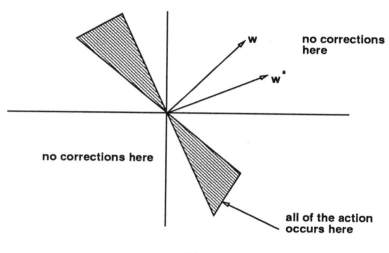

Figure 10

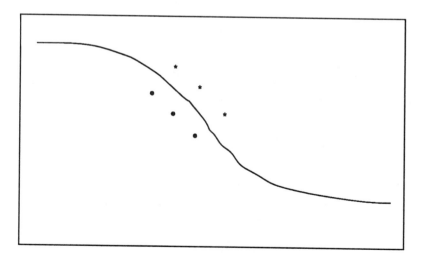

Figure 11

- confusion classes are by their nature near the boundary

- specialized non-linear mappings are fed again into multi-RCE for rapid classification

- note that these specialized mappings can be very different in different parts of the space

We note also that confusion class results can also be fed back to tune the original feature extractors so as to produce better separation.

This very brief summary only suggests the richness and variety of current efforts to enhance the efficacy of neural network architectures. What should be clear is that the question is no longer whether such architectures will prove to be useful. Rather this issue has become, which among these architectures, along with supporting hardware, is fastest, cheapest and/or most accurate. For a specific task, which is best.

Bibliography

[1] [Reilly 88] "GENSEP: A Multiple Neural Network Learning System with Modifiable Network Topology," Douglas Reilly, Christopher L. Scofield, Leon N. Cooper and Charles Elbaum. Abstracts of the First Annual International Neural Network Society Meeting, Boston 1988. Neural Networks, vol. 1, supplement 1, 1988.

[2] [Ahmad88] S. Ahmad and G. Tesauro, "Scaling and generalization in neural networks: A case study," in Proc. of the 1988 Connectionist Models Summer School, D.S. Touretzky, G.E. Hinton and T.J. Sejnowski, eds., Morgan Kaufmann Publishers, San Mateo, CA, 1989, pp. 3–10.

[3] [Blum89] A. Blum and R.L. Rivest, "Training a 3-node neural network is NP-complete," in Advances in Neural Information Processing Systems, D.S. Touretzky, ed., Morgan Kaufmann Publishers, San Mateo, CA, 1989, pp. 494–501.

[4] [Carroll 89] T.O. Carroll, H. Ved, D. Reilly, "Neural Network ECG Analysis" IJCNN, Washington, D. C., June 1989; Technical Report Nestor Incorporated.

[5] [Intrator90a] N. Intrator, "Feature extraction using an exploratory projection pursuit neural network," Ph.D. dissertation, Brown University, May 1990.

[6] [Intrator90b] N. Intrator, "Feature extraction using an unsupervised neural network," to appear in Proc. of the 1990 Connectionist Models Summer School, D.S. Touretzky, J.L. Elman and T.J. Sejnowski, eds., Morgan Kaufmann Publishers, San Mateo, CA, 1990.

[7] [Judd87] S. Judd, "Learning in networks is hard," in Proc. IEEE First Int. Conf. on Neural Networks, San Diego, CA, June 1987, vol. II, pp. 685–692.

[8] [Reilly82] D.L. Reilly, L.N. Cooper and C. Elbaum, "A neural model for category learning," Biol. Cybern., vol. 45, 1982, pp. 35–41.

[9] [Reilly87] D.L. Reilly, C.L. Scofield, C. Elbaum and L.N. Cooper, "Learning system architectures composed of multiple learning modules," in Proc. IEEE First Int. Conf. on Neural Networks, San Diego, CA, June 1987, vol. II, pp. 495–503.

[10] [Rumelhart86] D.E. Rumelhart, G.E. Hinton and R.J. Williams, "Learning representations by back-propagating errors," Nature, vol. 332, 1986, pp. 533–536.

[11] [Scofield87] C.L. Scofield, D.L. Reilly, C. Elbaum and L. N. Cooper, "Pattern class degeneracy in an unrestricted storage density memory," in Neural Information Processing Systems, Denver, CO, 1987, D.Z. Anderson, ed., American Institute of Physics, New York, NY, 1988, pp. 674–682.

[12] [Scofield88a] C.L. Scofield, "Learning internal representations in the Coulomb energy network," in Proc. IEEE First Int. Conf. on Neural Networks, San Diego, CA, June 1987, vol. I, pp. 271–276.

[13] [Scofield88b] C.L. Scofield, "Unsupervised learning in the N-dimensional Coulomb network," in Abstracts of the First Annual Int. Neural Network Society Meeting, vol. 1, suppl. 1, 1988, p. 129.

[14] [Scofield90] C.L. Scofield, "Neural network automatic target recognition by active and passive sonar signals," in Proc. of the Conf. on Neural Networks for Automatic Target Recognition, Tyngsboro, MA, May 1990.

[15] [Werbos74] P. Werbos, Beyond Regression: New Tools for Prediction and Analysis in the Behavioral Sciences. Ph.D. dissertation, Harvard Univeristy, 1974.

Neural Networks for Internal Representation of Movements in Primates and Robots*

Rolf Eckmiller, Nils Goerke, Jürgen Hakala
Division of Biocybernetics
Heinrich–Heine–Universität Düsseldorf, Germany

1 Introduction

Numerous physiological, behavioral, and theoretical studies in neuroscience suggest topographical arrangements of spatial and temporal information for motor control in various brain regions [3, 29]. Especially, the parietal cortex [2], the cerebellum [23], and various parts of the precentral cortex [19, 26] in higher mammals have been implicated in such internal representations of space and spatio–temporal events (trajectories) for motor control.

In contrast to neuroscience, the exploration of neural networks for robot motor control [16] does not require the analysis of existing (biological) systems, but rather the synthesis of technically feasible systems. However, the current knowledge of neuroscience may serve as an important 'concept source'. Afterall, the ability of a fly to generate obstacle–avoiding flight trajectories in a green house in real time or the motor skills of a tennis champion are not based on an algebraic–analytical representation of the various mapping operations as in conventional, software–driven computers for robot control, but on poorly understood geometric–topologically represented functions of dynamic neural networks [17].

This paper compiles recent data on the internal representation of

* Supported by Ministery for Research and Technology (BMFT) under grant, ITR 8800F6

space in the primate oculomotor system and on artificial neural networks for path planning, trajectory storage, and inverse kinematics for the motor control of a planar, redundant robot arm. The contributions exemplify the need to bridge the gap between 'Computational Neuroscience' and 'Neuroinformatics' for the mutual benefit of both neuroscience and computer science.

2   Eye Movement Control in Primates

A simple scheme of the horizontal foveal pursuit eye movement system in primates [8, 10] is given in Figure 1. The small hatched rectangle at the top indicates a target projection on the retina (open horizontal bar at the top of Figure 1) at an eccentricity r relative to the foveal center F. Since the goal of foveal pursuit is the continous minimization of the position error r, the occurance of significant eccentricities during pursuit (in the range of up to ± 3–5 degrees) typically indicates a recent difference between target– and eye velocity. Thus, the eccentricity r in the spatial domain can be detected by afferent visual neurons serving as eccentricity detectors (open triangles with tip down). The neural activity of these neurons can be interpreted as neural control signal to change the current eye velocity, or in other words as eye acceleration signal $\ddot{s}$, in the temporal domain. This processing stage is therefore named as spatiotemporal translator (STT).

The model in Figure 1 contains a hypothetical stage MPG as motor program generator under the assumption that foveal pursuit eye movements are based on internally generated pursuit velocity signals, which are continuously being updated by retinal position error signals r proportional to $\ddot{s}$. A neural network model for MPG has been recently proposed [11], which accounts for updating, neural prediction during temporary target disappearance, and memory. This MPG model with an activity peak travelling on a neural triangular lattice is not based on neurophysiological data. The MPG output is assumed here to be represented by gaze– and eye velocity coding neurons, which have been recently discovered in the monkey brain stem [10].

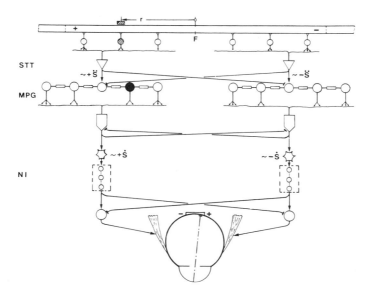

Figure 1: Model of the primate foveal pursuit system for horizontal eye movements. STT: spatiotemporal translator; MPG: motor program generator; NI: neural integrator.

The final processing stage in Figure 1 serves as neural integrator (NI) in order to transform a pure eye velocity control signal into a superposition of eye velocity and position control signals at the level of the oculomotor neurons, which participate in the neural control of one of the six (only two eye muscles for horizontal movements are shown in Figure 1) extraocular eye muscles. Based on neurophysiological data in trained monkeys, a model was recently proposed [9] describing the neural integrator as a cascade of neurons (indicated in Figure 1).

It should be noted that no other motor control system in vertebrates has received more scientific attention than the oculomotor system. However, many functional details and their structural basis are still unclear. The new research area of 'Computational Neuroscience' can be expected to improve this situation.

3 Arm Movement Control in Robots

Typical features of internal representations for robot motor control should include an internal model of the work space, inputs to receive various desired trajectories from different external sources, real–time correction on the basis of sensory information regarding obstacles, and mapping of corrected desired trajectories onto the corresponding real trajectory via modules for inverse kinematics and inverse dynamics of redundant robots.

This wish list has its origins in our current understanding of the features of various biological sensori–motor autonomous systems (animals) as well as in the growing expectations in industry (e.g.: health–, space–, defence–, computer industry) that such important features might be within reach of the currently available technologies. However, given the huge gaps in our theoretical understanding and technological abilities regarding even 'simple' biological motor systems, it seems prudent to begin with limited technical designs as experimental test beds. For this reason, we chose a redundant planar robot arm with 4 joints (4–joint machine = 4JM) to explore alternative neural network topologies for motor control [12, 14, 15].

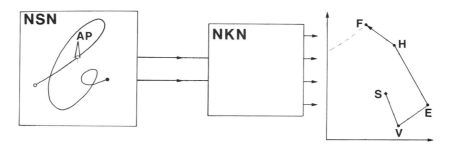

Figure 2: Scheme of motor control of a 4–joint machine with two neural net modules. NSN serves for path planning, storage, and generation of desired trajectories by means of travelling activity peak (AP) on the surface of a neural lattice. NKN maps desired trajectories onto control signals for the four actuators of the 4JM.

Figure 2 gives a scheme of two suggested neural net modules, one for path planning (neural space net = NSN) and one for processing of the inverse kinematics (neural kinematics net = NKN) together with the 4JM, which moves fingertip F in the x/y plane. The following two paragraphs describe recent studies on artificial neural nets for these two functional modules.

3.1   Artificial Neural Nets for Internal Representation of Desired Trajectories

3.1.1   Internal Representation with Neural Nets

Biological neural nets as information processing systems typically generate actions of a motor system as final output. During evolution of the brain, internal representations for many sensory and motor signals appeared. It is common experience, that a desired motor trajectory is independent of the actual orientation or the final joint configuration of the corresponding motor system (a written signature looks the same on a horizontal table, a vertical blackboard or the ceiling, although the final motor commands sent to arm and hand muscles are quite different).

Several artificial neural networks for representation of time dependent events have been suggested in the literature: adaptive neural oscillators as adjustable central pattern generators [7], sequential networks that learn sequences of definite actions [24], embedding fields [20], and modified Hopfield nets [1]. All these networks have in common, that the whole network continuously changes its configuration while generating a given time function. The information is stored in the synaptic weights and the time delays between neurons.

In our approach the information is represented in the neural net as the spatial location of an activity peak travelling over the network structure, for storage or retrieval of a desired trajectory [15, 18]. Adequate network topologies could be lattices, clusters or linear neuron chains, depending on the given motor task (e.g.: grasping, singing, or writing). To perform the mapping operation from instantaneous impulse rate to spatial location [31], we chose pulse processing neurons (see also [4, 6]), with dynamic features similar to biological neurons.

3.1.2   Realization with a Pulse Processing Neural Network

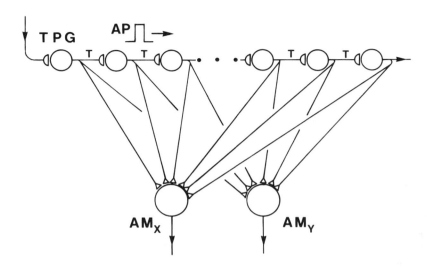

Figure 3: Proposed network structure, capable of learning 2–dimensional trajectories; Temporal Pattern Generator (TPG) realized as linear neuron chain (horizontal sequence of open circles); AP: travelling Activity Peak; Activity Memory (AM$_{X,Y}$), one neuron for each dimension.

In the proposed model the problem of generating temporal sequences is subdivided into two parts, which can be implemented by two neural network subsections with different topology, the Temporal–Pattern–Generator (TPG) and the Activity–Memory (AM). The TPG represents the time course as spatial location of a travelling peak of neural activity. Subsequently, the AM–network modulates the TPG output activity according to the transfer function of the AM–neurons, thus generating a given desired trajectory. The synaptic weights (open triangles) connecting the TPG to the AM–network specify the generation of a temporally varying instantaneous impulse rate. Two different learning schemes have been used to adapt the appropriate synaptic weights during learning of specific desired trajectories.

A possible realization of the proposed network structure (an alternative model has been proposed elsewhere [15]) is shown in Figure 3.

The TPG–module is realized by a linear chain of neurons, which propagates the output from one neuron to the next via synaptic connections (open semi–circles) with time delay (T). Thus, an impulse (AP) initiated at the input neuron is propagated along the TPG chain, activating one neuron after the other.

An AM network (Figure 3) consists for example of two pulse processing neurons $(AM_{x,y})$ with large numbers of synaptic connections from the chain of TPG neurons. An AM neuron assembles the sequence of incoming weighted unit pulses from the TPG, indicated in Figure 4 as Netto input. This input is subsequently transformed into a membrane potential (MP) similar to biological neurons. The pulse train at the output (bottom trace in Figure 4) is generated on the basis of the MP according to a given transfer function of the AM neuron.

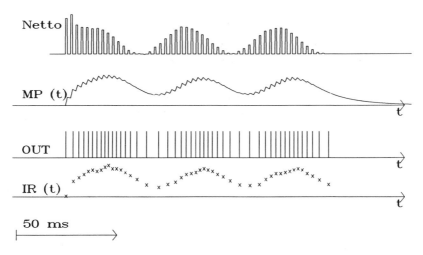

Figure 4: Time dependent processes of an AM neuron: Netto: weighted input pulses to represent postsynaptic potentials (EPSP) of synapses with adaptive weights; MP: membrane potential; OUT: pulse train with sinusoidal modulation of AM output; IR: instantaneous impulse rate of the pulse train OUT.

The synaptic weights at the AM neuron can be adapted during a supervised learning phase (e.g.: delta rule or a modified Hebb learning rule). After only a few (5–9) complete presentations (one AP has traveled along the entire TPG chain from left to right) of the teacher signal (sinusoid as desired MP time course), the desired activity time course is learned by the network. The time dependent events at one of the AM neurons (Figure 3) after learning a sinusoidal time series are shown in Figure 4. The generation of 2–D trajectories can be achieved by simultaneous use of two AM neurons (AM_x for x–component and AM_y for y–component).

3.2 Artificial Neural Nets for Coordinate Transformation

3.2.1 Basic Ideas

In robot control several types of coordinate transformation have to be performed. Often, the coordinate transformation (in general terms a mapping operation) requires that input and output do not have the same number of dimensions. A typical example is the inverse kinematics of redundant manipulators.

For real world problems specific constraints and mechanisms are introduced to avoid joint limits and to achieve cyclic behaviour for periodic trajectories. Since the conventional solutions [25] are computationally extensive, we developed a neural net solution with the potential of real time processing.

Artificial neural nets (e.g. [28]) often need a large amount of training data, and the number of training cycles for a satisfying solution are growing exponentially with the complexity of the task. Even if a–priori knowledge about the system is available, often it cannot be used to preshape the chosen neural net topology. The neural net presented here, is capable of performing the mapping task without learning. The functional proporties of this neural kinematics net (NKN) with several layers are based on neurons with local receptive fields; all neurons of a given class have the same characteristics and are assembled as 2–dimensional neural lattices.

3.2.2 Inverse Kinematics Solution

The inverse kinematics problem is addressed here (Figure 2) for a 4–joint machine (4JM) with joint limits [12, 13, 14]. A small movement of fingertip F in two dimensional space is considered as a typical trajectory element. The movement of fingertip F for each subsequent trajectory element is processed locally. For the proposed local mechanism, we use information about current joint position and desired movement direction (see: paragraph 3.2.4).

The first processing step of this NKN mechanism yields eight vectors, two for each joint [13, 14] as possible movement contributions of the four actuators in F assuming the same small rotations at each joint. The first chosen contribution vector is the one closest to the desired direction for the given trajectory element. A fixed, non–iterative selection process specifies the other three vectors. Subsequently, the contribution vectors must be rescaled twice to adjust the vectorial sum to the desired direction and then to the desired length [13, 14].

The local processing mechanism of NKN produces solutions, which are cyclic for periodic trajectories and keep the joint speed within acceptable limits. Oscillations in some regions of the working area were avoided by incorporating the recent history of the joint movements. Specifically, a change of sign for joint velocities is only allowed, if it has not been changed during several previous steps [21].

Our NKN model for inverse kinematics requires large numbers (at least several thousands) of neurons, which can perform AND–operations between two inputs. Recent data on both sensory and motor maps [5, 30] suggest that these assumed features are biologically plausible.

The NKN neurons are topographically ordered in layered structures, with the ability to perform local operations on inputs spawned from the respectively adjacent layer above. Depending on the layer and neural class, these neurons encode a specific location in space or a specific variable by their activity. Since receptive fields are used, the description of weight–space is equivalent to that of receptive field properties. These receptive field properties depend on a separate, tuning input. This allows for example, to chose the direction of a direction–sensitive neuron by means of a second input. The transfer–function of the neurons is sigmoidal.

The following two paragraphs describe the structure and function of several neural net sub–modules of the NKN.

3.2.3   Neural Net for Position Model

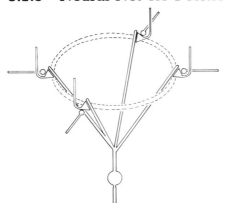

Figure 5: Neural Position Encoder NPE as element of position model (POM). NPE function is based on an AND–operation of limb length information (embedded in a ring–shaped receptive field) and angle–input provided as pre–synaptic tuning signal.

The Position Model (POM) [12, 13, 14] is a sub-module of the NKN. POM consists of four layers; in each layer the varying position of one joint is represented (see Figure 7 for a similar sub–module POM*): rotation angle information of stationary joint S is fed into the top layer for virtual joint V (see Figure 2), which in turn provides position and angle information to specify the position of the adjacent joint E in the next layer and so on, such that in layer four the position of fingertip F is represented.

The key element of POM is the Neural Position Encoder (NPE), which provides connections from a given layer to the next one below. NPEs have overlapping receptive fields and a given layer of NPEs is capable of monitoring a joint position (e.g. E) on the basis of three types of information:

- position of the adjacent joint closer to stationary joint S (here: V), provided as output from the POM layer above,

- length of the corresponding limb (here: V–E) given as radius of the ring–shaped receptive field of all NPEs in this layer (see: Figure 5 and left part of Figure 6), and

- angle between the corresponding limb (here: V–E) and the reference direction (3 o'clock) given as sum of the rotation angles along the chain of joints (here: sum of rotation angles a_S and a_V), which are continuously monitored by angle detecting sensors.

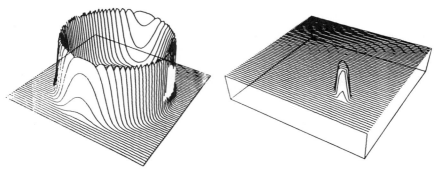

Figure 6: Sub–threshold radially–symmetric receptive field of NPE (left); supra–threshold receptive field of NPE following an AND–operation between angle input and limb–length input (right).

As shown in Figure 5, an NPE receives two types of input signals. The vertical inputs specify the current location of neural activity of NPEs in the layer above. The horizontal inputs specify the corresponding limb angle. For sake of simplicity only a few synaptic and pre–synaptic connections are shown in Figure 5, thus distinguishing only between four possible angles. The real number of synapses is defined by the desired position– and angle resolution.

The function of POM can be briefly described as follows: let's assume that only a few neighboring NPEs in layer V are active and send their activity as vertical input to NPEs in layer E. The fact that the next joint E is always at a fixed distance (V–E) apart from joint V, is embedded in the ring–shaped receptive field of all NPEs in layer E. The task of the NPEs in layer E requires to find the position, which corresponds to the current angle of limb V–E (with regard to 3 o'clock). This angle signal is sent as horizontal pre–synaptic input in one direction (open hexagonals in Figure 5) and contacts only those few neighboring synapses of the selected NPE, which are located on a straight line between signal source and receptive field center.

The resulting receptive field of NPE is a single peak (Figure 6 right). This AND–operation of raising a small portion of the receptive field of one particular NPE to supra–threshold levels, is based on limb length information (receptive field radius) and angle–input. The exact position of a given joint is represented by the sum of weighted locations of a small number of neighboring NPEs.

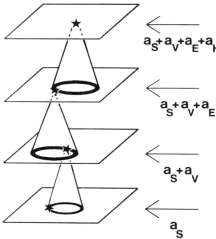

$a_S+a_V+a_E+a_H$

$a_S+a_V+a_E$

a_S+a_V

a_S

Figure 7: Inverse Position Model (POM*) with tuneable receptive fields. Black rings: ensemble of sub–threshold NPEs for a given joint position in the layer above. Stars: Supra–threshold NPEs corresponding to joint positions.

3.2.4 Neural Net for Inverse Kinematics

Implementation of the whole inverse kinematics process requires an inverse position model (POM*), which starts the process described above at fingertip F and ends at shoulder joint S (Figure 7). F is considered as stationary center of the new reference coordinate system. The conical projection beams from a given joint position (star) indicate the location of all NPEs with the appropriate distance to the next joint position. The horizontal input signals to the various layers of POM* (Figure 7) indicate rotation angles (e.g. a_S) of the various joints.

This design allows direct access to angles and distances between fingertip F and each of the joints. POM* contains additional classes of neurons with receptive field properties of distance detectors (D–neurons) and angle–detectors (A–neurons), which are capable of directly monitoring all distances between F and any joint as well as all angles of the direction from F to any joint relative to the reference direction (3 o'clock).

POM* allows to specify the possible movement contributions for each joint for any position of 4JM. The various output signals from POM* serve to select the sequence of four contributing vectors (see: 3.2.2). After rescaling the four contributing vectors so as to achieve a vectorial sum of desired direction and length [13, 21], the actual joint-angle signals are fed back to the POM* as basis for processing the next trajectory–element.

NKN operates without learning, since for each single step, function and position of each neuron is pre–defined. The proposed local operation of finding variable solutions for the inverse kinematics incorporates a–priori knowledge, which could hardly be found with adaptive neural net topologies by means of the currently popular learning rules.

Pre–shaping neural net topologies on the basis of geometrical and theoretical a–priori knowledge is a powerful method in neuroinformatics [17] and can be combined with neural net adaptation during a learning phase. There are conceptual similarities between this kind of neural net design and building clockwork automata (since about 1300) [27].

Bibliography

[1] D. Amit, *Storage and Retrieval of Temporal Sequences*, in: Modeling Brain Function, D. Amit, Cambridge University Press, Ch.5, pp.215–270

[2] R.A. Andersen, G.K. Essick, R.M. Siegel, *The Encoding of Spatial Location by Posterior Parietal Neuron*, Science, 1985, 230, pp.456–458

[3] R.J. Baron, *The Cerebral Computer*, Hillsdale, L. Earlbaum

Publ., 1987

[4] J.R. Beerhold, M. Jansen, R. Eckmiller, *Pulse-Processing Neural Net Hardware with Selectable Topology and Adaptive Weights and Delays*, in: Proc. IEEE, Int. Joint Conf. Neural Networks, San Diego, June 1990, Vol.II, pp.569–574

[5] Y. Burnod, R. Caminiti, P. Johnson, P. Granguillaume, I. Otto, *Model of Visuo–Motor Transformations performed by the Cerebral Cortex to Command Arm Movements at Visual Targets in the 3–D Space*, in: Advanced Neural Computers (R. Eckmiller ed.), Elsevier, North Holland, 1990, pp.33–42

[6] S. Canditt, R. Eckmiller, *Pulse Coding Hardware Neurons that can learn Boolean Functions*, in: Proc. IEEE, Int. Joint Conf. of Neural Networks Washington, January 1990, Vol.II, pp.102–105

[7] K. Doya, S. Yoshizawa, *A Neural Network Model of Temporal Pattern Memory: Adaptive Neural Oscillator Using Continuous–Time Back–Propagation Learning*, Neural Networks, 2, pp.375–386

[8] R. Eckmiller, *Neural Control of Foveal Pursuit versus Saccadic Eye Movements in Primates – Single Unit Data and Models*, IEEE Transactions and Systems, Man, and Cybernetics, SMC–13, 1983, pp.980–989

[9] R. Eckmiller, *The Transition Between Pre–motor Eye Velocity Signals and Oculomotor Eye Position Signals in Primate Brain Stem Neurons During Pursuit*, in: Adaptive Processes in Visual and Oculomotor Systems, E.L. Keller and D.S. Zee (eds.), Pergamon Press, 1986, pp.301–305

[10] R. Eckmiller, *Neural Control of Pursuit Eye Movements*, Physiological Reviews, 67, 1987, pp.797–857

[11] R. Eckmiller, *Computational Model of the Motor Program Generator for Pursuit*, J. Neurosci. Meth., 21, 1987, pp.127–138

[12] R. Eckmiller, *Concept of a 4-Joint Machine with Neural Net Control for the Generation of 2-Dimensional Trajectories*, Neural Networks, 1, Suppl.1, 1988, pp.334

[13] R. Eckmiller, *Neural Networks for Generation of Eye and Arm Movement Trajectories*, in: Neural Programming, M. Ito (ed.), Karger, Basel, 1989, pp.173-187

[14] R. Eckmiller, J. Beckmann, H. Werntges, M. Lades, *Neural Kinematics Net for a Redundant Robot Arm*, Proc. IEEE, Int. Joint Conf. Neural Networks, Washington, June 1989, Vol.II, pp.333-338

[15] R. Eckmiller, *Neural Nets for Sensory and Motor Trajectories*, IEEE Control Systems Magazine, 9, 1989, pp.53-60

[16] R. Eckmiller (ed.), *Advanced Neural Computers*, Elsevier, North Holland, 1990

[17] R. Eckmiller, *Concerning the Emerging Role of Geometry in Neuroinformatics*, in: Parallel Processing in Neural Systems and Computers, R. Eckmiller, G. Hartmann, G. Hauske (eds.), Elsevier, North Holland, 1990, pp.5-8

[18] N. Goerke, M. Schöne, B. Kreimeier, R. Eckmiller, *A Network With Pulse Processing Neurons for Generation of Arbitrary Temporal Sequences*, in: Proc. IEEE, Int. Joint Conf. Neural Networks, San Diego, June 1990, Vol.III, pp.315-320

[19] A. P. Georgopoulos, *On Reaching*, Ann. Rev. Neurosci., 9, 1986, pp.147-170

[20] S. Grossberg, *Some Networks That Can Learn, Remember, and Reproduce any Number of Complicated Space-Time Patterns*, in: J. Mathematics and Mechanics, Vol.19, No.1, July 1969, pp.53-91

[21] J. Hakala, R. Steiner, R. Eckmiller, *Quasi-local Solution of Inverse Kinematics of a Redundant Robot Arm*, in: Proc. IEEE,

Int. Joint Conf. Neural Networks, San Diego, June 1990, Vol.III, pp.321–326

[22] J.M. Hollerbach, K.C. Suh, *Redundancy Resolution of Manipulators with Kinematic Redundancy*, in: Proc. IEEE Int. Conf. Robotics & Automation, 1986, pp.9–14

[23] J.C. Houk, A.R. Gibson, *Sensorimotor Processing through the Cerebellum*, in: New Concepts in Cerebellar Neurobiology, J.S. King (ed.), Alan Liss Inc., 1987, pp.387–416

[24] M.I. Jordan, *Supervised Learning and Systems with Excess Degrees of Freedom*, COINS Technical Report 88–27, MIT Press, Cambridge, Nov. 1988

[25] C.S.G. Lee, *Robot Arm Kinematics, Dynamics and Control*, IEEE Computer, 15, 1982, pp.62–80

[26] R. Lemon, *The Output Map of the Primate Motor Cortex*, TINS, 11, 1988, pp.501–506

[27] K. Maurice, O. Mayr (eds.), *The Clockwork Universe – German Clocks and Automata 1550–1650*, Neale Watson Academic Publ., New York, 1980

[28] D.E. Rumelhart, G.E. Hinton, R.J. Williams, *Parallel Distributed Processing*, D.E. Rumelhart, J.L. McClelland (eds.), MIT Press, Cambridge, Ch.8, 1986, pp.318–362

[29] J.F. Soechting, F. Lacquaniti, C.A. Terzuolo, *Coordination of Arm Movements in Three-dimensional Space. Sensomotor Mapping during Drawing Movement*, Neuroscience, 17, 1986, pp.295–311

[30] D.L. Sparks, J.S. Nelson, *Sensory and Motor Maps in the Superior Colliculus*, Trends in Neuroscience, 10, 1987, pp.312–317

[31] D.C. Tam, *Temporal-Spatial Coding Transformation: Conversion of Frequency-Code to Place-Code via a Time-Delayed Neural Network*, Proc. IEEE, Int. Joint Conf. of Neural Networks, Washington, January 1990, Vol.I, pp.130–133

Recognition and Segmentation of Characters in Handwriting with Selective Attention

Kunihiko Fukushima   and   Taro Imagawa
Faculty of Engineering Science, Osaka University

Keywords: Neural network, Character recognition, Segmentation, Characters in handwriting, Selective attention.

1 Introduction

Machine recognition of individual characters in handwriting is a difficult problem. It cannot be successfully performed by a simple pattern matching method, because each character changes its shape by the effect of the characters before and behind. In other words, even the same character is scripted differently when it appears in different words, in order to be connected smoothly with the characters in front and in the rear.

One of the authors previously proposed a "selective attention model", which has the function of segmenting patterns, as well as the function of recognizing patterns [1],[2],[3]. When a composite stimulus consisting of two patterns or more is presented, the model focuses its attention selectively to one of them, segments it from the rest, and recognizes it. After that, the model switches its attention to recognize another pattern. The model also has the function of associative memory and can restore imperfect patterns. These functions can be successfully performed even for deformed versions of training patterns, which have not been presented during the learning.

We have modified the model and extended its ability to be able to recognize characters in handwriting [4]. This paper briefly introduces the new model and offers a preliminary result of computer simulation.

2   Structure and the Behavior of the Model

The basic framework and behavior of the new model are similar to those of the original model for selective attention [2],[3]. Since a detailed explanation of the original model has already appeared in several papers, we will explain the framework of the model briefly below, and will discuss the parts which are modified from the original model in more detail.

Readers who are already familiar with the original model can skip reading subsections 2.1, 2.3, and 2.5. Main differences from the original model are as follows: The mechanism for the control of the search area, which will be discussed in subsection 2.6, has been newly introduced. The method of gain control and switching attention, which will be discussed in subsections 2.4 and 2.7, has been modified. The new model has a four-staged network instead of three, and the u_S-cells of the first stage have fixed input connections, which are not modifiable, as will be discussed in section 2.2.

2.1   Framework of the Model

The model is a hierarchical multilayered network, and consists of a cascade of many layers of neuron-like cells. The cells are of the analog type: their inputs and outputs take non-negative analog values.

The network has backward as well as forward connections between cells. Figure 1 shows how the different kinds of cells, such as u_S and u_C, are interconnected in the network. Each circle in the figure represents a cell. Although the figure shows only one of each kind of cells in each stage, numerous cells actually exist arranged in a two-dimensional array. We will use notation u_{Cl}, for example, to denote a u_C-cell in the l-th stage, and U_{Cl} to denote the layer of u_{Cl}-cells. The L-th stage is the highest stage of the network. We have $L = 4$ in the model discussed in this paper.

The signals through forward paths manage the function of pattern-recognition, while the signals through backward paths manage the

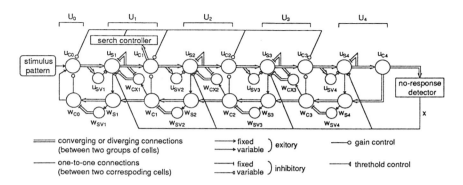

Figure 1: Hierarchical network structure illustrating the interconnections between different kind of cells.

function of selective attention and associative recall.

2.2   Forward Paths

If we consider the forward paths only, the model has almost the same structure and function as the model "neocognitron" [5],[6], which can recognize input patterns robustly, with little effect from deformation, changes in size, or shifts in position.

Cells u_S are feature-extracting cells. They correspond to S-cells in the neocognitron. With the aid of subsidiary inhibitory cell u_{SV}, they extract features from the stimulus pattern. The u_S-cells of the first stage have fixed input connections and extract line components of various orientations. In all other stages higher than the first, u_S-cells have variable input connections, which are reinforced by unsupervised learning.

The u_C-cells, which correspond to C-cells of the neocognitron, are inserted in the network to allow for positional errors in the features of the stimulus. Each u_C-cell has fixed excitatory connections from a group of u_S-cells which extract the same feature, but from slightly different positions. Thus, the u_C-cell's response is less sensitive to shifts in position of the stimulus patterns.

During this process, local features extracted in a lower stage are gradually integrated into more global features. This structure of the network is effective for endowing the network with robustness against deformation in pattern recognition.

The layer of u_C-cells at the highest stage, that is, layer U_{CL}, works as the recognition layer. The response of the cells of this layer shows the final result of pattern recognition. Even when two patterns or more are simultaneously presented to the input layer U_0, usually only one cell corresponding to the category of one of the stimulus patterns is activated in the recognition layer U_{CL}. This is partly because of the competition between u_S-cells by lateral inhibition, and also because of the attention focusing by gain control signals from the backward paths, which will be discussed below.

2.3   Backward Paths

The cells in the backward paths are arranged in the network making a mirror image of the cells in the forward paths. The forward and the backward connections also make a mirror image to each other, but the directions of signal flow through the connections are opposite.

The output signal of the recognition layer U_{CL} is sent back to lower stages through backward paths, and reaches the recall-layer W_{C0} at the lowest stage of the backward paths. The backward signals are made to be transmitted retracing the same route as the forward signals. This is because the cells in the backward paths are made to receive gate signals from the corresponding cells in the forward paths. Guided by the gate signals from the forward paths, the backward signals reach exactly the same positions at which the input pattern is presented.

As mentioned above, usually only one cell is activated in the recognition layer U_{CL}, even when two or more patterns are presented to the input layer U_{C0}. Since the backward signals are sent back only from the activated recognition cell, only the signal components corresponding to the recognized pattern reach the recall-layer W_{C0}. Therefore, the output of the recall-layer can also be interpreted as the result of segmentation, where only components relevant to a single pattern are selected from the stimulus. Even if the stimulus pattern which is now recognized is a deformed version of a training pattern, the deformed pattern is segmented and emerges with its deformed shape.

2.4 Gain Control

The forward cells receive gain-control signals from the corresponding backward cells, and the forward signal flow is facilitated by the gain-control signals from backward cells. More specifically, the gain of each u_C-cell in the forward paths is controlled by a signal from the corresponding w_C-cell.

The method of gain control is somewhat different in the new model from that in the original model. When the w_C-cell is activated, the gain between the inputs and the output of the u_C-cell is increased. (In the original model, the gain of a u_C-cell is decreased when the corresponding w_C-cell is not activated). Thus, only the forward signal flow in the paths in which backward signals are flowing is facilitated.

Since the backward signals are usually sent back only from one activated recognition cell, only the forward paths relevant to the pattern which is now recognized are facilitated. This means that attention is selectively focused on only one of the patterns in the stimulus.

A u_C-cell which receives a strong gain control signal becomes fatigued. It cannot maintain high gain without receiving a large gain-control signal. Once the gain control signal disappears, the gain of the u_C-cell drops rather rapidly, and cannot recover for a long time. This effect of fatigue is effectively used in the model for switching attention to another pattern. It is effective in preventing the model from recognizing the same character twice.

2.5 Threshold Control

When some part of the input pattern is missing and the feature which is supposed to exist there fails to be extracted in the forward paths, the backward signal flow is interrupted there and cannot go down any further. In such a case, the threshold for extracting features is automatically lowered around that area, and the model tries to extract even vague traces of the undetected feature. More specifically, the fact that a feature has failed to be extracted is detected by w_{CX}-cells from the condition that the cells in the backward paths are active but that the corresponding cells in the forward paths are not (Figure 1). The signal from w_{CX}-cells weakens the efficiency of inhibition by u_{SV}-cells, and virtually lowers the threshold for feature-extraction by u_S-cells. Thus, u_S-cells are made to respond even to incomplete features, to which, in the normal state, no u_S-cell would respond.

Once a feature is thus extracted in the forward paths, the backward signal can then be further transmitted to lower stages through the path unlocked by the newly activated forward cell. Hence, a complete pattern, in which defective parts are interpolated, emerges in the recall-layer. From this pattern, noise and blemishes have been eliminated, because no backward signals come back for components of noise or blemishes in the stimulus. Thus, the output of the recall-layer W_{C0} can be interpreted as an auto-associative recall from the associative memory.

A threshold-control signal is also sent from the no-response detector shown at far right in Figure 1. When all the recognition cells are silent, the no-response detector sends the threshold-control signal to u_S-cells of all stages through path x shown in Figure 1, and lowers their threshold for feature-extraction.

2.6   Control of Search Area

The original model of selective attention can recognize and segment patterns correctly when the number of simultaneously presented patterns is small, but not always when too many patterns are presented simultaneously. In the new model, a search control signal is applied to the network so as to restrict the number of patterns processed simultaneously. The signal controls the search area for the recognition. The search area has a size somewhat larger than the size of one character. It is not necessary to control the size and the position of the area so accurately because the selective attention model by itself has the ability to segment and recognize patterns.

The position of the search area is shifted to the place in which a larger number of line extracting cells are activated. To be more strict, the output of u_{C1}-cells are filtered by a spatial filter with Gaussian distribution, and the place of maximal activity is detected. The center of the search area is moved to this place.

As shown in Figure 1, the search control signal is applied to u_C-cells and controls the gain of u_C-cells in a similar way to the gain control signal from w_C-cells. Both the search control signal and the gain control signal control the gain of u_C-cells simultaneously: the effect of these two signals are multiplied to control the gain of u_C-cells. In the present simulation, the search control signal is applied to all U_C layers except U_{CL}, and decreases the gain of the u_C-cells.

The boundary of the search area is not sharply restricted; the gain of the u_C-cells are controlled to decrease gradually around the boundary. Since the present model has been designed to recognize a character string written in a single line only, the spatial distribution of the gain is controlled to be Gaussian in the horizontal direction, but is uniform in the vertical direction.

2.7 Switching Attention

Once a character has been recognized and segmented, the attention is switched to recognize another pattern. To be more exact, there is a detector in the network which determines the timing of attention switching. The detector monitors the following two conditions: whether the number of activated recognition cells u_{CL} is only one, and whether the total activity of layer U_{CL-1} has nearly reached a steady state. When both of these conditions are simultaneously satisfied, the detector send a command to switch attention.

Once a command to switch attention is given to the network, the backward signal flow is cut off for a short period. Since the gain control signal from w_C-cells disappear, the gain of u_C-cells falls to the level determined by the degree of fatigue of the cells. The effect of the threshold control signal is also reset at this moment.

In order to find a new position, to which the search area is to be moved, the output of u_{C1}-cells are filtered by a spatial filter with Gaussian distribution again, and the place of maximal activity is

Figure 2: Five training patterns used for learning.

sought. The search control signal is extinguished during this process. Once the place of maximum activity is detected, the search area is moved to the place, and the process of recognition and segmentation is restarted.

3   Computer Simulation

A preliminary experiment was performed with computer simulation to check the ability of the model. The input layer of the model has a rectangular shape, and consists of 57×19 cells.

The network was trained with unsupervised learning in a similar way as for the original model [2],[3]. The five training patterns shown in Figure 2 were repeatedly presented to the network during the training phase. The size of each training pattern is 19×19. These characters were presented only in this shape, and anything like a deformed version of them was not presented.

The connecting strokes between characters changes their shapes considerably, depending on the combination of characters. Sometimes, when a character is placed in front of or at the end of a character string, a connecting stroke might disappear there. In order to decrease the effect of such deformation, the tail ends of the connecting strokes of each training pattern are made to fade away as shown in Figure 2, rather than chopped off abruptly.

Figure 3(b) shows how the response of layer W_{C0} of the network changes with time, when a handwritten character string shown in Figure 3(a) is presented to the input layer. Time t after the first presentation of the character string is indicated in the figure. It can be seen from this figure that character 't' is first recognized and segmented (at time $t = 0$), then follows 'a' ($t = 2$) and 'e'

(a) A character string presented to the input layer.

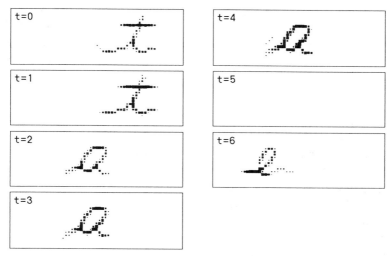

(b) Time course of the response of layer W_{C0}, in which the result of segmentation appears.

Figure 3: An example of the response of the model.

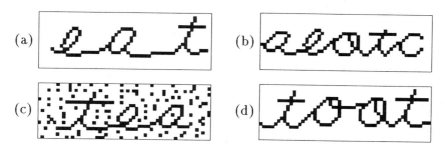

Figure 4: Some examples of input character strings which have been successfully recognized and segmented.

($t = 6$). Although the characters in the input string are different
in shape from the training characters shown in Figure 2, recognition
and segmentation of the characters have been successfully performed.

Figure 4 shows some examples of input character strings which
have been successfully recognized and segmented. It should be noted
here that Figure 4(a) is the same character string as Figure 3(a), but
is written in a different styles of writing. In spite of the difference
in shape, the string was also processed correctly. As shown in Figure 4(d), recognition and segmentation can be successfully performed
even for a string which contains two of the same character 'o' with
somewhat different shapes.

4   Discussion

We have modified the original model of selective attention and extended its ability to be able to recognize characters in handwriting.
The computer simulation showed that the recognition and segmentation of characters can be successfully performed even though each
character in a handwritten word changes its shape by the effect of
the characters before and behind.

However, the present results have been obtained only for a small
number of training patterns. It is a future problem to test the performance of the model with a larger number of training patterns, and
to fix the problems which might arise.

Bibliography

[1] K. Fukushima, *A neural network model for selective attention in
visual pattern recognition,* Biological Cybernetics, **55**[1], pp. 5–
15 (Oct. 1986).

[2] K. Fukushima, *A neural network model for selective attention in
visual pattern recognition and associative recall,* Applied Optics,
26[23], pp. 4985–4992 (Dec. 1987).

[3] K. Fukushima, *A neural network for visual pattern recognition,*

Computer (IEEE Computer Society), **21**[3], pp. 65–75 (March 1988).

[4] T. Imagawa and K. Fukushima, *Recognition of continuous writing of English words with the mechanism of selective attention,* (in Japanese), JNNS'90 (1990 Annual Conference of Japan Neural Network Society), Tokyo, Japan, p. 74 (Sept. 1990).

[5] K. Fukushima, *Neocognitron: A self-organizing neural network model for a mechanism of pattern recognition unaffected by shift in position,* Biological Cybernetics, **36**[4], pp. 193–202 (April 1980).

[6] K. Fukushima, *Neocognitron: A hierarchical neural network capable of visual pattern recognition,* Neural Networks, **1**[2], pp. 119–130 (1988).

Adaptive Acquisition of Language

A. L. Gorin, S. E. Levinson,
A. N. Gertner and E. Goldman
AT&T Bell Laboratories

1 Introduction

1.1 Problem and Goals

Automated speech recognition (ASR) technology has reached a level of performance such that it is commercially viable for certain carefully chosen applications. However, for even the most elementary of tasks, capabilities fall far short of human performance. We believe that the enormous potential benefit of ASR will not be realized until its performance much more nearly approximates that of humans. Indeed, active research efforts worldwide are aimed squarely at that goal.

Present ASR technology is predicated upon constructing models of the various levels of linguistic structure assumed to compose spoken language. These models are either constructed manually or automatically trained by example. A major impediment is the cost or even the feasibility of producing models of sufficient fidelity to enable the desired level of performance.

The proposed alternative is to build a device capable of acquiring the necessary linguistic skills *in the course of performing its task.* We call this *learning by doing,* and contrast it with *learning by example.* The purpose of this paper is to describe some basic principles and mechanisms upon which such a device might be based, and to recount a rudimentary experiment evaluating their utility for that purpose.

Understanding how to construct such devices would yield valuable technological payoffs. Automated training and on-line adaptation would greatly reduce the human labor required to engineer ASR systems for complex environments. Furthermore, we will see that a system which learns by doing must accept unconstrained input, detect and recover from errors, and then learn from those errors. Such a system must deal with the world as it actually presents itself, rather than how the system designer thought it would be.

1.2 Language Conveys Meaning

A survey of the ASR research literature reveals that work is almost exclusively devoted to transcription, the process of converting speech to ordinary text. If pressed, however, we suspect that most researchers in ASR would acknowledge that the ultimate value of the transcription is the intelligence that can be extracted from it. Meanwhile, they continue to concentrate their efforts on transcription, with the intention of later combining their results with others who are working on message understanding. Implicit in this division of labor is the assumption that transcription and understanding are distinct processes connected at a simple orthographical interface. Also assumed is that the requisite highly faithful models of acoustic, phonetic, prosodic and syntactic structure can actually be derived from the speech signal alone, exclusive of its intended meaning.

We argue that these unwritten suppositions are wholly unjustified and, thus, that all attempts to separate transcription and understanding will lead to machines whose performance fall far short of human capabilities. Spoken language, the original natural language, evolved in order for humans to convey important messages to each other. Thus, ab initio, speech and meaning, code and message, were inextricably bound and any attempt to understand one without the other will lead, at best, to an incomplete and inadequate conception of spoken communication.

For example, information theory tells us that by building redundancy into a code, the error rate of decoding can be reduced. This has led to some research into how to exploit semantic redundancy to achieve a more accurate transcription of the speech signal. This turns the whole communication process on its head. The role of the redundancy is to make the message, not its transcription, robust. Meaning is not present so that we can accurately recognize words, but rather linguistic structure useful in order to facilitate the extraction of meaning.

The common definition of language [Web87] includes "words, their pronunciation, and the methods of combining them ... a systematic means of communicating ideas." This suggests an operational definition of language acquisition, namely gaining the capability of extracting the intended information from a natural language message. This viewpoint is in contrast to much of the research on automated language acquisition, which focuses on discovering syntax, oftentimes specifically to the exclusion of meaning.

A paradigm for communication is that the originator's goal is to effect some transformation in the state of the recipient [Fod75]. We say that the recipient correctly *understands* a communication if the desired transformation indeed takes place (that is, the intended meaning was extracted from the message). In this work, we consider machines which can perform some set of meaningful actions, and where a person's goal in communication is to induce the machine to perform one of those actions. The concept of a machine and its set of actions is quite general. One example might be a telephone switch, where the action is to create a telephone channel connecting one or more parties. Another example might be an information processing system, where the action is to retrieve information from a database. Yet another example might be a robotic device, whose actions comprise manipulation of its physical environment.

We formalize this concept of understanding as follows. For any particular task, the goal is to map input messages into meaningful action. The set of all possible input messages we call language, and the mapping we call understanding. This is an operational definition of *understanding,* essentially partitioning the language into semantic equivalence classes for a designated task. Although one might desire a deeper definition of understanding, we are satisfied with the notion that the machine *understands* if it consistently does as it is told over a sufficiently broad range of messages. This concept can be generalized to cover actions which are predicated on changes in internal state, by mapping message *sequences* into meaningful action.

1.3 Learning by Doing

Automated training is clearly a desirable feature for a speech recognition system, and has been the focus of much work at the acoustic, phonemic, lexical and syntactic levels of linguistic structure. When training is to continue over time, the behavior is referred to as adaptation or learning. These concepts are distinct albeit related. Adaptation implies a modification in response to a changing environment, while learning implies an improvement in capability [Web87].

Learning by example involves presenting the system with both input *and* the desired output. This paradigm is illustrated in Figure 1a, which depicts the traditional method of supervised training. In this paradigm, a set of patterns and their true identities are presented to the machine. The decision rule classifies each input pattern on the basis of the distortion between it and a prototypical pattern of each class. The distortion is a smooth function of the continuous parameters of the decision rule, so that it can be minimized in a principled manner. Under certain very general conditions, this minimization will result in a lower probability of classification error. This process can be repeated with additional training examples until the classification is as accurate as possible. *All* present speech recognition systems are trained in this manner, which in no way depends on the *meaning* of the patterns. Note that the distortion error is measured in some parameter space and may contain many bits of information about the fidelity of the decision rule.

One encounters a fundamental obstacle when attempting to apply the *learning by example* paradigm to a system which learns during the course of performing its task. That obstacle is the assumption that the system is continually provided with both the input and the *true* output. After all, if the user needs to constantly utilize an alternative communication channel to provide the system with the desired output, then what is the point of utilizing the system to begin with? Thus, the learning by example paradigm is useful only in a special learning mode, namely where a teacher is available who continually provides both the input on one channel and the desired output on a second channel.

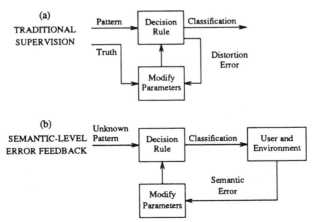

Figure 1: Adaptation and Learning

A paradigm which overcomes this obstacle is depicted in Figure 1b, which we call *learning by doing*. As in the previous case, this is an error feedback system but there the similarity ends. In this case, only the *stimuli themselves* are presented to the system. A classification is effected and an action is taken. This action is then judged by the user as to its appropriateness to the task and environment. This single bit of information (i.e. that the action was acceptable or not) is then used to modify the parameters of the classifier. We denote this a *semantic-level error feedback*. Note that for complex action spaces, there may be a multitude of acceptable responses. Initially, the system can merely guess at the meaning of the input. As more stimuli are received over time, however, the system should improve its proportion of appropriate responses. This is the basis on which we intend to build a speech understanding system.

We have envisioned three criteria with respect to which the propriety of a system response might be judged. The simplest is that the user of the system will inform the system immediately and explicitly whether or not the response was appropriate. The second, somewhat more subtle, is that the user informs the system implicitly of the sufficiency of its action in the course of subsequent dialog. Third, and most complex, the system has more than one input channel (e.g. speech and vision) and can autonomously judge the correctness of its own responses by correlating the decisions reached independently from each input channel. It is our goal to build a system with all three of these mechanisms. In this paper, we study only the first plus a greatly simplified version of the second.

1.4 Constrained-Action Tasks

In order to incorporate our theories in a speech understanding system, it is necessary to define an appropriate task. Because our proposed system is so different in concept from existing systems, we cannot adopt any of those presently under study. The precise reason why a different task is necessary is summarized in Figure 2.

There are presently only a few examples of *complete* speech understanding systems, all of which operate on tasks of the form shown in Figure 2a. In these tasks, the semantic and pragmatic domain is quite rich and as such comprises a significant portion of the semantic structure of the entire language. Two examples are the airline reservation task [Lev80] and the tourist's city guide [Zue90]. In order to perform at an acceptable level, such systems require greatly constrained input, for example a severely restricted vocabulary and/or a rigid artificial syntax.

In the experiments which we conducted, exactly the opposite approach

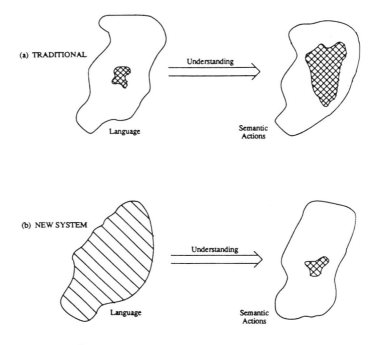

Figure 2: Language Conveys Meaning

was taken, as illustrated in Figure 2b. Our task, which we describe below, has a very restricted semantic domain. That is, the system can perform only a few simple actions. However, we make *no restrictions whatsoever* on the language used to specify the desired action to the system. Moreover, our system will build its language model *from zero* in the course of performing its task. Thus we say that, in a rudimentary sense, it adaptively acquires language.

1.5 Mechanisms

Our operational definition of language acquisition is to gain the capability of extracting the intended information from a natural language message. We formalized this as learning an *understanding* function which maps input messages to machine actions. We propose to construct this mapping by building associations between message components and appropriate machine responses. In particular, we investigate connectionist decision rules whose connection weights are those associations. We envision several levels of complexity in the network architecture. The simplest builds associations between words which occur in the input message and machine actions. The second is to include an intermediate layer comprising *phrase nodes*, building associations between phrases and machine actions. The third, most complex, is to include in the intermediate layer nodes corresponding to non-terminal symbols of an underlying grammar. In this work, we study only the first plus a special case of the second.

A novel training algorithm is introduced, which does *not* require any gradient search. The connections weights are defined in terms of mutual information, leading to rapid, single-pass and order-invariant learning. In addition to these practical properties, this information-theoretic network has several intriguing theoretical characteristics. For example, although *no* gradient is computed, it can be shown that the information-theoretic adaptation step is guaranteed to decrease the single-step error function [Gor89a].

We have introduced the concept of *learning by doing*, embodied in a feedback control system with semantic-level error feedback. We propose to implement a human-machine dialog by such a control system, where the user input is interpreted as a message sequence intended to induce the machine to perform some particular action. The dialog is said to *converge* when the semantic-level error feedback is zero, that is when the machine has responded in a manner judged to be appropriate. Given such a weak error-feedback, one needs be concerned with convergence rate. It can be shown that, under certain conditions, such dialogs converge exponentially quickly (cf. Section 5).

1.6 A Rudimentary Experiment

The utility of these principles and mechanisms is demonstrated and evaluated by applying them to an elementary inward-call-management task, the object of which is to connect a caller to the department of a large organization appropriate to his inquiry. Initially, the system knows *nothing* about the language for its task. There is no vocabulary, no grammar, and no semantic associations. In the course of directing incoming calls the system acquires a vocabulary, learns the meaning of words and some rudimentary grammatical relationships relevant to its task. In particular, meaning is acquired by building associations between words and actions. The rudimentary grammar is implicit within associations developed between word-pair occurrences and actions. The above-mentioned mechanisms are used, namely a connectionist network embedded in a feedback control system which adjusts the connection weights of the network based on the success or failure of the machine's behavior as evaluated by the caller's reaction to it.

An experimental evaluation of the system has been conducted using typed rather than spoken input. The system was tested by 12 subjects over a two month period. Over 1000 conversations were held, during which the machine acquired a vocabulary of over 1500 words. Subsequent tests showed that the learning was stable, in that it retained 99% of the knowledge it had acquired in the interactions.

1.7 Summary

The principles outlined above constitute the foundations of a theory of syntax and semantics, and the experiment a rudimentary demonstration and evaluation of that theory. The first principle is that the purpose of language is to convey meaning, and that language acquisition involves gaining the capability of decoding that meaning. The second principle is that language is to be acquired during the course of performing meaningful tasks. The mechanisms proposed to implement these principles involve a connectionist network to model the structure of the perception to meaning mapping, and a feedback control system to govern the learning of the map parameters.

Adherents of conventional theories of language will no doubt object that such a simple theory is completely inadequate to explain the complex cognitive aspects of language such as reasoning and detailed syntactic structure. While it is true that the very small network used in our experiments is incapable of expressing the whole range of cognitive behavior of humans, this in no way invalidates our theory. We claim that intelligence in general, and linguistic competence in particular, are emergent characteristics. That is, when there are enough networks of the type we describe, and of a sufficiently large size and all working in concert, then intelligent behavior will result. We further assert that what we call intelligence is not the result of highly developed reasoning skills, but mostly derives from the workings of multiple sensory inputs and an array of vast but simple mechanisms of the type described herein, augmented by a very limited reasoning ability that is acquired later in life, long after the perception to meaning mappings have been well established.

The contents of this paper are as follows. Section 2 reviews the background literature for the ideas presented herein. Sections 3 and 4 define the information-theoretic decision network and training algorithm, and briefly review some of its theoretical properties. In particular, Section 3 presents a single-layer *bag-of-words* network, and Section 4 a multilayer network which captures a *rudimentary syntax*. Section 5 defines the inward-call management task and dialog control mechanism. Section 6 describes the experimental procedure and results, including some insights into methodology for evaluating systems which *learn by doing.* Section 7 provides a conclusion plus a description of our plans for future work.

2 Background

In this section we review the literature as it relates to the principles and mechanisms proposed in the previous section. Some readers may desire to proceed directly to the technical discussion in Section 3, returning to this section in a second reading.

2.1 Language and Meaning

Chomsky makes a fundamental distinction between competence and performance, defining competence as "the speaker-hearer's knowledge of his language," and performance as "the actual use of language in concrete situations" [Cho65] (pp. 4). By 'knowledge of his language', he means knowledge of the underlying system of rules which are put to use in actual performance. This system of rules is to be encoded in a grammar, which assigns structural descriptions to sentences.

Primarily concerned with linguistic competence, Chomsky describes a language acquisition device as "an input-output device that determines a particular generative grammar as 'output,' given primary linguistic data as input," where "primary linguistic data consists of signals classified as sentences and non-sentences, and a partial and tentative pairing of signals with structural descriptions" [Cho65] (pp. 32, 38). Language acquisition would proceed by searching through the set of possible grammar hypotheses, selecting those which are compatible with the primary linguistic data and which optimize some empirical evaluation criteria such as simplicity.

Building upon such a viewpoint, much of automated language acquisition research focuses on the discovery of syntactic structure, wherein the goal is to develop a theory which predicts the set of (possibly infinite) grammatical sentences in a language from a finite number of observations. The literature on this subject is vast, and we do not attempt a survey of methods for acquiring linguistic competence. We mention, however, the paper of Fu and Booth [Fu75] which surveys algorithmic methods of grammatical inference for finite state and context-free grammars, including generalizations to higher-dimensional and stochastic grammars. We also mention Langley's paper [Lan82] on the AMBER system, both for its intrinsic merit and in that it provides a survey of previous models of language acquisition. He divides the research broadly, into those systems that take advantage of semantic feedback and those that do not. In most cases, the goal of those systems is to acquire syntactic structure, and semantic feedback is exploited to that end.

The grammatical inference procedures described by Fu and Booth [Fu75] first construct the canonical grammar. Given a set of examples S drawn from a language, the canonical grammar parses exactly that set S. To provide generalization, they survey methods for 'backing away' from the canonical grammar, in particular via the technique of derived grammars. These methods yield grammars which parse supersets of S, thus providing generalization. They explore a variety of heuristics for searching the set of derived grammars, in particular via providing negative examples S^-. It is accepted, however, that children are rarely provided with such negative examples. (For example, see MacWhinney's preface in [Mac87].) One would thus prefer alternate mechanisms for pruning the search. The need for heuristic pruning is not merely a search issue, but also necessary because of fundamental limitations on the learnability of languages from positive examples alone, as described by Gold [Gol67].

A principled method of controlling such searches is to exploit meaning. Humans do not learn language in a vacuum, but rather during the course of daily living. Clark provides a succinct, albeit possibly extreme, argument for the role of meaning in human language acquisition. Her *Principle of Contrast* is embodied in: "Different words mean different things. That is, wherever there is a difference in form in a language, there is a difference in meaning ... It is by virtue of this property that language maintains its usefulness as a medium of communication" [Cla87] (pp. 1). There has been much debate in the literature over the role of semantics in human language acquisition. We do not wish to become embroiled in that discussion, so instead refer the interested reader to the literature, embodied for example in the collection of papers by Wanner and Gleitman [Wan82], by MacWhinney [Mac87], or by Moore [Moo73].

In those experimental systems which do exploit semantic information for language acquisition, the standard approach is to represent meaning symbolically, attempting to make the representation isomorphic to some subset of reality. Anderson's work on LAS [And77] is a good example of this approach. He represents scene descriptions (meaning) as associative networks in a variant of the HAM propositional representation. His UNDERSTAND command accepts a sentence as input and produces a HAM-encoded meaning as output. The LEARNMORE command accepts a sentence/meaning pair which it exploits to modifying the underlying ATN. Another, more recent, example of a system which acquires language by correlating linguistic and non-linguistic input is Siskind's MAIMRA system [Sis90].

We argue, however, that representing meaning in some symbolic form, no matter how complex the symbolism, incorrectly reduces the *understanding* issue to that of language translation (i.e. simply transforming one symbolic representation into another), thus begging the actual question. When one person speaks with another, how can he know whether the intended message was received? We argue that the correct approach is the equivalent of a Turing Test: Evaluate whether the communication was correctly understood on the basis of whether the recipient responds in an expected and appropriate manner. For example, if one requests, from a cashier, change of a dollar in quarters, then one evaluates whether the message was understood by examining the returned coins.

To the authors' knowledge, the principle that understanding involves mapping input messages to appropriate machine actions has not been exploited in the construction of language acquisition devices (although it exists in the psycholinguistic literature). It has been exploited, however, in the programming of robotic devices by Brooks [Bro86]. In that work, the robots operate via a mapping from stimuli to action, where stimuli comprises sensory data and action comprises physical motion. Wiener [Wie61] (pp. 134) describes how one might construct a cybernetic device which exhibits negative phototropism (light avoiding motion) based on an association between input stimuli and machine action. In both of these robotic examples, however, the associations were preprogrammed rather than learned.

2.2 Learning as a Feedback Control System

Learning by example involves presenting a machine with input/output pairs. One can model many of the derived learning procedures as a feedback control system, where the actual output is compared to the desired output, then system parameters are modified to reduce that distortion error. We do not attempt a survey of learning and adaptation methods based on this principle, but will mention a few examples. The application of such methods to training speech recognizers is described in [Lev85] [Jua90], to adaptive filters in [Wid76], and to echo canceling by [Son67]. Learning boolean propositions, by example, is described by Valiant [Val84] and Pitt [Pit88]. As described in the introduction, however, learning by example encounters obstacles if applied to our problem of learning spoken language during the course of performing a task.

Narendra and Thathachar [Nar74], describe an alternate learning paradigm, in their survey of *learning automata,* wherein a stochastic automaton is embedded in a feedback control system. The output of the automaton is one of a finite number of actions. Its input includes a penalty value, which is produced stochastically by the environment in response to its action. The automaton's goal is to modify the distribution of its output actions so as to minimize the expected value of the penalty. They compare this method to stochastic hillclimbing, observing that although both approaches are iterative, they are quite distinct, since updating is done in the parameter space in one, and probability space in the other: "The automata methods have two distinct advantages over stochastic hillclimbing methods in that the action space need not be a metric space (i.e. no concept of neighborhood is needed), and since at every stage any element of the action set can be chosen, global rather than local optimum can be obtained" (pp. 324).

Although it is not obvious whether or not our approach could be characterized as a learning automaton, we share with those efforts the concept that learning is driven by a penalty function, (in our case a semantic-level error signal), in contrast to hillclimbing methods wherein the error function is a distortion measure in a continuous parameter space. This distinction also arises in reinforcement learning [Bar90] and actor-critic learning [Wil90].

2.3 Connectionism, Language and Mutual Information

There are a variety of formalisms which have been explored as the basis of machine intelligence, including statistical decision theory [Dud73], rule-based systems [Win84] and connectionism [Rum86]. Although the borders between these formalisms are often vague, connectionism is distinguished by its biological motivations and its viewpoint that intelligence is an emergent property, i.e., intelligent behavior can result from the interaction of large numbers of simple mechanisms working in concert.

There has been much research investigating connectionist methods for natural language processing. Allen and Riecken [All89], for example, utilized back-propagation training of a temporal network for the purpose of learning pronoun reference and response generation. Jain and Waibel [Jai90] investigated a recurrent network which learns to parse sentences. McClelland and Kawanoto [McC86] describe methods for assigning roles to constituents. None of this activity, to the authors' knowledge, has addressed the problem of learning to *understand,* in our sense of mapping input messages to machine action.

Mutual Information (MI), which we utilize as a connection weight in our decision networks, is a well-known statistical method of measuring association [Tho69]. The general form of our proposed connectionist network allows for intermediate nodes representing phrases or non-terminal symbols. Methods based on MI have been proposed for acquiring both. Church has utilized MI to automatically determine word associations [Chu89], Sproat has developed algorithms for automatically determining word units based on MI [Spr 90], and Magerman describes how to use MI to discover constituent boundaries [Mag90]. Jelinek describes MI methods for clustering words into parts-of-speech equivalence classes [Jel90]. MI-based decision rules for information retrieval, which is a particularly important, albeit complex, action space, is described by VanRijsbergen [Van77]. Related methods using correlation-based association measures are described by Salton [Sal89].

The conceptual distance between rule-based and connectionist methodology may eventually diminish. For example, Smyth and Goodman [Goo89a] [Smy90] have explored methods based on MI for guiding rule induction in databases. They propose methods for parallel rule firing and combination of resultant inferences, leading to a reformulation of the rule-based system as a connectionist network, with nodes corresponding to rule clauses and connection weights corresponding to a confidence measure on the rules. Their connection weights are exactly the ones which we use, although the estimation procedures may differ [Goo89] [Goo90].

We conclude this background section by observing that although the intellectual foundation of our work is drawn from several disparate fields, to the authors' knowledge the combination of ideas presented here is unique in its application to the construction of a language acquisition device.

3 An Adaptive Network for Mapping Sentences to Semantics

Consider a system whose input is unrestricted text and whose output is one of a finite set of semantic actions. In this and the subsequent section, we define and describe a medium-grain connectionist decision network and an adaptive, sequential training procedure that implements such a system. In particular, the input to the supervised training procedure is a set $S = \{\langle \text{sentence}, \text{action} \rangle\}$ of ordered pairs comprising a sentence and an associated semantic action. One can straightforwardly generalize the procedure to also learn from negative examples. It will become clear, in Section 5, how this method is incorporated into a system which *learns by doing* rather than *by example.*

It is illustrative to compare this approach to that described by Watt [Wat68]. As we do, he views the collection of sentences which connote the same action in a given context as an equivalence class. With the goal of deriving habitable languages, he defines criteria by which to select a simplest single exemplar from each equivalence class. This differs from our approach, where we instead attempt to model the within-class variation of the equivalence classes.

The input to the network is unrestricted text drawn from some alphabet of symbols, denoted A. A subset of the alphabet, denoted A_d, is reserved for delimiters, so that a word is defined as any input subsequence which is delimited by elements of A_d. For example, the alphabet can be $\{a - z\} \cup$ {space, comma, period} wherein a word is a sequence of letters delimited by spaces or punctuation. Another example is an alphabet of phonetic symbols [Lev89], with a silence symbol as a delimiter, corresponding to a speech recognition system which understands sequences of isolated words. We postpone, however, the issues of connected-word recognition to future work.

Let c_k, $1 \leq k \leq K$, denote the semantic actions, and v_m, $1 \leq m \leq M$, denote the vocabulary words. We first consider a single layer network, as shown in Figure 3, for mapping an input sentence $s = \langle v_{m_1}, v_{m_2} \ldots v_{m_L} \rangle$ to a semantic action $c_{k_0}(s)$, where L is the length of the sentence s. In Section 4, we will extend this to a second-order multi-layer network which captures a rudimentary syntax. The input layer comprises medium-grain nodes that detect the presence of a vocabulary word v_m in the input sentence s, producing an output o_m between 0 and 1. (In this implementation, words are counted only once, no matter how often they occur. It is straightforward to extend the outputs to actually count the number of occurrences.) These nodes are medium-grain in the sense that they execute some function which detects the presence of a word in the sentence. The simplest such function is a matching function which produces an output of 1 if a particular symbol sequence is observed, else produces an output of 0. A more sophisticated function is one which produces an output o_m equal to the probability that word v_m is in the sentence. In the case of speech input, this could be a wordspotting algorithm such as the one described by Wilpon et al. [Wil89] which detects the occurrence of a word embedded within continuous speech. The training and recognition procedures described here are independent of the internal structure of these medium-grain input nodes. These outputs o_m are combined by each of the semantic nodes in the second layer to produce activations a_k according to the following standard formula

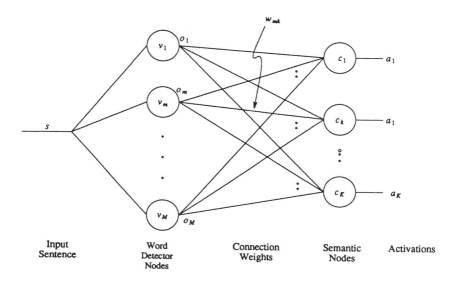

Figure 3: A Single-Layer Network for Mapping Sentences to Semantic Actions

[Rum86],

$$a_k = \sum_{m=1}^{M} o_m w_{mk} + w_k, \tag{3.1}$$

where the w_{mk} are connection weights and the w_k are biases. At this time, we do not utilize any non-linear thresholding. The input sentence is then understood as connoting that semantic action c_{k_0} whose activation a_k is maximum,

$$k_0 = \arg\max_k a_k. \tag{3.2}$$

Rather than viewing the weights and biases as abstract parameters, we give them explicit meaning via the following definitions.

$$w_{mk} = I(c_k, v_m) = \log \frac{P(c_k|v_m)}{P(c_k)}, \tag{3.3}$$

$$w_k = \log P(c_k), \tag{3.4}$$

where $I(c_k, v_m)$ is the mutual information [Tho69] between the single word v_m and the semantic action c_k. This definition of connection weight is

intuitive, and will be shown also to be quite useful experimentally in subsequent sections. It will be shown to be advantageous, as compared to
gradient search techniques, because it exhibits rapid learning, requires only
a single pass through the training data, is order invariant, and automatically modifies the step-size based on the number of observations that have
impacted a particular connection weight. To aid in understanding its theoretical properties, we present a proposition showing that under certain
restrictive assumptions the network provides a maximum a posteriori decision rule. Except in such cases, the network is *not* performing a maximum
a posteriori decision rule, but is still interesting and useful in and of itself. This proposition is related to the observation, by Minsky and Papert,
that the maximum likelihood decision rule, for independent inputs, can be
viewed as a linear perceptron [Min88] (pp. 203).

Proposition. If the words v_{m_i} in the sentence $s = \langle v_{m_1} v_{m_2} \cdots v_{m_L} \rangle$ are
independent, and if the outputs o_m of the first layer are restricted to 0 or
1, then the activations $a_k = \log P(c_k|s)$.

Proof.

$$P(c_k|s) = \frac{P(s|c_k)P(c_k)}{P(s)}$$

$$= \frac{\left[\prod_{i=1}^{L} P(v_{m_i}|c_k)\right] P(c_k)}{P(s)} \quad \text{via the independence hypothesis,}$$

$$= \prod_{i=1}^{L} \left[\frac{P(c_k|v_{m_i})P(v_{m_i})}{P(c_k)}\right] \frac{P(c_k)}{P(s)}$$

$$= \prod_{i=1}^{L} \left[\frac{P(c_k|v_{m_i})}{P(c_k)}\right] \cdot P(c_k) \cdot \frac{\prod_{i=1}^{L} P(v_{m_i})}{P(s)}.$$

The term $\frac{\prod_{i=1}^{L} P(v_{m_i})}{P(s)}$ is equal to 1 via the independence hypothesis, and
the claim follows by taking the logarithm of each side of the above formula,
yielding

$$\log P(c_k|s) = \sum_{i=1}^{L} I(v_{m_i}, c_k) + \log P(c_k). \tag{3.5}$$

Thus, $a_k = \log P(c_k|s)$ via formulas 3.1-3.4 when the outputs o_m are
boolean. ∎

An advantage of these definitions of weight and bias is that they can be directly estimated from counts, which can in turn be sequentially accumulated. The simplest estimate of the probabilities in formulas (3.3) and (3.4) is via computation of the relative frequencies,

$$\hat{P}_1(c_k|v_m) = \frac{N(v_m, c_k)}{N(v_m)}, \tag{3.6}$$

$$\hat{P}_1(c_k) = \frac{N(c_k)}{N_T}, \tag{3.7}$$

where $N(v_m)$ denotes the number of observations of the word v_m, $N(c_k)$ denotes the number of observations of sentences in class c_k, $N(v_m, c_k)$ denotes the number of observations of the word v_m in sentences of class c_k, and $N_T = \sum_{k=1}^{K} N(c_k)$ denotes the total number of sentences observed in all of the K classes. Note that both estimates are well-defined probability measures, in the sense of having values between 0 and 1 and summing to unity.

These estimates converge asymptomatically, but suffer from quantization noise for small numbers of observations. A standard method for smoothing in the presence of a small number of observations is via interpolating the measured relative frequencies with a prior belief. Our prior belief of $P(c_k)$ is $\frac{1}{K}$, given K possible semantic actions, yielding an estimate

$$\hat{P}_2(c_k) = (1 - \alpha)\frac{1}{K} + \alpha\hat{P}_1(c_k), \tag{3.8}$$

where α is an interpolation weight ($0 \le \alpha \le 1$) defined as

$$\alpha = \frac{N_T}{m_\alpha + N_T}, \tag{3.9}$$

and where m_α is a parameter (> 0) representing the mass of our prior belief that the classes are equiprobable. Thus, if $N_T = 0$, then $\hat{P}_2(c_k) = \frac{1}{K}$. If $N_T \gg m_\alpha$, then $\hat{P}_2(c_k) \approx \hat{P}_1(c_k)$.

Our prior belief of $P(c_k|v_m)$ is $P(c_k)$, i.e., that the semantic action c_k is independent of the word v_m. Thus, we estimate

$$\hat{P}_2(c_k|v_m) = (1 - \beta)\hat{P}_2(c_k) + \beta\hat{P}_1(c_k|v_m), \tag{3.10}$$

where β is an interpolation weight ($0 \le \beta \le 1$) given by

$$\beta = \frac{N(v_m)}{m_\beta + N(v_m)} \tag{3.11}$$

and where m_β (> 0) represents our prior belief that c_k is independent of v_m. For example, if a word has never been observed, then the estimate $\hat{P}_2(c_k|v_m) = P_2(c_k)$, which implies a zero connection weight w_{mk}. Again note that the estimates in (3.8) and (3.10) provide well-defined probability measures.

We digress to examine the range of values for the term $\hat{I}_2(c_k, v_m) = \log \frac{\hat{P}_2(c_k|v_m)}{\hat{P}_2(c_k)}$, which is our estimate of the connection weights thus far. From formulas 3.6, 3.8 and 3.10, we observe that

$$\frac{\hat{P}_2(c_k|v_m)}{\hat{P}_2(c_k)} = (1 - \beta) + \frac{\beta}{\hat{P}_2(c_k)}\left[\frac{N(v_m, c_k)}{N(c_k)}\right]. \tag{3.12}$$

This expression is greater than or equal to $(1-\beta)$, with equality iff $N(v_m, c_k) = 0$, i.e. iff the word v_m has never been observed in class c_k. Thus

$$\hat{I}_2(v_m, c_k) \geq \log \frac{m_\beta}{m_\beta + N(v_m)}. \tag{3.13}$$

This lower bound for $\hat{I}_2(v_m, c_k)$ is always less than or equal to 0, with equality iff $N(v_m) = 0$. As the number of observations, $N(v_m)$, increases, the lower bound goes to $-\infty$. Alternatively, $\hat{I}_2(v_m, c_k)$ is bounded above by the positive number $-\log \hat{P}_2(c_k)$.

The interpolations, $\hat{P}_2$, provide smoothed estimates when the number of observations of a word or class is small, on the order of m_α or m_β respectively. One discovers, however, that even with hundreds of observations, the estimates can still be noisy, especially for those words with zero connections. For example, although a word v_m may have no semantic significance, it may appear unevenly in the K classes. We are thus motivated to center clip the estimates: If the estimate is less than some threshold distant from our prior belief of it, then clip it to that prior. Let q denote that threshold. Therefore:

$$\hat{P}_3(c_k) = \begin{cases} \hat{P}_2(c_k) & \text{if } \left|\hat{P}_2(c_k) - \frac{1}{K}\right| > q \\ \frac{1}{K} & \text{otherwise.} \end{cases} \tag{3.14}$$

$$\hat{P}_3(c_k|v_m) = \begin{cases} \hat{P}_2(c_k|v_m) & \text{if } \left|\hat{P}_2(c_k|v_m) - \hat{P}_3(c_k)\right| > q \\ \hat{P}_3(c_k) & \text{otherwise.} \end{cases} \tag{3.15}$$

Appropriate settings of the center clip parameter can accelerate unlearning of false hypotheses. This is a particularly simple center clipping scheme. One enhancement would be to choose different q's in (3.14) and (3.15). Another would be to scale the left and right clipping thresholds asymmetrically, proportional to the different sizes of the left and right intervals about the priors.

The probability estimates of formulas (3.14) and (3.15) are then inserted into equations 3.3 and 3.4 to provide estimates of the weights and biases. Observe that the weights and biases are thus totally determined by the count measurements $N(v_m)$, $N(c_k)$, and $N(v_m, c_k)$, plus the prior mass and clip threshold parameters. Since counts can be accumulated sequentially, then the estimates of the weights can be adaptively and sequentially updated with each new input.

In order to accelerate the unlearning of false semantic connections, one can appropriately set a center clipping threshold such that a single counterexample drives the probability estimate back to the prior, and thus the connection weight to zero. Let us illustrate this phenomenon via a small simulation. Consider a 3-class problem, with equiprobable classes, and prior mass $m_\beta = 1$. Now consider a word v_1 which appears only in class c, i.e., $\hat{P}_1(c|v_1) \equiv 1$. Via formulas 3.10 and 3.11, $\hat{P}_2(c|v_1) = \frac{.33 + N(v_1)}{1 + N(v_1)}$, where $N(v_1)$ is the number of occurrences of word v_1. Figure 4 illustrates this function for $0 \leq N(v_1) \leq 3$, showing its asymptotic yet slow approach to unity. Consider now another word v_2 with zero semantic connections, (i.e. asymptotically $\hat{P}_1(c|v_2) = .33$), but which occurs first in class c, then in some other class, then again in class c. Figure 4 also illustrates $\hat{P}_2(c|v_2)$. Center clipping with $q = .30$ yields $\hat{P}_3(c|v_2)$, serving to accelerate the separation of the two curves, thus accelerating the unlearning of the false hypothesis that v_2 has a non-zero semantic connection. This technique is used, for example, in the experiments of Section 6, with $m_\alpha = m_\beta = 1$ and $q = .30$. In that case, a single occurrence suffices to learn a positive semantic connection, and a single counterexample suffices to unlearn a false hypothesis.

It follows directly from the definition of the training procedure that it is sequential, requires a single pass through the data, is invariant to the data order, and has a single asymptotic solution. We will show, experimentally, that it also provides rapid learning, acquiring new words and their meaning from single observations. These properties are in striking contrast to those of stochastic gradient algorithms, which can require multiple iterations through the data to converge, is highly sensitive to data order, and is guaranteed to converge only to some local minimum of the error function. The sequential nature of the two learning procedures leads one to ask if there is any relationship between the information-theoretic adaptation step and the stochastic gradient. Although it is beyond the scope of this paper, it can be shown that there is indeed such a relation. In particular, for fixed class priors, the information-theoretic adaptation vector has the

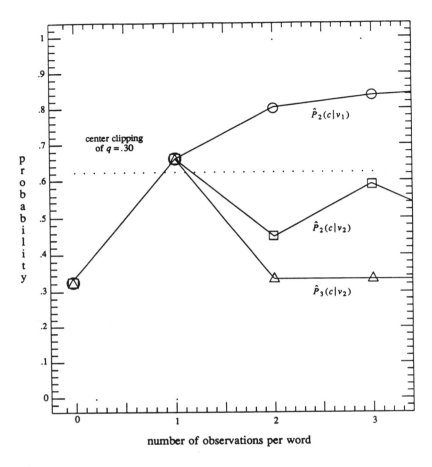

Figure 4:   Center Clipping Accelerates the Unlearning of False Semantic Connections

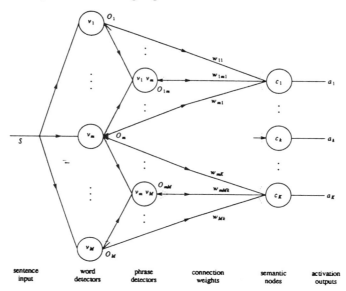

Figure 5: A Multi-Layer Network for Mapping Sentences to Semantic Actions

same sign, in each coordinate, as the negative gradient of the single-step error function. Furthermore, for non-zero input vectors, the information-theoretic adaptation step is guaranteed to decrease the single step error function [Gor89a].

4 A Multi-Layer Network with a Rudimentary Syntax

We now extend the network of the previous section to extract meaning via learning associations between phrases and machine actions. As before, consider a vocabulary $V = \{v_m\}_{m=1,M}$ of M words, and a sentence $s = \langle v_{m_1} v_{m_2} \cdots v_{m_L} \rangle$ of length L which connotes one of K semantic actions $\{c_k\}_{k=1,K}$. Consider a multi-layer network as in Figure 5, where the first layer is the same as the previous section, comprising nodes which are word detectors, whose output O_m is a value between 0 and 1 according to the presence of word v_m. The second layer comprises phrase detectors, where in this paper we consider only phrases comprising two adjacent words, with output O_{mn} a value between 0 and 1 according to the presence of the adjacent word-pair $v_m v_n$ in the sentence s. The inputs to the phrase detectors for $v_{m_1} v_{m_2}$ are the outputs of the first layer word detectors for v_{m_1} and v_{m_2}. There are many methods of combining such inputs to obtain an output for the adjacent-wordpair node, which we need not specify for now. The simplest case is for noise-free input, in which outputs are either 0 or 1. In that situation, we would simply utilize a network that implements the boolean *and* function with a *time delay* of one word [Tan87].

The activation a_k for a semantic action c_k is given by a linear combination of the outputs,

$$a_k = w_k + \sum_{m=1}^{M} O_m w_{mk} + \sum_{m=1}^{M} \sum_{n=1}^{M} O_{mn} w_{mnk}, \qquad (4.1)$$

where we define information-theoretic connection weights as follows, with 4.2 and 4.3 identical to 3.3 and 3.4.

$$
\begin{aligned}
w_k &= \log P(c_k), &\qquad (4.2)\\
w_{mk} &= I(v_m, c_k), &\qquad (4.3)\\
w_{mnk} &= I(v_m v_n,\ c_k) - I(v_m, c_k) - I(v_n, c_k). &\qquad (4.4)
\end{aligned}
$$

The event $v_m v_n$ comprises the adjacent co-occurrence of the two words in the sentence S. As before, the expression $I(A, B)$ denotes the mutual information between two events [Tho69], defined as

$$I(A, B) = \log \frac{P(A|B)}{P(A)}. \qquad (4.5)$$

The connection weight from the second-order nodes, given in formula (4.4), is the *excess* mutual information of the word-pair over the individual words. This decision network can clearly be generalized to include intermediate nodes corresponding to n-tuples, to non-adjacent words or even to non-terminal symbols.

The single layer network of the previous section was deficient in being insensitive to word-order. The following proposition shows that if the word order is not relevant in the input data, then this multi-layer network reduces to the single-layer network. It is essentially a proof of a well-known property of mutual information, but is included for completeness.

Proposition. If the occurrences of the vocabulary words v_m and v_n are independent, then the connection weights from their word-pair node are all zero, i.e. $w_{mnk} = 0$ for all k. (This holds true even for a network with nodes corresponding to non-adjacent words.)

Proof. First observe that via Bayes rule

$$P(c_k|v_m v_n) = \frac{P(v_m v_n|c_k)\ P(c_k)}{P(v_m v_n)}, \tag{4.6}$$

which by the independence hypothesis implies that

$$P(c_k|v_m v_n) = \frac{P(v_m|c_k)P(v_n|c_k)P(c_k)}{P(v_m)P(v_n)}. \tag{4.7}$$

Applying Bayes rule to formula (4.7), one obtains

$$P(c_k|v_m v_n) = \frac{P(c_k|v_m)P(c_k|v_n)}{P(c_k)}. \tag{4.8}$$

Combining this with the definition of mutual information in formula (4.5) yields the well-known relation

$$\begin{aligned}
I(v_m v_n, c_k) &\equiv \log \frac{P(c_k|v_m v_n)}{P(c_k)} \tag{4.9} \\
&= \log \frac{P(c_k|v_m)P(c_k|v_n)}{P(c_k)P(c_k)} \\
&\equiv I(v_m, c_k) + I(v_n, c_k).
\end{aligned}$$

Finally, from the definition of w_{mnk} in formula (4.4), this implies the desired result that $w_{mnk} = 0$. ∎

Corollary. If the words in the sentence are independent, then the multi-layer network reduces to the single-layer network of the previous section.

This is a particularly interesting result because it runs counter to typical experience. Systems with large number of parameters often encounter difficulty when faced with simple input data. Not so with the multi-layer network, which both theoretically and experimentally adapts itself to simple problems quite well.

We showed that under certain assumptions, the single-layer network was equivalent to a *maximum a posteriori* decision rule. We obtain a similar result for this multi-layer network. Notice however, that the hypotheses are rarely true, and in particular not true for our experimental system. This result is interesting because it provides insight into the network's characteristics. We emphasize that, in general, it is *not* computing a *maximum a posteriori* decision.

Proposition. *If* the words are unambiguous, so that all first-layer outputs are 0 or 1, and *if* the language generating the sentences is first-order Markovian, *then* the multi-layer network is equivalent to a *maximum a posteriori* decision rule.

Proof. Let $s = \langle v_{m_1} v_{m_2} \cdots v_{m_L} \rangle$ be a sentence of length L comprising the word v_{m_l} in position l. Let c_k be a semantic action. First observe that via Bayes Rule

$$P(c_k|s) = P(s|c_k)P(c_k)/P(s). \tag{4.10}$$

Now, it is true in general that

$$
\begin{aligned}
P(s|c_k) &= P(v_{m_1} v_{m_2} \cdots v_{m_L} |c_k), \\
&= P(v_{m_L}|v_{m_1} v_{m_2} \cdots v_{m_{L-1}} \text{ and } c_k)P(v_{m_1} v_{m_2} \cdots v_{m_{L-1}}|c_k), \\
&= \left[\prod_{l=2}^{L} P(v_{m_l}|v_{m_1} v_{m_2} \cdots v_{m_{l-1}} \text{ and } c_k)\right] \cdot P(v_{m_1}|c_k). \tag{4.11}
\end{aligned}
$$

Invoking the Markovian assumption of this proposition yields

$$P(s|c_k) = \left[\prod_{l=2}^{L} P(v_{m_l}|v_{m_{l-1}} \text{ and } c_k)\right] \cdot P(v_{m_1}|c_k). \tag{4.12}$$

Transforming this formula via a logarithm then provides

$$\log P(s|c_k) = \sum_{l=2}^{L} \log P(v_{m_l}|v_{m_{l-1}} \text{ and } c_k) + \log P(v_{m_1}|c_k). \tag{4.13}$$

Consider now the semantic-conditional transition probabilities $P(v_{m_l}|v_{m_{l-1}} \text{ and } c_k)$, which we will recast in terms of mutual information measures. Observe that

$$
\begin{aligned}
P(v_{m_l}|v_{m_{l-1}} \text{ and } c_k) &= \frac{P(v_{m_{l-1}} v_{m_l} \text{ and } c_k)}{P(v_{m_{l-1}} \text{ and } c_k)} \tag{4.14} \\
&= \frac{P(c_k|v_{m_{l-1}} v_{m_l})P(v_{m_{l-1}} v_{m_l})}{P(c_k|v_{m_{l-1}})P(v_{m_{l-1}})} \\
&= \frac{P(c_k|v_{m_{l-1}} v_{m_l})}{P(c_k)} \frac{P(c_k)}{P(c_k|v_{m_{l-1}})} P(v_{m_l}|v_{m_{l-1}}).
\end{aligned}
$$

From the definition of mutual information in formula 4.5, we then infer that

$$
\begin{aligned}
\log P(v_{m_l}|v_{m_{l-1}} \text{ and } c_k) &= I(v_{m_{l-1}} v_{m_l}, c_k) - I(v_{m_{l-1}}, c_k) \\
&\quad + \log P(v_{m_l}|v_{m_{l-1}}). \tag{4.15}
\end{aligned}
$$

This formula provides a relationship between the class-dependent and class-independent transition probabilities. Combining formulas (4.13) and (4.15) yields

$$\log P(s|c_k) = \sum_{l=2}^{L} I(v_{m_{l-1}} v_{m_l}, c_k) - \sum_{l=2}^{L} I(v_{m_{l-1}}, c_k)$$
$$+ \sum_{l=2}^{L} \log P(v_{m_l}|v_{m_{l-1}}) + \log P(v_{m_1}|c_k). \quad (4.16)$$

Again invoking the Markovian assumption, observe that

$$\log P(s) = \sum_{l=2}^{L} P(v_{m_l}|v_{m_{l-1}}) + \log P(v_{m_1}), \quad (4.17)$$

which when combined with formula (4.16) yields

$$\log P(s|c_k) = \sum_{l=2}^{L} I(v_{m_{l-1}} v_{m_l}, c_k) - \sum_{l=2}^{L} I(v_{m_{l-1}}, c_k)$$
$$+ I(v_{m_1}, c_k) + \log P(s). \quad (4.18)$$

To obtain an expression for $P(c_k|s)$, we combine formulas (4.10) and (4.18) to yield

$$\log P(c_k|s) = \sum_{l=2}^{L} I(v_{m_{l-1}} v_{m_l}, c_k) - \sum_{l=2}^{L} I(v_{m_{l-1}}, c_k)$$
$$+ I(v_{m_1}, c_k) + \log P(c_k). \quad (4.19)$$

This completes our expansion of the log probability. We now expand the definition of a_k and show equality. Utilizing formulas (4.1) through (4.4), and the assumption that the outputs are zero or one according to the unambiguous occurrence of the words, we obtain

$$a_k = \sum_{l=2}^{L} [I(v_{m_{l-1}} v_{m_l}, c_k) - I(v_{m_{l-1}}, c_k) - I(v_{m_l}, c_k)]$$
$$+ \sum_{l=1}^{L} I(v_{m_l}, c_k) + \log P(c_k),$$
$$= \sum_{l=2}^{L} I(v_{m_{l-1}} v_{m_l}, c_k) - \sum_{l=2}^{L} I(v_{m_{l-1}}, c_k)$$
$$+ I(v_{m_1}, c_k) + \log P(c_k). \quad (4.20)$$

Comparing formulas (4.19) and (4.20) implies

$$a_k = \log P(c_k|s),$$

proving our proposition that selection of the semantic action c_{k_0} such that $k_0 = \arg\max_k a_k$ is equivalent to a *maximum a posteriori* decision rule. ■

The information-theoretic connection weights are defined in terms of single and joint probabilities, which are in turn estimated using counters and smoothing parameters. In particular, the conditional probabilities that are necessary to compute the second-order connections in formula (4.4) can be estimated from measured relative frequencies via

$$\hat{P}_1(c_k|v_m v_n) = \frac{N(v_m v_n, c_k)}{N(v_m v_n)}, \qquad (4.21)$$

where $N(v_m v_n, c_k)$ is the number of observations of the word-pair $v_m v_n$ in the class c_k; and $N(v_m v_n)$ is the total number of observations of the word-pair $v_m v_n$ in all classes. We denote these as $\hat{P}_1$, indicating that it is a first estimate.

As for the first-order connections, the smoothing procedure for the word-pair probabilities interpolates the measured relative frequency, $\hat{P}_1$, with a prior belief. As the prior belief, before a word-pair has ever been observed, we assume that the two words in the word-pair are independent.

Based upon this assumption, we obtain a second estimate

$$\hat{P}_2(c_k|v_m v_n) = (1 - \beta)\frac{\hat{P}_2(c_k|v_m) \cdot \hat{P}_2(c_k|v_n)}{\hat{P}_2(c_k)} + \beta\hat{P}_1(c_k|v_m v_n), \qquad (4.22)$$

where β is an interpolating parameter defined via

$$\beta = \frac{N(v_m v_n)}{m_b + N(v_m v_n)}, \qquad (4.23)$$

and m_b is a parameter represents our prior belief of occurrence class c_k conditioned on word-pair $v_m v_n$. The value of m_b affects the connection weights w_{mnk} in the multi-layer network. By changing the value of m_b we can change contribution of the connection weights w_{mnk} of the word-pair and transform the performance of multi-layer network to that of the single-layer one.

The interpolation $\hat{P}_2(c_k|v_m v_n)$ provide smoothed estimates when the number of observations of a word or a word-pair are small. As for the single-layer network, we also center clip these estimates to obtain $\hat{P}_3(c_k|v_m v_n)$.

5 A Conversational-Mode System

We now describe a conversational-mode system which demonstrates and evaluates our proposed principles and mechanisms. We restrict ourselves to constrained-action tasks. That is, one can ask the machine to perform one of a small number of actions, but is allowed total freedom in making such requests. As described in the introduction and illustrated in Figure 2, this differs from conventional systems in that the semantic actions are highly constrained, while the language is unconstrained. By adding a semantic action connoting *Outside my domain of actions*, then *any* sentence can be mapped to an appropriate action.

The application scenario chosen is inward call management: a customer calls a large organization and first encounters an operator whose function is to forward the call to one of several departments. In particular, we consider a store which has three departments: furniture, clothing and hardware. The input to the system is unconstrained text, connoting one of three possible semantic actions: forwarding of the call to one of the three departments. An example input might be *"I want to buy a new dining room set"*, whence the appropriate semantic action is to connect the caller to the furniture department.

We now describe the human-machine dialog subsystem, which is implemented as a control system with a semantic-level error feedback. Consider a dialog where the person's goal is to induce the machine to perform a desired action. In this implementation, the connection weights are held constant during the dialog, and adapted before commencing the next dialog.

The initial user input is a natural language request for the machine to execute the desired action. This communication is denoted s_0. The machine's response is to indicate its understanding of the request, denoted N_0. The person then responds with a message which is a mixture of a control message (judging the appropriateness of the machine's proposed action) and possibly additional clarifying communication. This control system is illustrated in Figure 6.

Let s_l denote the lth user input, $a(s_l)$ the semantic activation array produced by the network of Section 4, and $e(s_l)$ (for $l \geq 2$) the error component of the messages. In this implementation, the values of $e(s_l)$ are 0 or $-\infty$. Let N_l denote the machine response after the lth input message.

Define a total activation array at each stage of the dialog as

$$A_1 = a(s_1) \tag{5.1}$$

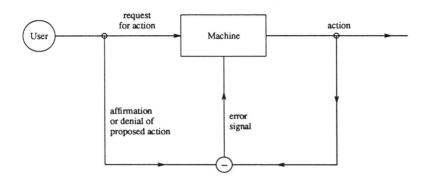

Figure 6: A Conversational Model Providing Semantic-Level Supervision

$$A_l \;=\; (1-\alpha)A_{l-1} + \alpha\, a(s_l) + \begin{bmatrix} 0 \\ \vdots \\ e(s_l) \\ \vdots \\ 0 \end{bmatrix} \leftarrow \text{position } N_{l-1}, \quad (5.2)$$

where α is a gain parameter between 0 and 1. In this implementation, we set $\alpha = 1/l$. If the components of A_l are denoted A_{lk}, then the machine's response after the lth input is to propose action N_l given by

$$N_l = \arg\max_k A_{lk}. \qquad (5.3)$$

The dialog *converges* when $e(s_l) = 0$, at which point action N_{l-1} is executed. The dialog can be terminated and the user *connected to a supervisor* if it continues too long without convergence (an idea which will be quantified shortly). If the dialog converges, then the network is provided with one or more (depending on dialog length) positive examples for adaptation. If the dialog fails to converge, then the negative examples could be exploited for adaptation, (although learning from failures was not implemented in the experiments of Section 6). Thus, a system which *learns by doing* is used to provide positive and negative sentence/action pairs to the network training procedure.

One could explore extensions of this system via variants on $e(s_l)$ and α. In particular, setting $e(s_l)$ to some finite value would allow the dialog to recover from noisy supervision or changes of intent. A more flexible α would allow for an extended dialog with a sequence of goals.

One can consider the probability that such a dialog converges in l steps. A naive convergence model can be derived as follows. Let p be the probability of error on the first user input (i.e., the probability of an unacceptable machine response). In such an event, hypothesize that the second input will comprise an independent paraphrasing of the request, so that probability of error is again p. In such case, if $P(l)$ denotes the probability that a dialog converges ($e(s_l) = 0$) in l steps, then

$$P(l) = p^{l-1}(1 - p). \tag{5.4}$$

It is difficult to experimentally evaluate the validity of (5.4) on this current task, because of the small number of possible actions. However, preliminary experiments on a similar system with 15 actions by Miller [Mil89] verify this exponential decay.

Three sample dialogs with the system are shown below. The first dialog shows a situation where the machine arrives at the correct answer immediately. It anecdotally demonstrates that this is *not* a keyword-based system, as the machine has learned to balance the connections of the semantically significant words *table* and *stain*. Observe that lack of user response is interpreted as affirmation. The second dialog shows a situation where the machine encounters an unknown word, that was key to the semantic interpretation. Error recovery proceeds via the dialog control model of formulas 5.1-5.3, and nodes are created in the network for newly observed words. The third dialog shows, anecdotally, how that unknown word has been learned by the system from the previous interaction. Observe that this newly learned word is understood in a different context than in which it was learned, although *no* word-level supervision was provided.

The activation outputs of the first and second best choices are compared to decide whether to respond confidently (as in Sessions 1 and 3) or hesitantly (as in Session 2).

SOME CONVERSATIONS
Session One

Machine: HELLO.
            THIS IS THE J.C. BELL DEPARTMENT STORE.
            WE SELL FURNITURE, CLOTHING AND HARDWARE.
            HOW MAY I HELP YOU?

User: *Where can I get some stain for my redwood table?*

Machine: I WILL CONNECT YOU TO THE HARDWARE
            DEPARTMENT.

User:

Operator: HELLO, THIS IS THE HARDWARE DEPARTMENT.
            MAY I HELP YOU?

Session Two

Machine: HELLO.
            THIS IS THE J.C. BELL DEPARTMENT STORE.
            HOW MAY I HELP YOU?

User: *I need a blue tuxedo.*

Machine: MAYBE I SHOULD CONNECT YOU TO THE FURNITURE
            DEPARTMENT?

User: *No, a tuxedo is something that you wear.*

Machine: I WILL CONNECT YOU TO THE CLOTHING DEPART-
            MENT.

User: *Ok, let's try that.*

Operator: HELLO, THIS IS THE CLOTHING DEPARTMENT.
            MAY I HELP YOU?

Session Three

Machine: HELLO.
            THIS IS THE J.C. BELL DEPARTMENT STORE.
            HOW MAY I HELP YOU?

User: *I want to buy a tuxedo because I'm getting married tomorrow.*

Machine: I WILL CONNECT YOU TO THE CLOTHING
            DEPARTMENT.

User:

Operator: HELLO, THIS IS THE CLOTHING DEPARTMENT.
            MAY I HELP YOU?

6   Experimental Results

An experiment was performed in which 12 users conducted typed conversations with the system over a two month period. Initially, the system knew nothing about the language for its task. It had *no* vocabulary, *no* grammar and *no* semantic associations. In the course of over 1000 conversations, the machine acquired a vocabulary of over 1500 words, their meaning in the context of this task, and a rudimentary grammar.

The machine was initially provided with the concepts of word, phrase and sentence, but with no instantiations thereof. A word was defined to be any character string delimited by blanks or punctuation, and a phrase defined to be any adjacent pair of words. Each time a new word or phrase was observed in an input message, a new node was created in the network of Figure 5. The only exceptions to this zero initialization were the words *no* and *ok*, whose semantic associations to the error function e of formula 5.2 were provided.

We report on several quantitative results of this experiment. First, we analyze how the vocabulary grows over time. Second, we show that there are but a few frequently occurring words, and that most words occur infrequently. In particular, the rank-frequency plots for both words and word-pairs are linear in the log-log domain, following Zipf's Law [Pie61] (pp. 238). One concludes that the machine is consistently faced with input messages containing unknown words and phrases.

How does one evaluate the performance of such a system, which is consistently encountering the unknown? A certain percentage of errors is inevitable, given its incomplete knowledge. (An old adage says that 'someone who claims never to make mistakes is either a liar or a fool'.) We thus evaluate such a device in two ways. First, when it does make a mistake, can it recognize the error and recover from it? Second, does it learn from the mistake?

Based on these ideas, we perform two experiments to evaluate the performance of the inward-call manager. First, we measure the probability of dialog convergence in one, two or three interactions, illustrating the error recovery capability during the *learning by doing* operation. Second, we evaluate the stability of that learning, by measuring how well it remembers what it was taught.

6.1 Vocabulary Growth and Distribution

The vocabulary size was measured after each conversation, and is plotted in Figure 7. The system acquired over 1500 words and almost 3200 word-pairs during the course of the 1000 conversations. The vocabulary shows no sign of leveling off, increasing at a rate of approximately 1.2 new words per conversation, indicating that the system is nowhere near saturation.

The distribution of words is shown in Figure 8, on a log-log scale. Rank is defined as the number of times a word occurred, and frequency is the number of distinct words with that rank. There are only a few words which occur frequently, while most words occur infrequently. The linear behavior of the log-log plot is a general phenomena, known as Zipf's Law. The same behavior is exhibited by the rank-frequency plot of word-pairs in Figure 9.

Table 1 shows a list of the most frequently occurring words, and Table 2 the most frequently occurring word-pairs. One observes that most of these

word	count	word	count
I	541	my	177
a	417	for	169
you	259	want	141
need	250	some	136
to	238	sell	136

Table 1.   Most Frequent Words

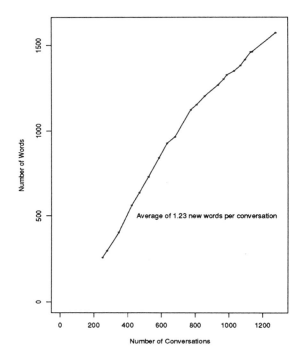

Figure 7: Vocabulary Growth

high-frequency words and phrases are semantically null for the task. Conversely, one can observe that many of the low-frequency words (of which there are many more, so we do not list them) are semantically significant. This again emphasizes the importance of being continually in a learning mode, i.e. of *learning by doing*.

6.2 Dialog Length

Table 3 shows the measured probability of a conversation converging in at most 1, 2 or 3 interactions. The 68% success rate on initial inputs is indicative of the introduction of over one new vocabulary word per conversation. The 2% of non-successful conversations concluded with a ma-

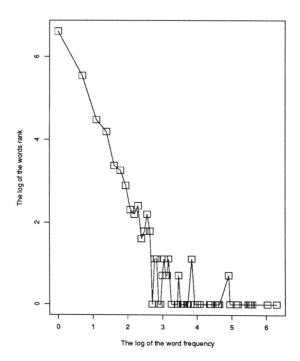

Figure 8:   Log-Log Plot of Word Rank versus Frequency

chine message *I'm sorry, I will have to connect you to a human operator, please hold on,* corresponding to the machine action for an *out-of-scope* request. Upon examination, we observed that some of these were actually out-of-scope, while others were due to noisy supervision. I.e., the machine proposed the correct action, but the user judged it inappropriate (either inadvertently, or maliciously to test robustness.) Although it did occur, we did not measure the other type of noisy supervision, in which a user judged an inappropriate response to be appropriate.

One can ask how such results will scale as the number of actions increase. In Section 5, we derived a naive dialog convergence model (formula 5.4) providing theoretical justification for predicting an exponential decay in probability of dialog length. Miller [Mil89], in an experiment involving 15 actions, obtained experimental results similar to Table 3 which furthermore

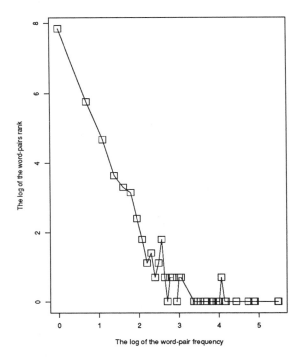

Figure 9: Log-Log Plot of Word-Pair Rank versus Frequency

follow this predicted exponential decay.

6.3 Stability

The next experiment measured the stability of the learning, i.e. how well did the machine remember what it was taught? This was done by testing on the training data. The network which resulted from the over 1000 conversations was tested, without additional adaptation, on the first input sentence from each of those conversations. Table 4 shows the probability of correct semantic action for both the single-layer and multi-layer networks, indicating that the rudimentary syntax-related information captured by the phrase-layer does indeed provide additional task-relevant knowledge.

word-pair	count
I need	243
do you	239
I want	134
you sell	131
need a	114

Table 2. Most Frequent Word-Pairs

Length	1	2	3
Probability of Success	68%	92%	98%

Table 3. Dialog Length

Interestingly, experiments also showed that during the learning mode, performance was the same for the two networks. By analogy, consider two students being taught new material by the same teacher. During their learning mode, both error and recover in approximately the same manner. When given final exams, however, one student remembers 99% of what he was taught, the other only 95%.

Network	Probability of Success
Single-Layer	95%
Multi-Layer	99%

Table 4. How Well the Network Remembers what it was Taught?

These results are similar to those obtained on several other tasks where the number of actions range between 2 and 15 [Gor89] [Ger89] [Mil89].

7 Conclusions

Existing Automated Speech Recognition technology is based upon constructing models of the various levels of linguistic structure assumed to comprise spoken language. These models are either constructed manually or automatically trained by example. A major impediment is the cost or even the feasibility of producing models of sufficient fidelity to enable the desired level of performance.

We have proposed an alternative, which is to build a device capable of acquiring the necessary linguistic skills *in the course of performing its task.*

We call this *learning by doing,* and have contrasted it with the traditional method of *learning by example.*

We have described some basic principles and mechanisms upon which such a device might be based. One of these principles is that the purpose of language is to communicate. This yields an operational definition of language acquisition, namely to gain the ability to extract information from a message. The second principle is to govern the learning by a feedback control system where the error signal is at the level of meaning. In particular, the error signal is a judgment of the appropriateness of the machine response.

We described a connectionist mechanism which builds associations between message components and machine actions, utilizing a novel training procedure in which the connection weights were defined as mutual information. We then defined a dialog control mechanism based on control system methods utilizing semantic-level error feedback. We recounted a rudimentary experiment which demonstrated and evaluated these principles and mechanisms on a text-based inward call manager, involving over 1000 conversations with 12 users. Starting with only the words *no* and *ok* in its vocabulary, it acquired a vocabulary of over 1500 words during the course of performing its task, and retained 99% of what it experienced.

Although the experiments conducted thus far are of a rudimentary nature, we consider them to be the early stages in a long-term study of automatic acquisition of intelligence by machines through interaction with a complex environment.

We envision several directions for future research. One direction is to utilize spoken rather than typed input to the system, exploring how its behavior changes when the input message is a stochastic process rather than a deterministic signal. Furthermore, in fluent speech, one will not be provided with explicit word boundaries. We anticipate such a system acquiring new words based on both acoustic and semantic consistency. A second research direction is to extend the feedback control system governing the human/machine dialog, allowing more sophisticated discourse, including multiple actions, changes of intent, and recovery from noisy supervision.

A third direction is to attempt tasks with a larger and more complex repertory of actions. Relationships among actions imply some useful model of how the machine and its environment interact. One can exploit such relationships in order to obtain improved generalization in the language acquisition process.

However, as the repertory of actions becomes more complex, one encounters a familiar impediment: the model is manually constructed, so that the cost and feasibility of obtaining high-fidelity representations limits performance. As in this current work, an alternative is to automatically acquire that model.

This motivates a fourth direction of future research, which is to explore how a machine might automatically acquire the model necessary to enable speech understanding for complex tasks. The model which people utilize when understanding speech is derived from interaction with their total environment, utilizing the five senses and proprioception as input and physical action as output. We conjecture that in order to acquire a model which will enable high-performance speech understanding for complex tasks, a machine must also possess such sensory-motor capabilities. We believe that the same principles and mechanisms described for language acquisition are applicable to this problem.

Acknowledgements

We thank L. R. Rabiner for his suggestion of exploring connectionist approaches to language learning, and M. S. Sondhi for many enlightening conversations on control theory. We also thank K. W. Church, F. Pereira, L. R. Rabiner and N. Z. Tishby for their review of this manuscript and many insightful comments.

Bibliography

[All89]   R. B. Allen and M. E. Riecken, "Reference in Connectionist Language Users," pp. 301–308, in "Connectionism in Perspective," (ed. R. Pfeifer et al.), North-Holland (1989).

[And77]   J. R. Anderson, "Induction of Augmented Transition Networks," Cognitive Science, Vol. 1, 1977, pp. 125–157.

[Bar90]   A. G. Barto and S. P. Singh, "Reinforcement Learning and Dynamic Programming," Proc. of The Sixth Yale Workshop on Adaptive and Learning Systems, pp. 83–86, August 1990.

[Bro86]   R. A. Brooks, "A Robust Layered Control System for a Mobile Robot," IEEE Journal of Robotics and Automation, Vol. RA-2, No. 1, pp. 14–23, March 1986.

[Cho57]   N. Chomsky, "Syntactic Structures," Mouton Publishers, Paris (1957).

[Cho65]   N. Chomsky, "Aspects of the Theory of Syntax," The M.I.T. Press, (1965).

[Chu89]   K. W. Church and P. Hanks, "Word Association Norms, Mutual Information and Lexicography," Proc. of 27th Meeting of the Association for Computational Linguistics, pp. 76–83. (Expanded version to appear in the Journal of Computational Linguistics, 1990.)

[Cla87]   E. V. Clark, "The Principle of Contrast: A Constraint on Language Acquisition," pp. 1–34 in "Mechanisms of Language Acquisition," (ed. B. MacWhinney), Erlbaum Publishers (1987).

[Dud73]   R. O. Duda and P. E. Hart, "Pattern Classification and Scene Analysis," Wiley (1973).

[Fod75]   J. A. Fodor, "Language of Thought," Crowell, New York (1975) pp. 103.

[Fu75]   K. S. Fu and T. L. Booth, "Grammatical Inference: Introduction and Survey — Parts 1 and 2," IEEE Trans. on Systems, Man and Cybernetics, SMC5 (1), pp. 95–111, SMC5(4), pp. 409–423.

[Fur83]   G. W. Furnas, T. K. Landauer, L. M. Gomez, S. T. Dumais, "Statistical Semantics: Analysis of the Potential Performance of Key-Word Information Systems," BSTJ Vol. 62, No. 6, July-August 1983.

[Fur85]   G. W. Furnas, "Experience with an Adaptive Indexing Scheme," Proc. CHI Human Factors in Computing Systems, April 1985, San Francisco, pp. 131–135.

[Ger89]   A. N. Gertner and A. L. Gorin, "A Multi-Layer Network for Adaptive Language Acquisition," AT&T Bell Laboratories Technical Memorandum, Dec. 1989, unpublished.

[Gol67]   E. M. Gold, "Language Identification in the Limit," Information and Control, Vol. 10, pp. 447–474 (1967).

[Goo89]   R. M. Goodman, J. W. Miller and P. Smyth, "An Information-Theoretic Approach to Rule-Based Connectionist Expert Systems," in "Advances in Neural Information Processing Systems," Morgan Kaufmann (1989).

[Goo89a]   R. Goodman and P. Smyth, "The Induction of Probabilistic Rule Sets — The ITRULE Algorithm," Proc. of the Sixth International Workshop on Machine Learning, 1989.

[Goo90]   R. M. Goodman, C. Higgins, J. Miller, P. Smyth, "A Rule-Based Approach to Neural Network Classifiers," to appear in the Proc. of the International Neural Network Conference, Paris, July 1990.

[Gor89]   A. L. Gorin and S. E. Levinson, "Adaptive Acquisition of Language," AT&T Bell Laboratories Technical Memorandum, August 1989, unpublished.

[Gor89a]   A. L. Gorin and S. E. Levinson, "A Neural Network with Information-Theoretic Connection Weights," AT&T Bell Laboratories Technical Memorandum, Dec. 1989, unpublished.

[Jai90]   A. N. Jain and A. H. Waibel, "Incremental Parsing by Modular Recurrent Connectionist Networks," in "Advances in Neural Information Processing Systems," (ed. D. S. Touretzky), Morgan Kaufmann (1990).

[Jel90]   F. Jelinek, "Self-Organizing Language Modeling for Speech Recognition," pp. 450–506, in "Readings and Speech Recognition," (ed. Waibel and Lee), Morgan Kaufmann (1990).

[Jua90]   B. H. Juang and L. R. Rabiner, "The Segmental K-Means Algorithm for Estimating Parameters of Hidden Markov Models," to appear in the IEEE Trans. on ASSP.

[Lan82]   P. Langley, "Language Acquisition Through Error Recover," Cognition and Brain Theory, 1982, 5(3), 211–255.

[Lev80]   S. E. Levinson and K. L. Shipley, "A Conversational-Mode Airline Information and Reservation System Using Speech Input and Output," Bell System Technical Journal, Vol. 59, No. 1, Jan. 80, pp. 119-137.

[Lev85]   S. E. Levinson, "Structural Methods in Automatic Speech Recognition," Proc. IEEE, Vol. 73, No. 11, pp. 1625-1650, Nov. 1985.

[Lev89]   S. E. Levinson, M. Y. Liberman, A. Ljolje, and L. Miller, "Speaker-Independent Phonetic Transcription of Fluent Speech for Large-Vocabulary Speech Recognition," Proc. ICASSP, pp. 441–444, May 1989.

[Mac87]   B. MacWhinney (ed.), "Mechanisms of Language Acquisition," Erlbaum (1987).

[Mag90]   D. M. Magerman and M. P. Marcus, "Parsing a Natural Language using Mutual Information Statistics," Proc. of the AAAI (1990).

[McC86]   J. L. McClelland and A. H. Kawanoto, "Mechanisms of Sentence Processing: Assigning Roles to Constituents of Sentences," in Parallel Distributed Processing, Vol. 2, Chapt. 19, (ed. J. L. McClelland and D. E. Rumelhart), MIT Press.

[Mil89]   L. Miller, A. L. Gorin and S. E. Levinson, "Adaptive Language Acquisition for a Database Query Task," AT&T Bell Laboratories Technical Memorandum, Dec. 1989, unpublished.

[Min88]   M. Minsky and S. Papert, "Perceptions: An Introduction to Computational Geometry," MIT Press, Cambridge, Mass. (1988).

[Moo73]   T. E. Moore (ed.), "Cognitive Development and the Acquisition of Language," Academic Press (1973).

[Nar74]   K. S. Narendra and M. A. L. Thathachar, "Learning Automata — A Survey," IEEE Trans. on Systems, Man and Cybernetics, Vol. SMC-4, No. 4, July 1974.

[Pie61]   J. R. Pierce, "Symbols, Signals and Noise," Harper (1961).

[Pit88]   L. Pitt and L. G. Valiant, "Computational Limitations on Learning from Examples," Journal of the ACM, Vol. 35, No. 4, pp. 965–984, October 1988.

[Rum86]   D. E. Rumelhart and J. L. McClelland, "Parallel Distributed Processing," Vol. 1 and 2, MIT Press (1986).

[Sal89]   G. Salton, "Automatic Text Processing," Section 10.3, Addison-Wesley (1989).

[Sis90]   J. M. Siskind, "Acquiring Core Meanings of Words," Proc. of the 28th Annual Meeting of the Association for Computational Linguistics, pp. 143–156, June 1990.

[Smy90]   P. Smyth and R. M. Goodman, "An Information-Theoretic Approach to Rule Induction from Databases," to appear in IEEE Trans. on Knowledge and Data Engineering.

[Son67]   M. M. Sondhi, "An Adaptive Echo Canceller," BSTJ Vol. 46, pp. 497–511, 1967, reprinted in "Speech Enhancement," (ed. J. S. Lim), IEEE Press (1982).

[Spr90]   R. Sproat and C. Shih, "A Statistical Method for Finding Word Boundaries in Chinese Text," to appear in Computer Processing of Chinese and Oriental Languages.

[Tan87]   D. W. Tank and J. J. Hopfield, "Neural Computation by Concentrating Information in Time," Proc. Nat. Academy Sci., pp. 1896–1900, April 1987.

[Tho69]   J. B. Thomas, "Statistical Communication Theory," Wiley (1969).

[Van77]   C. J. Van Rijsbergen, "A Theoretical Basis for the use of Co-Occurrence Data in Information Retrieval," Journal of Documentation, Vol. 33, No. 2, pp. 106–119, June 1977.

[Val84]   L. G. Valiant, "A Theory of the Learnable," Communications of the ACM, Vol. 27, No. 11, pp. 1134–1142, November 1984.

[Wan82]   E. Wanner and L. R. Gleitman, "Language Acquisition: The State of the Art," Cambridge University Press (1982).

[Wat68]   W. C. Watt, "Habitability," American Documentation, pp. 338–351, July 1968.

[Web87]   Webster's Ninth New Collegiate Dictionary, Merriam-Webster, 1987.

[Wid76]   B. Widrow, J. M. McCool, M. G. Larimore and C. R. Johnson, "Stationary and Nonstationary Learning Characteristics of the LMS Adaptive Filter," Proc. of the IEEE, Vol. 64, No. 8, August 1976.

[Wie61]   N. Wiener, "Cybernetics," 2nd edition, MIT Press, 1961.

[Wil90]   R. J. Williams and L. C. Baird, "A Mathematical Analysis of Actor-Critic Architectures," Proc. of the Sixth Yale Workshop on Adaptive and Learning Systems, pp. 96–101, August 1990.

[Wil89]   J. G. Wilpon, L. R. Rabiner, C. H. Lee and E. Goldman, "Automatic Recognition of Vocabulary Word Sets in Unconstrained Speech using HMMs," to appear in IEEE Trans. on ASSP.

[Win84]   P. H. Winston, "Artificial Intelligence," Addison-Wesley (1984).

[Zue90]   V. Zue, J. Glass, D. Goodine, H. Leung, M. McCandless, M. Phillips, J. Polifrone, and S. Seneff, "Recent Progress on the Voyager System," Proc. of the DARPA Speech and Natural Language Workshop, June 1990.

What Connectionist Models Learn: Learning and Representation in Connectionist Networks [1]

Stephen José Hanson
Siemens Corporate Research, Inc.
Princeton, NJ

David J. Burr
Bellcore
Morristown, NJ

1 Introduction

There have been historical tensions between the study of learning and the study of representation in psychology and artificial intelligence (AI). For over half a century behavioral psychologists addressed the problem of how knowledge was acquired from experience but ignored the problem of how knowledge and experience were represented internally (Skinner 1950). AI also initially focused on learning (Rosenblatt 1962), but soon turned almost exclusively to the study of representation (Minsky & Papert 1969). With the advent of cognitive psychology (e.g., Miller 1956), internal representation was on psychology's agenda too, but most of the work was still in the style of AI, inspired by the "computer metaphor" (Pylyshyn 1984). Meanwhile, except among behavioral psychologists, the problem of learning was receding into the background. Recently, a new approach, connectionism (Rumelhart & McClelland 1986), has offered not only an alternative "neural network metaphor," but a different style of computation, one that is especially suited to learning and allows the relationship between learning and representation to be studied directly for the first time.

According to popular accounts (Gardner 1985) and their sources (e.g., Miller 1987), the behavioral-to-cognitive shift that began in psychology

[1]This paper is reprinted from Hanson, S. (1990). What Connectionist Models Learn: Learning and Representation in Connectionist Neural Networks. *Brain and Behavioral Sciences*, 13(3), pp. 471-511. ©1990 Cambridge University Press. Reprinted with permission.

somewhere around 1956 took place partly because of the gradual pervasion
of psychologists' mental and personal lives by computers and partly because
none of the available answers to the question "what exactly is learned during learning?" proved to be satisfactory. Psychological phenomena turned
out to be too complex to be explained by existing theories. For example,
the crucial role of language in human learning far exceeded the explana-
tory scope of simple learning models, and language learning itself posed
uniquely cognitive as opposed to behavioral problems (Skinner 1957, and
Chomsky 1959). Yet even the combined resources of behavioral and cognitive psychology have so far proved unable to provide an integrated theory
of learning and representation; rather, as in AI, representation is now being
studied at the expense of learning.

The computer metaphor has had a profound and lasting effect on psychological modeling, as indicated by the proliferation of cognitive "flow-
charts" with rules in boxes linked by arrows. Many cognitive scientists
would agree with Anderson (1983) that "underlying human cognition is
a set of condition-action pairs called productions". This "rule-based" approach, although it provides an impressive array of tools for knowledge
representation, has unfortunately not proved useful for the study of learning. Its inadequacy is not evident when one studies toy problems, involving
only a small number of rules that need to be fine-tuned (Laird, Rosenblum
& Newell 1985; Schank 1975), but in more realistic tasks (e.g., expert systems, Lenat 1983), rule-based models face the characteristic problems that
tend to arise in AI research. A learning system should be able to acquire
and update its rules automatically on the basis of its existing rules while
learning to solve new problems. In practice, however, the existing rules
are often unable to handle new problems, which makes the entire system
very "brittle." The programmer must then typically introduce new rules
into the system and test their interactions, thereby creating a "bottleneck".
This need to keep intervening and revising on the part of the programmer
does not seem to be leading in the direction of a system that can learn
autonomously. The recurrent difficulties are all related to specifying the
size, nature and interdependencies of the rules whenever either the task or
the rules change (Langley 1983). The rule-based approach may not yet be
bankrupt when it comes to learning, but checks have bounced [2].

An interesting alternative to the rule-based approach has appeared recently: *Connectionism* consists of some old ideas about representation,

---

[2] The problem with the rule-based approach to machine learning is that the way
knowledge is represented is not integrated with the way the representation can be modified. There seems to be a general tradeoff between the complexity of the components
of the representation and how easily they can be changed while still preserving global
consistency throughout the representation.

spreading activation, semantic decomposition, and associative memory all packaged in something that looks like a cartoon brain with cartoon neurons, connected by cartoon synapses. Despite the demise of the *Perceptron* [3] (Rosenblatt 1962; Minsky & Papert 1969), neural network research has actually been alive and well and advancing at a steady if modest pace. Indeed, those who have been doing neural network modeling all along (Longuet-Higgins, Willshaw, Buneman 1970; Grossberg, 1976; Kohonen 1977; Anderson, Silverstein, Ritz, & Jones 1977) would no doubt view the recent meteoric rise of connectionism as a case of "disinhibition" rather than rebirth.

New learning methods (Ackley, Hinton, Sejnowski 1985; Rumelhart, Hinton, & Williams 1986) have played a significant role in disinhibiting connectionist modeling, but the relationship between the learning algorithms and the representations that may support them still remains largely unanalyzed. Nevertheless, in providing a framework for the study of learning and representation the new connectionism may in turn have disinhibited the behavioral science of the first half of the 20th century and made it possible to unify it with the cognitive science of the later half.

We will now present an overview of current connectionist models (henceforth "nets"), followed by a description of the goals of this target article and some specific hypotheses about learning and representation in such models. Then we will show how a geometric analysis of nets can provide a deeper understanding of pattern classification, distributed representations, and rule-based interpretations of network performance. Finally, we will show how data analytic methods can be applied to two large nets to determine just what it is that they have learned.

Nets can be created by independently varying certain features of what amounts to a simplified programming language. It is still somewhat controversial just which of these features are the critical ones, how they should be composed and what the corresponding computational powers of the net are. The features that will be singled out here are present in most nets, however, and provide reference points within the vast spectrum of possible nets, as the following taxonomy based on them will illustrate.

---

[3] The Perceptron was an early neural network model consisting of a set of modifiable weights interconnecting two layers of units, an input layer and an output layer. Such a system can only learn to discriminate stimuli that are "linearly separable," i.e., those that can be separated by a hyperplane in feature space.

2   Taxonomy of Connectionist Models

"Connectionist models" (nets) include a broad class of learning systems (Hinton 1987) that have the following three general features: They consist of (1) simple computing elements ("units"), arranged in various possible (2) architectures (e.g., "layers") with arbitrary patterns of interconnectedness, [4] and (3) recursive rules for updating the strength of the connections between the units. Many features of nets can be readily varied: This flexibility is an advantage to the modeler, but the potential variants it gives rise to are many and heterogeneous, and may appear only loosely related to one another. Certain core features nevertheless allow us to provide a taxonomy (Figure 1) and to explicate the novel computational aspects of the connectionist approach.

An example of a characteristic learning task for a net is categorization: Given a set of stimuli defined in an arbitrary feature space, a net can be asked to sort them into a predetermined set of categories. The net encodes each stimulus as a unique pattern of predefined features (i.e., the input representation is given). The activation of the input units in turn produces patterns of activity throughout the net. Some units (other than input units) can be treated as "output" units and still others as "internal state"s ("hidden units") of the net. Learning consists of changes in certain properties of the output units and the hidden units. In learning, the net can come to sort stimuli into "correct" categories, as indicated by properties of the output units. The properties in question will be discussed in detail in section 2.1.

The three general features singled out here – the computing elements, their architectures and their learning rules – are independent of the task they are performing. Consequently, when a particular kind of net is being designed for a particular task, its specific features are likely to be selected on an ad hoc rather than a principled basis, as in using a programming language. Hence when these features are used in psychological modeling there is always the possibility that they will have little to do with the behavioral or cognitive phenomena of interest. It is hoped that the more detailed computational analysis to be presented here will provide a better basis for selecting and interpreting nets as models for psychological processes.

A taxonomy that illustrates much (though by no means all) of the diversity of nets is shown in Figure 1. Its first level concerns the activation (or "transfer") function, which determines the kind of information one unit can signal to another. This may be linear or nonlinear. Nonlinear mod-

---

[4]Nets can be represented as arbitrary graphs of computing elements arranged in arbitrary topologies that may or may not include cycles.

els generate considerably more variable and complex performance. Linear models, on the other hand, can provide approximations that may help us understand what the nonlinear models are doing.

The second level of the taxonomy concerns the nature of the connections between units; these may be either "recurrent" – those that allow activation to flow (symmetrically or asymmetrically) through the net in arbitrary directions – or nonrecurrent (feedforward or acyclic) connections, which only allow activation to flow in one direction. Recurrence requires the activation function to be nonlinear (which is why "linear/recurrent" is the same as "linear/nonrecurrent" in Figure 1) and makes richer and more varied network behavior possible. [5]

At the next level of our taxonomy, the learning (or weight updating) rule is classified on the basis of properties of the input. If the stimuli are uncorrelated in feature space then a "Hebb" rule (or simple outer-product, Hebb 1949) can be used to learn or store the patterns in the net without interference. The Hebb rule modifies the correlation between the activities of units. It can be used in an "unsupervised" task, one in which no external feedback about correctness is provided. Under a weaker condition, one in which stimuli cannot be expressed as linear transformations of one another, an error-correcting rule such as the delta rule (Widrow & Hoff 1960) can be used to learn without interference. The delta rule uses the discrepancy between each unit's activity and the correct response to modify the correlation between units. (An unsupervised error-correcting system must somehow establish an internal criterion for correctness.)

The features of nets could be subclassified much further, but the last feature we will consider here is whether or not the connections between units compete with one another for activation strength. Many nets are based on competition between units, which can create groups of units that mutually reinforce each other through competition for activation from other units. Note that there are limits on the potential usefulness of taxonomies like the one in Figure 1 because what we know and want to know about nets will change over time. Nevertheless, the few features we have singled out here provide a framework for the arguments and analyses we will now present.

---

[5] Most of our analyses and conclusions will be independent of the presence or absence of extensive recurrence in the net. The introduction of dynamics can have significant effects on the computational properties of nets but will not be considered here. We will provide simple abstract foundations for network computation that account for most of the models in Figure 1; such a static analysis is a prerequisite for analyzing more complex cases. A number of recent models use recurrence (Pineda, 1988; Williams & Zipser 1988; Pearlmutter 1988; Singhal 1987).

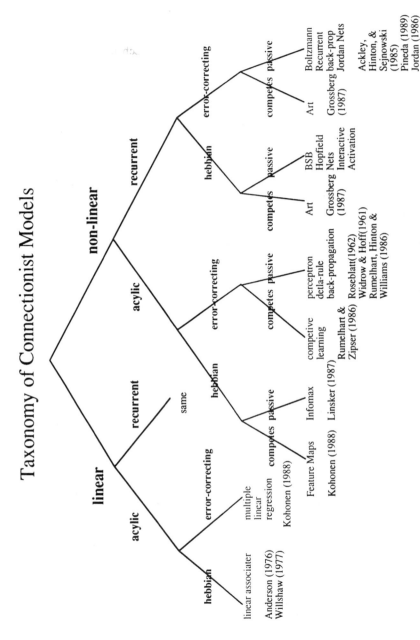

Taxonomy of Connectionist Models

Figure 1: Description on page 200

2.1 Units

At the heart of any net is a simple function that integrates information and transmits it from one set of units to another. Each unit has a distinct "fan-in", or set of input connections, which defines the input to that unit, plus a "fan-out," or set of output connections, which defines the output of that unit. In a net with recurrence, the input and output lines may be thought of as shared; it accordingly makes sense to think of a logical fan-in and fan-out to any such unit.

Figure 2 shows a typical unit with distinct fan-in and fan-out lines and associated functions (e.g., the fan-in is integrated by a summation function). The inset shows a fan-out that is associated with a *decision function*: a threshold step (Heaviside) function. Note that irrespective of whether the output is discrete or continuous over the activation range (as in the case of the popular *sigmoidal*, logistic, or *tanh* functions), a nonlinearity must be present. Both the Heaviside function,

$$a = H(\mathbf{f}) \tag{1}$$

where H is defined as

$$H = 1 \quad \text{if } \mathbf{f} \geq 0$$

$$H = 0 \quad \text{if } \mathbf{f} < 0$$

and the logistic,

$$a = \frac{1}{1 + e^{-\mathbf{f}}} \tag{2}$$

include a term which orients the fan-in function in feature space:

$$\mathbf{f} = \sum w_i u_i - \theta \tag{3}$$

Omitting threshold functions can seriously reduce the computational power of the net. What remains, however, is the sum of a large number of smooth continuous functions; this is known to be able to yield a powerful function approximator (as in Fourier analysis). It is possible to have nonlinear fan-in functions of the input that would allow the formation of complex partitions of feature space called "decision boundaries". One general form for such units is a polynomial of arbitrary order which can create arbitrary boundaries (see Figure 3 for example).

There are generalizations of fan-in functions which deviate from the usual dot-product function (linear in the decision boundary). One might

Typical UNIT in Network

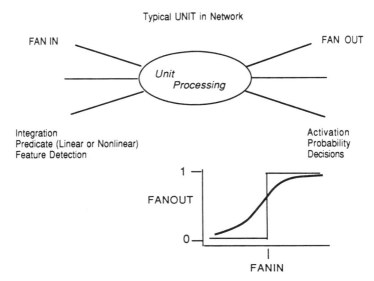

FAN IN

Unit
Processing

FAN OUT

Integration
Predicate (Linear or Nonlinear)
Feature Detection

Activation
Probability
Decisions

FANOUT

1

0

FANIN

Figure 2: Description on page 200

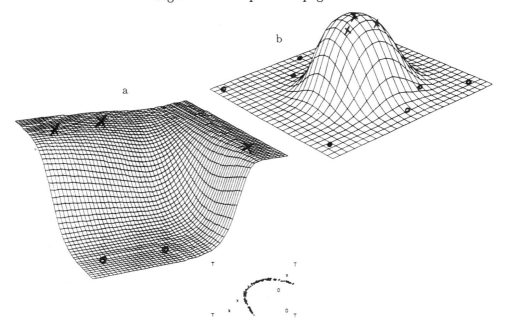

Figure 3: Description on page 200

think of these as analogous to complex "synaptic-dendritic" interactions within or between units (cf. Shepherd & Brayton 1987). In Figure 4, for example, we show five general cases of fan-in functions. The first case is linear; this is in a sense the most constrained function, in that there are no interactions with other units. The second, quadratic case weakens this constraint by allowing units to have more than one "axonal projection" (or connection) to a "dendrite." This allows interactions within the unit such that "synaptic" connections from the same unit can modulate each other. This sort of within-unit interaction is sufficient to produce quadratic boundaries or volumes like spheres (case three). Case four, polynomial units, allows further interactions between units on the same dendrite. These are the general, arbitrary-degree polynomials, including the *sigma-pi* case (Williams 1986; Maxwell, Giles & Lee 1988; Durbin & Rumelhart, 1989) and all possible decision conics, including hyperspheres (Cooper, 1962), hyperellipsoids and hyperhyperboloids (Specht 1967). The last and most general kind of fan-in function is an arbitrary decision volume based on still more general fan-in function.

As these fan-in functions become more complex, increasingly complex interactions are required at the neuronal level, with a corresponding need for more "neural" hardware to support them. Also, as the fan-in function of the individual unit is made more complex, fewer *network* properties are required to make the computation more general. In other words, individual units become more powerful at the expense of the interactive properties of the net as a whole.

This may be undesirable when one is modeling learning. For example, it is unclear how the degrees of freedom inherent in the shape of decision boundaries trade off with the complexity of learning such boundaries. A learning problem may be made worse as local node complexity is increased. This trade-off is analogous to the relationship between linear and nonlinear regression, where the nonlinearity increases the degrees of freedom in the model, allowing more flexibility in the accommodation of data, while making the parameter search problem harder and the fit of the model to the data potentially more arbitrary.

The fan-out function of a unit can also be varied, but with much less effect. What seems to be most important is the smoothness of the individual unit response. The output rate of real presynaptic neurons suggests a rationale for the existence and nature of fan-out functions. Biological neurons produce spikes at a rate that is a function of their stimulation. Their spike rate would be stochastic and might be well fitted as a Poisson process (Tomko & Crapper 1987):

Linear

$$\sum x_i w_{ij} \; + \; \theta_i$$

Quadratic

$$\sum x_i^2 w_{ij} \; + \; \theta_i$$

Spherical

$$\sum (x_i - w_{ij})^2 + \theta_i$$

Polynomial

$$\sum \sum x_i x_j w_{ijk} + x_i^{\alpha_i} + x_j^{\alpha_j} + \theta_k$$

General

$$\sum \Phi(\mathbf{x}, \mathbf{w})$$

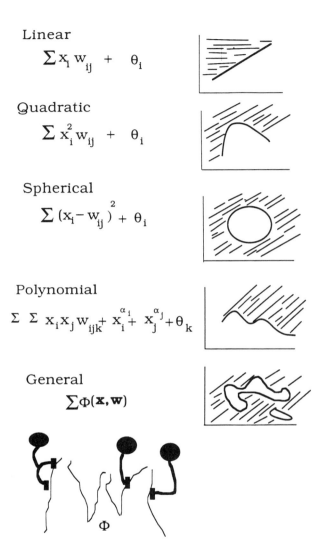

Figure 4: Description on page 200

$$P(k) = \frac{\lambda^k exp(-\lambda)}{k!} \qquad (4)$$

The latency between spikes (or the average interspike interval obtained by integrating over time) provides rate information that could be used by postsynaptic units. The specific sort of rate function one gets from such integration is a gamma distribution function, which is smooth and sigmoidal.

The logistic or hyperbolic tangent functions have been used in the fan-out of units in models like ART (adaptive resonance theory, Grossberg, 1987), brain-state-in-box (Anderson, 1976), Boltzmann machines (Ackley, Hinton & Sejnowski, 1985), CMAC (Albus, 1975), and back-propagation (Rumelhart, Hinton & Williams, 1986). The specific properties of either the gamma or the logistic as spike rate functions seem to be less important than the smoothness of the generalization surface as composed by such units. Equally important is the rate at which the surface falls off from some maximal point in the feature space. Many possible fan-out functions can be considered for various problems. For example, combining spherical regions with periodic decay can produce lateral inhibition effects and so-called *center-surround* or Marr-Hildreth units (Marr 1982). Such variations may have very specific applications to vision, audition or motor control. Different fan-out functions may be useful for different kinds of function approximation; whether or not particular function approximation classes are suited to particular problem domains is unclear.

Although, monotone increasing activation functions are suggested by analogy with the firing rate information received by postsynaptic units, a stronger reason for using such fan-out functions is that they can be shown to be used for composing real valued functions (cf. Williams 1986; Hornik, Stinchcombe & White, 1988; Cybenko 1988; Carroll & Dickenson 1989). Another critical aspect of the fan-out function is its role in categorization. The contours and smoothness of the output space will determine the relationship among stimuli – the clusters they may form and their distribution within each category. Fan-out functions can also be interpreted probabilistically, which can lead to deeper connections between neural modeling, multivariate statistics, and inductive inference (Golden 1988). Finally, the parameters of rate functions could also be varied to explore search strategies during learning (cf. Hanson 1990).

2.2   Learning

A central feature of connectionist modeling is learning. Connectionist learning is based on a broad class of parameter [6] search techniques that may
be recursive, nonparametric, nonlinear, biased, and perhaps even inefficient
(cf. Hinton 1987). At first glance these properties may not seem very desirable for learning systems. In the worst cases, they may lead to problems of
computational complexity (Judd 1988, Blum & Rivest 1989) Nonetheless,
it is important to keep in mind that we are interested in learning processes
that could actually occur in brains, not those that could exist in principle only when representative samples and detailed knowledge about the
stochastic nature of the environment are available.

   Three kinds of constraints on learning in biological systems could lead
naturally to the sorts of properties listed above:

1. Data are continuously available but incomplete; the learner must constantly update parameter estimates with stingy bits of data which
   may represent a very small sample from a possible population.

2. The conditional distributions of categories with respect to stimuli and
   their features are unknown and have to be estimated from samples
   that may be unrepresentative.

3. Local information (in time) may be misleading, wrong, or varying;
   this would result in a poor tradeoff between using data now as opposed
   to waiting for more, possibly flawed data, with small and revocable
   updates.

   This small sample of the many kinds of learning constraints faced by
real organisms in real environments suggests why *weak* learning methods
(those that assume very little about the environment) may be so important. Weak algorithms are common in AI; in statistics, assumptions about
normality or dependence between variables may be weakened or features
of large sample statistics may even be ignored. An organism that is born
with prewired information about the probability distributions and statistics
in its environment clearly has an advantage. This may work well for the
kinds of organisms (e.g., some insects) that have little or no environmen-
tal diversity or a very limited behavioral repertoire. But even the analysis

---

[6] The parameters are the weights and connectivity in the net. Parameter search or estimation refers to techniques which attempt to find particular values of the parameters of
a model in order to solve a specific problem or satisfy particular constraints. Parameters
can be chosen to optimize particular criteria, making the search more difficult.

of relatively simple foraging problems of lower mammals (Krebs, 1978) requires a dynamic way of updating information about patch location, density and variance that would quickly overwhelm any prewired system.

The problem of learning a language is likely to complicate this statistical estimation task enormously, enough to make many linguists conclude that much of the structure must somehow be prewired (the "poverty of the stimulus") (Chomsky 1980, Lightfoot 1989) In reality, however, the linguistic environments and data a learner encounter will be large and diverse. Innate species-typical constraints are more likely to be related to general invariant properties of the world – such as its three dimensionality, ambient temperature range, light-day cycle, or food patch distribution – rather than to specific activities (such as chess playing, tennis, or speaking English; cf. Shepard 1987).

2.3   Layers: Hidden Units

A new innovation in connectionist modeling has been the introduction of hidden units (Ackley, Hinton, Sejnowski 1985; Werbos 1974; Rosenblatt 1962, *A-units*). As already mentioned, these are neither input nor output units, but intermediate ones, providing a potential communication link between more task-specific units. In the mammalian nervous system *interneurons*, which are neither sensory nor motor, may perform a similar role (see Jones 1985, chapter 4).

It can be shown that the hidden units are primarily responsible for the increased computational power of the new connectionist networks, both their discriminant power (as indicated by the complexity of their decision boundaries in feature space) and their power to construct input-to-output mappings. At a more abstract level, hidden units allow the net to "invent" or construct "variables" (units that respond consistently to the same input category) and "predicates" (units that respond to a value of a variable with a consistent output) that may be useful in solving a problem the net has been given. For example, a net given various animals (represented for input as sets of features) and asked to sort them into arbitrary groups might invent a hidden unit selective for spotted, four-legged, meat-eating creatures, sorting them into category "P" at the output layer, if their prey was small and warm-blooded. In the hidden layer the network would have invented a "predator" variable, to which the token "tiger" might be bound. The output layer could then implement an "eat" predicate for the category assignment: "eat(predator, prey)".

Perceptron networks, which have no hidden layers, cannot construct variables and predicates. The Perceptron's output layer must operate directly on the linear combinations of the input features rather than on higher-order combinations of these extracted features. A network with hidden layers, on the other hand, can construct quantities X, Y, and Z and arbitrary Boolean combinations of them.

This makes explicit what we've stated before: The capabilities described above are like those of a standard programming language, except that in a net the processes are parallel and continuous rather than serial and discrete. Nonetheless, it is possible in principle for a net to implement any sort of classical computation [7] (McCulloch & Pitts, 1943).

It has been argued that connectionism merely provides an alternative hardware for implementing symbolic models (with the latter's characteristic properties of "productivity,", "systematicity," etc.; Fodor & Pylyshyn 1988). To answer this "mere implementation" argument, many connectionists have focused on unique properties of nets (e.g. subsymbolic or distributed representations; Rumelhart & McClelland, 1986; Smolensky, 1988), but although hidden units have special representational properties, these do not amount to a new kind of representational approach (see below). Instead, these properties turn out to be related to existing data reduction techniques in multivariate statistics and psychometrics. (Dunn-Rankin, 1983; Everit, 1975).

Hidden units do have a remarkable set of properties, for example:

1. Hidden units make possible representations that are selected by the constraints of the task (Ackley, Hinton, & Sejnowski 1985).

2. Hidden-unit representations (e.g. projections of feature space),though independent of the learning rule, can be affected in important ways by a judicious choice of learning rule (cf. Hanson & Burr 1987b, Baum & Wilczek 1987; Hinton 1987).

3. Hidden units are among the determinants of the "attractors" or "stationary points" [8] in activation space and of the net's capacity when dynamics (recurrence) are present (cf. Jordan 1986; Pineda 1988).

---

[7] Since networks with sufficient resources can implement any real valued or boolean function mapping (see below), it is trivial to equate a network of a certain size and type with any turing machine computing the same function. The net would be qualitatively different from the turing machine, however. In general, what functions nets can or cannot learn, and under what conditions, is not yet known and is a current area of intense research (See for example, Rivest, Haussler, Warmuth, 1989)

[8] Neural networks with recurrence can be described by a set of nonlinear differential equations; the solutions of such a system of equations are usually called the attractors or stationary points of the system.

4. Hidden units are projections (linear or nonlinear, depending on the fan-in function) of the input variables or features into a subspace. They may or may not form a basis set for the original input vectors but are important for orthogonalizing them.

5. There are formal similarities between hidden units and (1) components in principal component analysis, (2) dimensions in multidimensional scaling [9] (Shepard, 1962), and (3) families of latent structure and feature extraction techniques (Shepard, Romney & Nerlove, 1968; Duda & Hart, 1973). Hidden units, however, have virtually no constraints on the sorts of linear projections they may perform; they are "weak" feature extractors.

6. Hidden units allow a powerful sort of discriminant analysis to be performed: A single layer of a sufficient number of hidden units can be shown to construct nonconvex regions in either a continuous or a Boolean feature space (Hanson & Burr 1987a; Wieland & Leighton 1987).

7. Hidden units make a powerful continuous compositional process possible, one that is similar to Fourier analysis. With at least one layer of a sufficient number of hidden units [10] and a continuous, monotone fan-out function, any real valued function or mapping from R^n to R^m can be constructed. (Hornik, Stinchcombe & White 1988; Carroll & Dickenson 1989; Cybenko 1988).

Surprisingly, a Perceptron lacks all of these properties. An enormous increase in computational power seems to result from the relatively simple step of adding hidden units.

3   Distributed Representations, Consequential Categories and Explanation

We will make three related claims:

---

[9] There is a close analogy between MDS (multidimensional scaling) methods and nets with hidden units. The Shepard-Kruskal MDS algorithm (Kruskal & Shepard 1974) uses a measure of the error between estimated ranks of pairwise interstimulus similarities that is like a net parameterized with weights between each of the stimuli. Gradient descent is used not only to estimate these weights but concurrently to estimate an initially unknown dimensionality reduction of the given variables. Thus, the dimensions in MDS correspond to hidden units in a net.

[10] The last two points were established in the context of simple acyclic (feedforward) nets; they accordingly apply to any other models that include these very basic network topologies as a special case.

1. Distributed representations are not special in and of themselves and provide no new representational abilities that other knowledge representation schemes from AI or computer science do not have (cf. Smolensky 1988).

2. Networks with hidden units learn "consequential categories" (cf. Shepard 1987) – regions in feature space that result from stimulus generalization [11]. The region associated with the stimulus plus the local nieghborhood make up the consequential region. Networks with hidden units can reorganize the feature space into simple (consequential) regions and associate them with output categories; this mapping corresponds closely to what is meant by a rule in symbolic models.

3. Post hoc analyses of the way a network computes and represents information over subsets of hidden units (see section 5.2) can clarify imprecise or incomplete models of psychological phenonema and can help reveal important relations between learning and representation that are not taken into account in the rule-based approach.

Some of the known computational properties of the kinds of nets we have discussed will now be described. Then we will show how representation in nets can be analyzed using various multivariate techniques, in particular, cluster analysis and other weak data reduction methods. Finally, we will propose a hypothesis about the nature of the mapping between input and output in hidden unit networks that is more specific than the suggestion that it is "subsymbolic" (cf. Smolensky, 1988).

4 Representation in Connectionist Models

Learning and representation interact in nets that encode input information dynamically (by learning) in an intermediate or hidden layer of units. Recent critical analyses (Pinker & Prince 1988; Fodor & Pylyshyn 1987) have been concerned with whether and how symbols, rules and representations are encoded and used in nets. Much of the debate has been polemical rather than substantive, being based on high-level representational claims by some connectionists (Smolensky, 1988), and on an incomplete understanding of what nets can represent and how they compute.

---

[11] Consequential regions are stimulus generalization regions corresponding to a particular stimulus. If an organism is conditioned to respond to a wavelength of 550 nm we might ask what is the response associated with nearby wavelengths? Similar responses to nearby stimuli determine the consequential regions in feature space.

4.1 Representations that are Distributed, Local or Both

In hidden unit networks it is the strengths of the connections between units that do the representing. Everything the system has learned at any point is encoded in its weights. The behavior (e.g. the activity patterns) of the hidden layer [12] will be completely determined at any point by the weights passing activation to it or, equivalently, by weights connected to its fan-in (in the dynamical case this would be the logical fan-in).

Learning is likely to produce a distributed representation of the mapping between the input and output domain, partly because of the way the input features are mapped onto outputs and partly because of statistical characteristics of the data presented to the net. "Local" units can arise as a function of the nature of the categories and the network's decision functions.

Four kinds of representations are possible in a net (see Figure 5). First, information can be completely local: for a given set of stimuli, a single unit in the hidden layer becomes active and passes information to the output layer. This hidden unit might be thought of as passing categorical information to the output, recognizing a set of discrete, Aristotelian features (e.g., red and round or green and big) or probabilistic ones.[13] In the simplest kind of local representation, inputs are mapped consistently onto the correct category. This type of mapping can also be thought of as symbolic, in that specific localized constituents of the representation can be associated with specific operations appropriate for the category. Because these constituents are localizable in the network, the specific operations associated with them can be viewed syntactically (as in the standard AI approach). Feldman (1985), Waltz (Pollack & Waltz, 1982) and their students have used such "localist" nets to model semantics and language processing. The difference between a localist net and a hidden unit net with local units is that the latter can learn the features of the input domain that determine the input for the local hidden units.

In the second kind of local representation, hidden units are connected to a small subset of the input or output units that pick out some similar feature (e.g., they may represent a set of vowels or set of verbs; see section 5.2) that the network has discovered can be "used" for correct categorization. This type of representation is local in the hidden layer because of clustering over

---

[12] For nets with complete unit-unit connections or nets with feedback between units, the special case of the feedforward/intermediate unit connectivity provides only one aspect of a richer sort of computation that might occur in other parts of the net. We are once again simplifying for clarity.

[13] Or "polymorphous" features, i.e. at least two of the following: red, round, green, big; see Hanson & Bauer 1986; 1989.

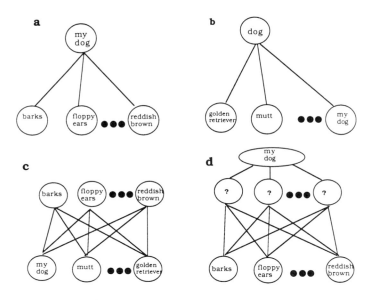

Figure 5: Description on page 200

some set of of symbols (or features) in the input (or output) representation. It might be thought of as a "supersymbol".

In the third form of representation, some set of hidden units is uniformly connected to some set of input or output units. In such a *distributed representation* a single input causes many hidden units to become activated. This kind of representation has also been referred to as "subsymbolic" (Smolensky, 1988), presumably because many hidden units are involved in coding information in the input or the output. The features in the input representation have been chosen a priori and are not modifiable. Such a fixed lexicon of input features is like the finite set of semantic elements into which the world is "carved" in some symbolic models (cf. Schank, 1975).

Fourth and last, distributed representations may be created by a set of hidden units that is not fixed a priori. Such nets can encode an unknown feature representation, with each hidden unit responding to one or more aspects of features in the input representation. If the input representation is local (one unit per symbol) then the subset of hidden units can be said to be "distributing" the symbol into a set of hidden unit features. This is similar to the way psychometric models attempt to recover unknown stimulus similarity functions on the basis of weaker invariants in the data set (e.g. "ranks", Shepard, Romney, Nerlove 1968).

The four cases we have discussed, involving both local and distributed representations, do not really differ from symbolic representations (Fodor, 1988), nor do they provide any radically new insights about representation that symbolists have not already thoroughly considered. Representations using features are neither new nor difficult to characterize; they date back to Aristotle. What distinguishes connectionist representations from other kinds of representation? Note that in the fourth kind of connectionist representation inputs are being mapped onto (unknown) feature representations based on the "consequence" (see footnote 10) of the category response. Distributed models differ from localist ones in which feature representations for the input are chosen apriori (as they are in most AI approaches) in that the relation between the inputs and features is made accessible to the learning rule [14] Based on the connection strengths, it now becomes obvious (to the net at least) what makes up the input stimulus. Moreover, the representation that determines its composition is readily accessible, visible, and shared [15] among all other stimuli in the domain.

This visibility or accessibility of the distributed representation is what distinguishes it from localist/symbolist/AI representations, in which the information encoded has been committed to the representational language. This is also one of the reasons why learning is so natural in nets: Symbolic models must somehow inform their learning algorithm about what aspects of the representation were responsible for some error or correct response ("the credit/blame assignment problem" Minsky 1961). Even worse, the "hidden" information embedded in the symbolic model's representational language for describing and manipulating the stimuli must be tracked down and made visible to the learning algorithm.

So the real difference between the symbolic and the connectionist approach is not in the type of representation but in the distributed representation's commitment to learning. In connectionism, simple feature representation is used in a novel way to make the learning process integral to the representational system. This language is "discovered" through the selection and recombination of previously defined and possibly arbitrary input features during learning. This focus on learning makes it crucial to understand the internal properties of network computation. In a sense, the usual representational question has been turned on its head: Instead of asking

---

[14] This is also true for the outputs, which, from the hidden layer's point of view, are shared and accessible in the output domain.

[15] This leads to the problem of how to extend the the net's feature "lexicon." Any representation scheme which uses features must encounter this problem at some time or another. Something must be fixed in the learning model, either the features or the similarity function. This reminiscent of the tensions between geometric (Shepard 1962) and feature models (Tversky 1977) in mathematical psychology.

what the representation for a cup or a chair is, connectionists want to know under what conditions a *useful* representation for a cup or chair would be learned.

4.2   From McCulloch and Pitts to Category Learning

Complex categorzation problems involving nonlinear boundaries (e.g. the "exclusive-or" predicate) have been an important obstacle for connectionist learning, partly because of the vague idea that neural nets should be able to compute logical functions similar to the ones out of which computers are built. McCulloch and Pitts (1943) showed that a neural unit computing a "majority logic" or "polymorphy" logic (m out of n) could be used, in principle, to implement any logical function. Note that this demonstration concerns what can be represented, not what can be learned.

Figure 6a shows the kind of solution McCulloch and Pitts may have had in mind for the exclusive-or predicate. There are two NOR gates and one AND gate (which might actually involve more than a single unit at each node). When the data from the table are inserted into the x and y input lines, the second layer responds as shown. Then the entire output of the net produces the XOR or *difference* response shown at the far right.

Exclusive-or turns out to be a topologically difficult categorization problem, one that must be solved using a hidden layer, because the patterns with the greatest Hamming distance between them must be assigned to the same category. Consequently, the net must construct a "metafeature" out of the original input bits, one that might be thought of as signaling "same" or "different". The problem is also one in which there is no linear separability (i.e., a single linear function of the input cannot in principle separate one category from the other). However, as shown in Figure 6b, *two* linear functions [16] of the input bits can successfully categorize the samples into the two requisite output categories. Figure 6c illustrates the effects of learning in terms of output categories in a three dimensional output or "performance surface" (the response of the ouput unit to all possible inputs) that was learned in 400 trials through the four patterns of the exclusive-or using five units with logistic fan-out function. Note the local warping around the two linear segments on either side of the valley in the performance space. The thresholds help locate and orient the line segments in the output space and allow arbitrary positioning of such boundaries.

---

[16] This can also be done with one hidden unit if there are two direct connections between input and output.

a

McCulloch & Pitts (1943)

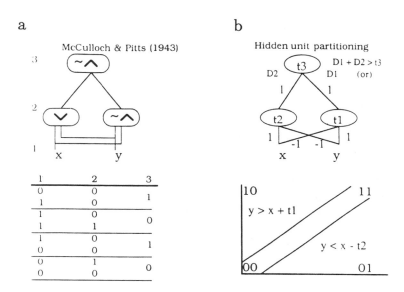

b

Hidden unit partitioning

1	2	3
0	0	1
1	0	
1	0	0
1	1	
1	0	1
0	0	
0	1	0
0	0	

c

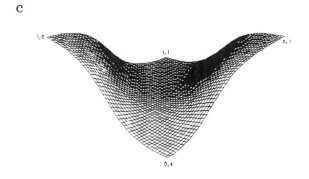

Figure 6: Description on page 200

4.3   The Geometry of the Fan-In and Activation

We will now describe how mappings occur between a set of input and output values in the typical hidden unit net, showing how it can construct mappings between input features and output classification regions. There is a general relation between what supervised learning networks can compute and simple linear discriminant analysis (Duda & Hart 1973; Nilsson 1965). The hidden unit net performs a linear discriminant analysis in which partition boundaries have been graded and are combined piecewise ("nonlinear discriminants"). We will demonstrate that networks with hidden units learn to produce associative maps and to classify patterns. They accomplish this by doing a nonlinear partitioning of an input space and associating these regions with an independent output space. The fan-in function, as discussed previously, completely determines the nature of the boundary segment in the performance space [17]. The simplest and most typical case is a linear function of the inputs to the unit.

As pointed out earlier, the particular choice of neural unit has implications for both the learning and the representational abilities of the net. It is precisely their smoothness and nonlocality which make graded activation units desirable in network learning algorithms. Units differ in the way they partition the pattern space into regions. The linear unit produces a single hyperplane partition of the space: several units together can produce a polygonal boundary (2-D), a polyhedron (3-D), or a hyperpolygon in N dimensions. A graded unit uses hyperplanes which warp the space locally about the linear segment which partitions the space into roughly high, medium and low regions. Several units can act together to produce smoothly curved boundaries; these are important in representing natural data, which usually have continuous smooth distributions. As we have seen, it is also possible to vary the choice of integration (fan-in) function in order to produce different types of partition boundaries.

4.4   Elemental Partitioning Regions: Constructing Connectionist Variables

It is instructive to examine first how a step neuron partitions a space. We will use a simple example of a four-neuron net to illustrate how neurons act together and produce piecewise linear boundaries. The example is done in the $x - y$ plane so activation surfaces can be illustrated clearly.

In Figure 7a, note that the lowest layer of neurons (L1, L2, and L3)

---

[17]Though all examples are illustrated in 2-D space, the results extend readily to higher dimensional spaces where planar regions generalize to hypervolumes.

corresponds to the lines in Figure 7b, and that the weights of each neuron define the corresponding line. Each neuron decides on which side of its line the input point lies. If the point indicated by the cross is input, then L1, L2 , and L3 will all turn on. Since the combined input to neuron α (3.0) exceeds its threshold, α also turns on. α is acting in this configuration like an AND gate. Note that any point in the region interior to the triangle will turn α on, and any point exterior to the triangle will turn α off. An XOR function could be realized by simply changing the threshold to 0.5. Activation patterns are shown in Figure 7cd for linear threshold units and in Figure 7ef for graded units. Notice the pronounced smoothing of the corners with graded units.

In the graded unit the predicates are continuous; they are like continuous Booleans. Of course, another particular activation function may be chosen to make the gradients steeper. Note that the second layer distorts the surface features by enhancing the middle bump and flattening the surrounding terrain. Flattening is not perfect, as with step activation, and some artifacts remain. Notice the ripples in the floor region of Figure 7f, which are absent in Figure 7e.

Surprisingly, if a nonconvex bounded region containing boundary concavities and/or holes is needed, then a single layer is often sufficient (Wieland and Leighton 1988). It is possible to take a cut out of any closed region with sets of hidden units, thus "sculpting the surface." An example is shown in Figure 8, in which two triangular regions are embedded in one larger triangular region (using six hidden units), producing a single nonconvex combination of the smaller triangular regions. Generally, unless the target geometry requires hyperplane cuts that are linearly dependent (thus reducing the degrees of freedom), a single layer of hidden units is sufficient for arbitrary feature space partitioning (Pavel, 1988).

The general property of neural models we have been discussing is *not* just their ability to model Boolean sentences. Rather, all neural models described earlier are capable of spatial partitioning and of constructing arbitrary continuous regions. Since neural models can use such arbitrary partitioning to solve problems and create associative maps, multiple units will often be involved in representing spatial regions. Knowledge is accordingly represented as distributed patterns of activation. This distributed knowledge is primarily due to the collaboration of simple neural fan-in functions solving spatial problems that require more than one line segment (e.g. cluster boundaries, Boolean combinations). Only when a single hyperplane is sufficient to solve the problem is it possible for the knowledge to be local, i.e. related to a single unit. Otherwise nets will tend to have distributed representations. The distributed-local representation issue is

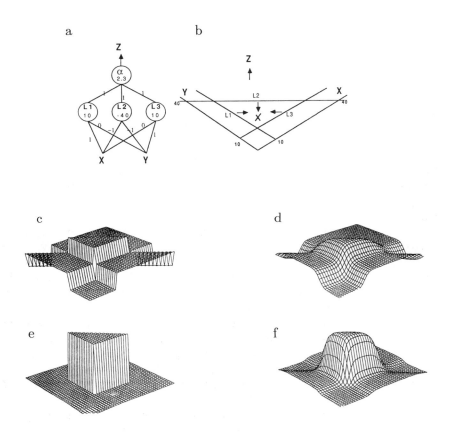

Figure 7: Description on page 200

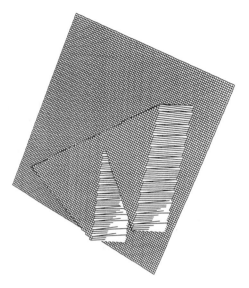

Figure 8: Description on page 201

directly traceable to the complexity of the fan-in functions.

4.5 Boundary Complexity and Dichotomization Capacity

The nature and computational power of distributed representations can be made quite precise in terms of a net's categorization abilities. This was done years ago in the context of work on decision functions and linear inequalities (motivated by early work done on neural nets in the 1950s) by a number of different authors (Cover 1965; Cooper 1962; Winder, 1962; Koford 1962). We will review some of these results here and briefly discuss some of their implications for representation in nets.

As suggested earlier, a general form for partition boundaries in neural nets is a polynomial of arbitrary degree (although other general forms are possible). Using this form will allow us to discuss the categorization capacity of nets with hidden units. If we consider the fan-in function to be an rth order polynomial, a convenient general form is the following recursion:

$$d^r\mathbf{x} = (\sum_{q_1=1}^{n} \sum_{q_2=q_1}^{n} \cdots \sum_{q_r=q_{r-1}}^{n} w_{q_1 q_2 \ldots q_r} x_{q_1} x_{q_2} \ldots x_{q_r}) + d^{r-1}(\mathbf{x}) \qquad (5)$$

Here n is the dimension of the feature space and r is the degree of the polynomial. For example, in the two-dimensional case (r=2), we get the general second-degree equation.

$$d^2(\mathbf{x}) = w_{11}x_1^2 + w_{12}x_1x_2 + w_{22}x_2^2 + w_1x_1 + w_2x_2 + w_0 \qquad (6)$$

which can produce arbitrary conics, like the hyperspheres and hyperquadratics discussed earlier. For large n and r, very complex boundaries can be formed in feature space, with a concomitant rapid increase in the number of degrees of freedom (N_{df}) of the model neuron:

$$N_{df} = \frac{(n+r)!}{r!n!} \qquad (7)$$

A reasonably general but arbitrary measure of the categorizing power of a net is the number of ways dichotomies can be formed with the decision boundary given a set of stimuli. For example, Figure 9 shows four points in a two dimensional feature space. Notice that line segment 1 separates three of the stimuli from the fourth. Given that there are two possible category assignments, each boundary could lead to two possible categorizations; consequently, the seven boundary segments allow 14 possible categorizations of the four stimulus points. There are actually 16 or 2^4 possible dichotomies, two of which are apparently not linear dichotomies (these correspond to "exclusive-or"). The general measure of categorizing power, or the number of linearly separable dichotomies (C), can be written as (Cover 1965):

$$C(k,n) = 2\sum_{j=0}^{n-1} \frac{(k-1)!}{(k-1-j)!j!} \quad k > n+1 \qquad (8)$$

Note the dramatic growth in C as a function of n, the number of dimensions. For example, with only 25 stimuli in a five-dimensional feature space, there are 25,902 linear dichotomies. Consequently, arbitrary categorizations can be found more easily in higher dimensions. In fact, the probability that a dichotomy chosen at random will be linearly implementable is just the ratio of the category power measure to the number of possible dichotomies of k stimuli (2^k).

$$P(C) = \frac{C(k,n)}{2^k} \quad k > n+1 \qquad (9)$$

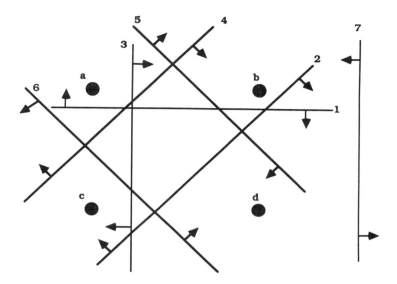

Figure 9: Description on page 201

For $k <<= n + 1$ this probability is 1.0. Thus, if we have at least one more dimension than stimuli, we are guaranteed to be able to linearly separate the stimuli according to any arbitrary categorization. As n gets large, for $k > 2(n + 1)$ this probability is near zero. Consequently, it seems reasonable to think of the value $2(n + 1)$ as a capacity for the linear net.

This capacity will vary as a function of the complexity of the decision boundary as well as the number of hidden units. It is always possible to use equation 8 to compute the dimensionality of a nonlinear fan-in net or a linear fan-in hidden unit net [18] in terms of the dimensionality of the linear net. For example, with eight stimuli in two dimensions there are (substituting $N_{df}=3$ from Eq. 8 for n in Eq. 9), 58 linear partitions. For a second order polynomial, which can include spherical and quadratic units, N_{df} is increased to six. Thus, in these transformed coordinates the category power equation results in 240 partitions for the second order polynomial. This increases the likelihood of arbitrary category partitioning from 23

This analysis of network capacity has two implications: First, more

---

[18] Given a nonlinear fan-out, such as the logistic, it will be obvious from considering the first few terms of the Taylor expansion of the exponential that high order polynomials of terms and cross-terms are available just at the hidden layer of a multilayer net of sigmoid fan-out, linear fan-in units.

dimensions (weights, hidden units etc...) are always better for solving arbitrary categorization problems. There is a sharp increase in categorization ability near the capacity $2(n + 1)$, however. At and beyond this point, categorization is a certainty. Unfortunately, there is also an inevitably dramatic increase in the number of possible solutions to any categorization problem. Generalization suffers because of the large number of available solutions that may not be effectively equivalent in their ability to correctly categorize. Thus, it is important to manage the network resources (weights, fan-in complexity, hidden unit number, fan-out complexity..etc..) so as to balance the categorization power as nearly as possible with the capacity of the net. Alternatively, it may be productive to develop algorithms in which the capacity itself would appear as a parameter to be optimized. In this way the net could dynamically alter its own dimensionality.

In some recent work the concept of costs has been applied to network learning (Rumelhart 1987, Hanson & Pratt 1989, Mozer & Smolensky 1989, Chauvin 1989). In general, one can find constraints that will tend to "pare down" the hidden units from a set that is sufficient for performing a task to one that is only necessary. Further research (see also Baum & Haussler, 1988; Valiant, 1984) will be needed to sort out the efficacy and applicability of such constraints. There is experimental evidence for the existence of an optimal or critical number of hidden units that depends on the given task (Burr 1988).

4.6   Rules and Variables

Now that we have analyzed the kinds of network computation that are possible, we would like to extend this to how *variables* can be constructed in the hidden layer (as previously discussed in section 4.6). A net can construct variables relevant to a classification task and can *bind* specific inputs in the learning sample to those variables. Such "variable bindings" are discovered during learning through exposure to the inputs and the categorization task; they allow the net to refer to or manipulate features of the input stimuli. If a system can construct functional classes of stimuli and associate them with functional classes of responses then it can be said to be constructing symbols and applying rules. Classes are the referents of the symbols that are constructed in the network as it learns; to compute the function on the class is equivalent to applying a rule in the context of the categorization task.

The net must be able to construct an internal "symbol" to refer to a set of inputs independently of other symbols for other sets of inputs. It must also be able to produce consistent outputs in response to these symbols. In other words, the net must learn to recognize stimuli from a category and to generate a response identifying the category. This kind of category-recognition/response-mapping is analogous to condition-action pairs in traditional rule-based systems. Thus the net is asked to define, over a set of input-target stimulus pairs:

$$< \text{class}_i \text{of inputs} > \rightarrow < \text{class}_i \text{of outputs} >$$

The predicate on the left side of this mapping is what allows the net to categorize a set of inputs by their features. Analogously, a class of inputs produces a set of consequential (generalization) regions in feature space. In addition, a class of outputs is produced from a set a consequential regions in the hidden unit space. During learning the net can be thought of as mapping one set of generalization regions from the feature space onto another from the hidden unit space.

On the basis of what we showed earlier, a net can learn very specific features of every input sampled. These are equivalent to an arbitrary Boolean sentence such as a k-term disjunctive normal form [19] (k-DNF). Two aspects of learning make it difficult for the net to learn a k-DNF, however. First, most network learning rules tend to extract common features and small n-tuple feature relations ("low order" features) first before learning exceptions, simply because error can be reduced better on the basis commonalities than on the basis of exceptions. Second, a network can only store an exception by using at least one partition (hidden unit). Hence if the number of hidden units is small (say $<< 2(N + 1)$) the net will probably be unable to "waste" resources over the entire sample while reducing error. The net must begin by extracting generalities and can only then consider storing exceptions using the partition boundaries that remain. The nature of hidden unit projections and their relation to sampling from the input-output pairs is still not understood.

4.7 Summary of Connectionist Computational Properties

Some general properties can be abstracted from the standard case we have considered (simple fan-in functions, recursive parameter estimation, and hidden layers). Before we turn to the internal details of specific nets, here is a summary of this section's main points:

---

[19]k-DNF is a logical form representing tokens as k conjunctive terms connected by disjuncts.

1. Whether network representation is distributed or local depends on the complexity of the fan-in function and the geometry of the spatial classes in feature space. If the fan-in function is linear, the geometry of the feature space is likely to require solutions based on more than one hyperplane and, as a side effect, distributed representations.

2. A single hidden layer with a sufficient number of hidden units is necessary and sufficient to represent any complex, arbitrary decision region. Consequently there is no arbitrary computational limit on what is possible to represent (nothing corresponding to the Minsky & Papert [1969] limit on the Perceptron).

3. Finding the minimum number of hidden units for any problem will depend on constraints related to task-specific architectural resources. The generalization ability of the net is intimately related to the number of hidden units or the dimensionality of the learning system.

4. Connectionist "rules" are composed from the generalization regions based on the spatial partitioning capacities of nets and on task constraints. Rules are thus mappings of input classes onto output classes discovered through exposure to conditional input and appropriate outputs.

5   Summary and Conclusions

We have tried to show that nets provide a unique framework for the study of learning and representation – phenomena that have been dissociated in psychology for over 30 years and have only recently reappeared jointly in cognitive science. Nets turn out to be capable of representing arbitrarily complex functions. Rules and symbols can be constructed from components that arise naturally out of the classification power of the net. We have countered Fodor and Pylyshyn's (1988) criticism that nets are merely an alternative hardware for implementing symbol systems by showing how the integration of learning and representation in nets provides a unique approach to modeling cognitive and behavioral data. Design principles related to representation are complemented by acquisition principles related to learning.

Our preliminary exploration of the the interaction between learning and representation, raises many questions:

- What constraints on representation ensure that a system will learn in a given task?

- How does a learning system manage its resources dynamically?

- Can constraints be introduced that produce one sort of representation but not another?

- How can we distinguish learning properties that are related to biological complexity rather than computational complexity?

Connectionism may or may not succeed in integrating learning and representation, but it is clear that some such synthesis will be needed for a full understanding of behavior and cognition. Networks force the modeler to confront the problem of sensory encoding and learning simultaneously; in AI systems these are dissociated. A network's performance reflects sensory constraints that mediate its interaction with the world, connecting its internal states to external events ("symbol grounding," Harnad 1990). The three basic features of the learning/representation interaction are (1) unit complexity, which determines the elementary operations in feature space, (2) network connectivity, which restricts the class of functions the net can represent, and (3) the learning rule, which selects input/output functions based on the properties of the input data. These three features provide a simple programming language in which symbols and rules arise out of the interaction between simple learning procedures and representational elements as they are shaped by the tasks the network learns to perform.

Acknowledgements

We would like to thank Charlie Rosenberg and Terry Sejnowski for supplying us with the weights from early versions of NETtalk and for interesting discussions about the internal analysis of nets. Charlie Rosenberg was instrumental in identifying various properties of units in NETtalk. We would also like to thank the Bellcore Connectionist group and members of the Princeton Cognitive Science Lab for providing a stimulating and lively environment for the development of many of the ideas in this paper. Finally we would like to thank a number of annonymous reviewers for suggestions that improved the organization of the paper and Stevan Harnad for extensive editorial help on the paper.

Figure Legends

Figure 1: Taxonomy of Connectionist models. A hierarchy of network types classified on the basis of four dichotomous features: (1) linearity vs nonlinearity; (2) recurrence (dynamics) vs absence of recurrence; (3) hebbian rules vs error-correcting rules; (4) passive vs competitive synapses. These four features classify most of the major connectionist models.

Figure 2: Typical Connectionist Threshold Unit. Shown in inset is a smoothing of the threshold (Heaviside function). Unit i transfers fan-in information to fan-out information. Fan-in of units has distinct integration functions which can be associated with the geometry of the feature space. Fan-out of units has distinct output functions which can be associated with the smoothness of the output space and can be interpreted probabilistically.

Figure 3: Polynomial and Spherical units performing an arbitrary pattern recognition. (3a) The response surface of a polynomial unit performing the categorization task of separating "x"s from "o"s located arbitrarily in a feature space. The inset shows the polynomial ridge projected into two dimensions. (3b) The response surface of a spherical unit performing an arbitrary categorization task of separating "x"s from "o"s. Note that a linear solution of this problem would require at least three units.

Figure 4: Five types of units derived from variations in fan-in function complexity (for details, see text). Note that volumes (3,5) in the feature space require interactions either within or between "synapses" and "dendrites" and can involve multiple units, while dichotomies (1,2,4) require only single units.

Figure 5: Examples of various sorts of local and distributed representations. (a) First example shows a completly local representation, (b) the next example is a local representation of a category, "dog", (c) the third case shows a distributed representation, where a number of hidden units can code for a single input, (d) and finally in the fourth case also shows a distributed representation, however with hidden units which can code for possibly arbitrary feature combinations in order to represent the concept.

Figure 6: McCulloch & Pitts and category partitioning. (6a) Construction of XOR circuit out of Boolean components. (6b) Actual connectivity for a network solving the XOR problem using linear units and partitioning the feature space into two regions for eventual recombination through the output unit. (6c) Response surface of the network shown in 5b after learning 400 sweeps through the four patterns.

Figure 7: Geometry of Linear Units in Feature Space. In the panels shown a closed region is constructed using only linear dichotomies in a two dimensional feature space (X,Y). L1-L3 represent partitions created by 3 individual hidden units. The output (α) of the network is shown in the third dimension (Z). (7a) Network connectivity creating a simple closed region. (7b) The partitioning in feature space of the three hidden units from network shown in 7a. (7c) Response surface of network in 7a prior to thresholding at output level. (7d) Response surface after thresholding at output. (7e) Output surface with logistic output prior to thresholding. (7f) Response surface after thresholding, notice artifacts due to the smoothing and recombination of the three logistic units.

Figure 8: Non-convex region designed with a single hidden layer containing six hidden units. Using the same approach as in figure 7 a arbitrary non-convex region can be created by carefully placing dichotomies in the two dimesional feature space. For example, the two connected triangular regions consist of 2 hidden units bounding the large triangle, 2 hidden units bounding the inner cut and 2 bounding the back edge (2 are required on the back edge for one to turn on the figure on the left and one to turn off the figure on the right). Similar to figure 7, each hidden unit is thresholded to "sculpt" the surface into its final form.

Figure 9: Number of different ways four points can be partitioned into dichotomies. Four points (a-d) in "general position" in a 2 dimensional plane can be linearly separated into 14 arbitrary categories. The hyperplanes are shown in the figure with 2 possible orientations.

Bibliography

[1] Ackley, D., Hinton, G. E., and Sejnowski, T. J. (1985) A Learning Algorithm for Boltzmann Machines, Cognitive Science, 9,1, 147-69.

[2] Albus, J. S., (1975) A new approach to manipulator control: The cerebellar model articulation controller (CMAC), American Society of Engineers, Transactions G (Journal of Dynamic Systems, Measurement and Control) 97(3):220-227.

[3] Anderson, J. A., Silverstein, J. W., and Ritz, S. R., Jones, R. S. (1977) Distinctive features, categorical perception, and probability learning: some applications of a neural model, Psychological Review, 84, 413-451.

[4] Anderson, J. A. (1976) Brain-State-in the Box model. Cognitive Science.

[5] Anderson, J. R., (1983) The Architecture of Cognition, Harvard.

[6] Baum, E. B. and Wilczek (1987) Supervised learning of probability distributions by neural networks. D. Anderson (Ed.) American Institute of Physics, New York.

[7] Baum, E. B. and Haussler, D. (1988) What size net gives valid generalization? D. Touretzsky (Ed.) Advances in Neural Information Processing Systems 1, Morgan-Kaufman.

[8] Blum, A. & Rivest, R. (1989) Training a 3-Node Neural Network is NP-Complete. D. Touretzsky (Ed.) Advances in Neural Information Processing Systems 1, Morgan-Kaufman.

[9] Burr, D. J. (1988) Experiments on Neural Net Recognition of Spoken and Written Text, IEEE Trans. on Acoustics, Speech and Signal Processing, Vol. 36, No. 7.

[10] Carroll, S. M. & Dickenson, B. (1989) Construction of neural nets using the Radon transform. In Proceedings of the International Joint Conference on Neural Networks, pp. 607-611.

[11] Chauvin, Y. (1989) A backpropagation network with optimal use of hidden units. D. Touretzsky (Ed.) Advances in Neural Information Processing Systems 1, Morgan-Kaufman.

[12] Chomsky, N. (1959) A review of B.F. Skinner's Verbal Behavior. Language 35:26-58.

[13] Chomsky, N. (1980) Rules and Representations. New York: Columbia University Press.

[14] Cooper, P. (1962) The hypersphere in pattern recognition. Information and Control, 5, 324-346.

[15] Cover, T. M. (1965) Geometrical and Statistical Properties of Systems of linear inequalities with applications to pattern recognition. IEEE Trans. Electronic Computers, Vol. EC-14,3, pp. 326-334.

[16] Cybenko (1989) Approximation by superposition of a sigmoidal function. Math. Control Systems Signals, in press.

[17] Duda, R. O., and Hart, P.E., (1973) Pattern Classification and Scene Analysis, New York: J. Wiley.

[18] Durbin, R. and Rumelhart, D. E. (1989) Product units: A computationally powerful and biologically plausible extension to backpropagation networks. Neural Computation 1, 133-142.

[19] Dunn-Rankin (1983) Scaling Methods. Hillsdale, N.J.: Erlbaum.

[20] Elman, J., (1987) Learning Word Classes. IEEE Neural Networks conference, San Diego.

[21] Everitt, B., (1975) Cluster Analysis, Heinemann Educational Books, London.

[22] Feldman, J. (1985) Connectionist Models and Their Applications. Cognitive Science Special Issue,9,1.

[23] Fodor, J. (1988) Personal communication, Princeton.

[24] Fodor, J., and Plyshyn, Z. (1988) Connectionism and Cognitive Architecture: A critical analysis, Unpublished Manuscript.

[25] Gardner, H. (1985) The Mind's New Science, Basic Books: New York.

[26] Gorman, P. R., and Sejnowski T. (1988) An Analysis of Hidden Units in a Sonar Recognition Task, Neural Networks.

[27] Golden, R., (1988) A unified framework for connectionist systems, Biological Cybernetics, 59, 109-120.

[28] Grossberg, S. (1976) Adaptive Pattern Classification and Universal Recoding, I: Parallel Development and Coding of Neural Feature Detectors. Biological Cybernetics, 23, 121-134.

[29] Grossberg, S. (1987) Competitive Learning: from interactive activation to adaptive resonance. Cognitive Science, 11,1,23-64.

[30] Hanson, S. J. (1990) The Stochastic Delta Rule. Physica D, in press.

[31] Hanson, S. J. and Bauer, M. (1986) Conceptual Clustering, Machine Learning and Polymorphy, in L. Kanal and J. Lemmer (Eds.) Uncertainty in Artificial Intelligence, North Holland: Amsterdam.

[32] Hanson, S. J. and Bauer, M. (1989) Conceptual Clustering, Categorization, and Polymorphy, Machine Learning, 3: 343-372.

[33] Hanson, S. J. and Burr, D. J. (1987a) Knowledge Representation in Connectionist Networks, unpublished manuscript.

[34] Hanson, S. J. and Burr, D. J., (1987b) Minkowski-r Backpropagation: Learning in Connectionist Models with Non-Euclidean Error Signals, In the Proceedings of Neural Networks: Natural and Synthetic, D. Anderson (Ed.) , American Institute of Physics.

[35] Hanson, S. J. and Pratt, L. (1989) Some comparisons of constraints for back-propagation networks, In Advances in Neural Information Processing, D. Touretzsky (Ed.), Morgan-Kaufmann.

[36] Hanson, S. J. and Olson, C. R. (1988) A connectionist network that computes limb position in a head-centered coordinate frame, Society for Neuroscience Abstracts.

[37] Harnad, S. (1990) The symbol grounding problem, Physica D, in press.

[38] Hartigan, J. (1969) Clustering Algorithms, J. Wiley and Sons: New York.

[39] Hebb, D. O. (1949) Organization of behavior: A neuropyschological theory. New York: Wiley.

[40] Hinton, G. E., (1986) Learning Distributed Representations of Concepts, Cognitive Science Meeting, Amherst MA.

[41] Hinton, G. E., (1987) Learning Procedures for Connectionist Models, CMU Technical Report.

[42] Hornik, K., Stinchcombe, M. & White, H. (1988) Multi-layer feedforward are universal approximators, unpublished ms.

[43] Jones, E. G. (1985) The Thalamus, Plenum Press, NY, Chapter 4.

[44] Jordan, M. I., (1986) Serial Order: A Parallel Processing Approach, Center for Human Information Processing UCSD, Technical Report, May.

[45] Judd, J. S. (1987) Learning in networks is hard. In Proceedings of the First International Conference on Neural Networks, pp. 685-692, IEEE, San Diego, Cal., June.

[46] Kohonen, T., (1977) Associative memory-a system-theoretical approach. New York: Springer-Verlag.

[47] Koford, K. A. (1962) Adaptive Network Organization, Stanford Electronics Lab. Quart. Res. Rev., no. 3.

[48] Krebs, J. (1978) Optimal foraging: Decision rules for predators. In J. R. Krebs & N. B Davies (Eds.) Behavioral Ecology: An evolutionary approach. Sunderland, Mass.: Sinauer, 1978.

[49] Kruskal, J., and Shepard, R., (1974) A Nonmetric Variety of Linear Factor Analysis, Psychometrika, 39,2.

[50] Laird, J. E., Rosenbloom, P. S. and Newell, A. (1985) Towards chunking as a general learning mechanism Technical Report cmu-cs-85-110, Department of Computer Science, CMU.

[51] Langley, P., (1983) Representational Issues in Learning Systems, Computer, 16, 9, 47-51.

[52] Lenat, D. (1985) The role of heuristics in learning by discovery: Three case studies, In Michalski, R. S., Carbonell, J. G., Mitchell, T. M. (Eds.), Machine Learning, Tioga Publishing.

[53] Lightfoot, D. (1989) The child's trigger experience: "Degree-0: learnability". Behavioral and Brain Sciences, 12.

[54] Longuet-Higgens, C., Willshaw, D. J., and Buneman, O. P., (1970) Theories of Associative Recall, Quarterly Review of Biophysics 3, 2, 223-244.

[55] Luce, D. and Krumhansl, C. Measurement, Scaling and Pscyhophysics, In R.C. Atkinson, D. Lindzay, R. J.Herrnstein, D. Luce (Eds.) Steven's Handbook of Experimental Psychology, New York: Wiley Interscience.

[56] Marr, D. (1982) Vision. New York: Freeman.

[57] Maxwell, T., Giles, C. Lee, and Lee, Y. C. (1988) The generation of efficient representations in neural net architectures using high order correlations, In Neural Information Processing-Neural and Synthetic, D. Anderson (Ed.), American Institute of Physics.

[58] Miller, G. A., (1987) personal communication.

[59] Minsky, M. (1961) Steps towards artificial intelligence, Proceedings of the Institute of Radio Engineers, 49, pp. 8-30.

[60] Minsky, M. and Papert, S. (1969) The perceptron: Principles of computational geometry, MIT press.

[61] McCulloch, W. S. and Pitts, W., (1943) A Logical Calculus of the Ideas Imminent in Nervous Activity, Bulletin of Mathematical Biophysics, 5, 115-133.

[62] Mozer, M. & Smolensky, P. (1989) Skeletonization: A technique for trimming the fat from a network via relevance assessment. In D. Touretzsky (Ed.) Advances in Neural Information Processing Systems. Palo Alto, CA: Morgan Kaufman.

[63] Nilsson, N. J., (1965) Learning Machines: Foundations of Trainable Pattern-Classifying Systems McGraw-Hill, New York.

[64] Pavel, M. (1988) personal communication, Boston.

[65] Pearlmutter, B. (1989) Learning State Space Trajectories in Recurrent Neural Networks, CMU Technical Report, CMU-CS-88-191.

[66] Pineda, F. J. (1988) Generalization of backpropagation to recurrent and high-order networks, In Proceedings of the IEEE Conference on Neural Information Processing Systems-Natural and Synthetic, AIP.

[67] Pinker, S., and Prince, A., (1988) On Language and Connectionism: Analysis of a Parallel Distributed Processing Model of Language Acquisition, MIT Technical Report.

[68] Pollack, J., and Waltz, D., (1982) Natural Language Processing using Spreading Activation and Lateral Inhibition, In Proceedings of the fourth annual Cognitive Science Conference. Ann Arbor MI, 50-53.

[69] Pylyshyn, Z., (1984) Computation and Cognition: Toward a Foundation for Cognitive Science. Cambridge: MIT Press/Bradford.

[70] Rivest, R. & Haussler, D. and Warmuth, M. K. (1989) Proceedings of second annual Computational Learning Theory. San Mateo, CA.: Morgan-Kaufman.

[71] Rumelhart, D. E., (1987) personal communication.

[72] Rumelhart, D. E., Hinton, G. E., and Williams R., (1986) Learning Internal Representations by Error Propagation. Nature.

[73] Rumelhart, D. E., and McClelland, J. J. (Eds.), (1986) Parallel Distributed Processing: Explorations in the Microstructure of Cognition. Vol 1: Foundations. Bradford Books/MIT Press, Cambridge, Mass.

[74] Rosenblatt, F., (1962) Principles of Neuro-Dynamics, Spartan, Washington, D.C.

[75] Schank, R. C., (1975) Conceptual Information Processing, North Holland, Amsterdam.

[76] Shepherd, G. M. and Brayton, R. K. (1987) Logic operations are properties of computer-simulated interactions between excitable dendritic spines, Neuroscience, 21, 151,166.

[77] Shepard, R. N. (1989) Internal representation of universal regularities: A challenge for connectionism, In, L. Nadel, L.A. Cooper, P. Culicover, & R. M. Harnish (Eds.) Neural Connections and Mental Computation. Cambridge, MA: MIT Press/Bradford Books.

[78] Shepard, R. N. (1987) Toward a Universal Law of Generalization for Psychological Science. Science, 237.

[79] Shepard, R. N. (1962) The analysis of proximities: Multidimensional scaling with an unknown distance function. II. Psychometrika, 27, 219-246.

[80] Shepard, R. N., Romney, A. K. & Nerlove, S. B. (1972) Multidimensional Scaling New York: Seminar Press.

[81] Singhal, S. (1987) The completly connected neural network. Bellcore Technical Report, Bellcore, Morristown, N. J.

[82] Skinner, (1950) Are theories of learning necessary?

[83] Skinner, (1957) Verbal Behavior. New York: Appleton-Century-Crofts.

[84] Smolensky, P. 1988, On the Proper Treatment of Connectionism, Behavioral and Brain Sciences, 11, 1, pp. 1-59.

[85] Specht, D. F. (1967) Generation of polynomial discriminant functions for pattern recognition. IEEE Transactions Electronic Computers, Vol EC-16,3, pp. 308-319.

[86] Tomko, G. J. & Crapper, D. R. (1974) Neural variability: Nonstationary response to identical visual stimuli, Brain Research, 79, p. 405-418.

[87] Tukey, J. (1977) Exploratory Data Analysis. Reading Mass: Addison-Wesley.

[88] Tversky, A. (1977) Features of Similarity Psychological Review, 84, 327-352.

[89] Valiant, L. G., (1985) Learning Disjunctions of Conjunctions, Proc. Ninth International Joint Conference on Artificial Intelligence, 560-566, Los Angeles, CA, August 18-23.

[90] Werbos, P. J. (1974) Beyond Regression: New tools for prediction and analysis in the behavioral sciences. Dissertation Thesis, Harvard University.

[91] Widrow, B. and Hoff, M. E. (1960) Adaptive switching circuits 1960 WESCON Convention Record Part IV, 96-104.

[92] Wieland, A. and Leighton, R. (1987) Geometric Analysis of Neural Network Capabilities, Neural Networks Conference, San Diego.

[93] Williams, R. J. (1986) The logic of activation functions, In Rumelhart, D. E. & McClelland, J. L. (Eds.), Parallel Distributed Processing: Explorations in the Microstructure of Cognition. Vol 1: Foundations. Bradford Books/MIT Press, Cambridge, Mass.

[94] Williams, R. J. and Zipser, D. (1988) A learning algorithm for cotinually running fully recurrent neural networks, ICS Technical Report, 8805.

[95] Winder, (1962) Threshold logic, Ph.D. Dissertation, Princeton University, Princeton, N.J.

EARLY VISION, FOCAL ATTENTION, AND NEURAL NETS

Bela Julesz
Laboratory of Vision Research
Psychology Department
Rutgers University
New Brunswick, NJ 08903
and Division of Biology
California Institute of Technology
Pasadena, CA 91125

During the Spring, Summer and Fall of 1990, I wrote five articles on early vision and focal attention for five different disciplines. One manuscript for the ATR Workshop on Modeling Human Visual Perception and Cognition, Kyoto, is intended mainly for engineers in machine vision and AI. The other four manuscripts are as follows: Representations of Vision: Trends and Tacit Assumptions in Vision Research Symposium, (ECVP, Sep. 1990, Paris) entitled Some Strategic Questions in Visual Perception (Julesz, 1991a) is written for my colleagues in psychology. The third is written for physicists, the fourth for neurophysiologists and the fifth for philosophers interested in visual perception. The second article contains about forty strategic questions for vision research in addition to some metascientific ones, and I hope that with these questions I have started a trend and other colleagues will extend my list. The third, and most important one intended for physicists, is an elaborate review entitled Early Vision and Focal Attention, and was written at the request of the Editors of Reviews of Modern Physics (Julesz, 1991b). The fourth article (Julesz, 1991c) of mine is an open peer review in which I answer, among others, the philosopher John Searle on his recent idea that the brain cannot have unconscious processes. This paper will be published sometime next year in the journal Behavioral and Brain Research and I will quote from my answer at a few places here. My fourth article (Julesz, 1990), intended for neurophysiologists, entitled "Early vision is bottom-up except for focal attention," just appeared in Symposium #55: The Brain celebrating the 100th anniversary of the Cold Spring Harbor Laboratory. These five articles span a large audience in different disciplines, and while working on them permitted me to ponder over the state of psychobiology from five different perspectives.

I mention these articles to offer more detailed sources of my views on vision. I will also elaborate here on some of the issues which I discussed at the CAIP Neural Network Workshop on Oct. 16, 1990. I think the interested reader will find in these reviews several topics related to neural networks. Nevertheless, as a token of my appreciation of being invited to this excellent workshop I will make a few brief remarks based on my Kyoto talk, but with some modifications..

During my 32 year career at Bell Laboratories (now at Rutgers University and CALTECH) - doing basic research in visual perception and trying to transfer some of the gained knowledge into technology - I often came across some surprising confusions by leading engineers about the state of brain research. I found it amazing that engineers with excellent brains and great sophistication, usually conservative in assessing technological innovations, would believe in half-baked AI projects. Conversely, there are now interesting technological possibilities to be exploited that for various reasons have not been attempted. A point in case, out of my expertise, is automatic speech recognition, a field whose development I witnessed over a three decades. In spite of great progress, some of the fundamental principles of human speech recognition are still an enigma, and the prodigious feats of a human who can pick out and understand in noisy environment a speaker of his native tongue cannot be mimicked by any machine at present. In visual perception the abilities of some humans are even more enigmatic. Take for instance the art of a cartoonist, who with a few strokes can portray a faithful image of a face that all of us can immediately recognize.

Let me assure the reader that I will not ruminate over the mysterious processes of semantics, form recognition, and Gestalt organization that I avoided during my scientific life. After all, since 1960 when I introduced computer-generated random-dot stereograms, cinematograms, and textures into psychology with my coworkers, I was able to show that stereoscopic depth and motion perception, and preattentive texture discrimination are basically bottom-up processes and can operate without the higher- order top-down processes. These processes of early vision are now well understood psychologically and recently some of them can be even linked to neurophysiological findings. So I will illustrate my point with a few examples of early vision, but adding to it my researches in focal attention, an area I am now concentrating on with my collaborators over eight years.

Before I mention a few concrete examples, let me summarize the essence of my life-long research in two sentences: A) I have shown with random-dot stereograms that contrary to earlier assumptions, stereopsis is not local, but a global process. B). Using artificial texture pairs with controlled geometrical and statistical properties, with my collaborators we have shown that, contrary to prevailing beliefs, preattentive texture discrimination is not a statistical (global), but instead a quasi-local process, that depends on a few conspicuous features, which I called textons. As I noted already, these are mainly bottom-up processes and by adding to them the only top-down process, focal attention, one can explain most of the basic perceptual processes without having to invoke the enigmatic processes of memory and semantics.

Perhaps few concepts are as misused as the concept of the "scanpath". It is commonly believed by workers in machine vision, that scanning eye-movements follow a characteristic path as an observer scans an image and are revealing the strategic locals of observer's interest. Furthermore, some even believe that this scanpath would repeat itself when an observer repeatedly scrutinizes the same image. In my youth, even I toyed with the idea of an "eye-yoked" picturephone system, permitting the viewer to dial up a remote vidicon that would be yoked to the viewer's eye such that it would follow his gaze, and only the central foveal area of high spatial resolution had to be transmitted. It took me some time to realize that presenting to the center of gaze a sharp image was a necessary but not sufficient first step. As known already by Helmholtz (1896), and elegantly studied by Posner (1980) serial shifts of focal attention underlying scrutiny can take place rapidly without eye-movements. [An English translation of this pioneering contribution by Helmholtz is provided by Nakayama and Mackeben (1989) from the third German edition after a century delay, because all existing English editions are based on the first German edition and Helmholtz added this important observation only to later editions.] While evidence is indirect, based on different models the experimental results are interpreted, the "searchlight of attention" scans about 30-60 msec/item (Sternberg 1966, Weichselgartner and Sperling 1987, Treisman and Gelade 1980, Bergen and Julesz 1983).

Recently, Jukka Saarinen and I measured directly the scanning speed of focal attention by briefly presenting (with masking) numbers at random locations, and though observers could not correctly report the order in the sequence, they could follow and identify as many as four consecutive numbers at 30 msec/item rates with orders of magnitude less error than by chance (Saarinen and Julesz, 1991). Obviously this rate depends on the visibility of the texture gradients, and some parallel mechanism seems to facilitate serial search (Kröse and Julesz 1989, Wolfe and Cave 1990).

Because focal attention shifts take place about five times faster than eye-movements, and independently from eye-movements, eye-movements usually are directed to some gross "center of gravity" of some visual scene and the detailed element-by-element scrutiny is done by the fast moving aperture of the "searchlight" of attention. We (Sagi and Julesz, 1986) measured the size of this aperture of focal attention. Unfortunately, while eye-movements can now be measured with a 1 minarc accuracy (e.g. using the fourth-Purkinje image eye-tracker of SRI), the position of focal attention cannot be measured yet. At present the time constant of PET-scan is 1000 times slower than the rate of focal attention, and it is not yet conclusively proven that attention will increase the oxygen flow of those neural tissues that are engaged. Before some fast, non-invasive methods are found, we have no idea what the observer is looking at, except by asking him. Therefore, any scheme that wants to exploit an observer's scanpath of measuring eye-movements is doomed to failure.

Interestingly, this is quite analogous to a debate between Brewster ar d Dove, just after the invention of the stereoscope by Wheatstone in 1838. Brewster thought that depth perception is the result of "triangulations" by convergence eye-movements, until Dove (1841) demonstrated stereopsis in a brief flash of an electric-spark, too brief for any convergence movements to occur. Obviously, it was necessary to bring the left and right images in near alignment for the neural machinery of stereopsis to operate. But it was this neural machinery that was essence of stereopsis. The amount of the alignment necessary for stereopsis was studied by Panum, and is now called Panum's-fusional-area. Only a century later were we (Fender and Julesz, 1967) able to show (using binocular retinal stabilization with close-fitting contact lenses) that for random-dot stereograms the classical Panum's area could be extended by 20 times, in the order of 2 deg.arc. Again, what is the use of measuring observer's convergence movements when a vast area in depth is scrutinized by binocular-disparity-tuned neurons.

Recent advances in understanding focal attention have a great impact on connectionist neural networks. In these networks each neuron participates in learning and storing some information by a small amount as a result of changing the weights of connectivities to liked neurons. This learning is rather indirect, and memories are stored as the global interaction of slow changes in the interconnection of the participating neurons. While such networks are nowadays quite fashionable and represent great progress, nevertheless are very different of the action of the human brain. In addition of focal attention wondering over a visual scene, attention can also scrutinize many processes within the human brain. While the reader can follow my thoughts, his attention can easily wonder to many other thoughts in rapid succession, and return to this article. It is this rapid change of thoughts and mental processes that is so alien to algorithms and machines.

Because connectionism, particularly its representation by neural networks of the PDP-kind (Rumelhart and McClelland, 1986), are popular among physicists and engineers who are not familiar with facts of brain research but understand "Hamiltonians", "strange attractors", "thermal annealing", and so on, should be particularly on the alert. While the invention of "hidden layers" and convergence theorems of learning through "back-propagation" extended the processing power of "perceptrons" considerably, it should be noted that the simplest network with a hidden layer is the "exclusive OR" (with 3 gates) and to learn this logical function from scratch requires over 500 trials. Now, let us assume that the number of trials for learning a task increases monotonically (linearly, polynomially, or exponentially) with the number of gates. A special way of genetic learning (evolution) is to change the connectivity of neurons in a brain of a given species at each mutation. So, to develop the human brain with its 10^{15} gates (synapses) might require eons, and even at a high mutation rate, time of life on Earth is too short to accomplish this feat by PDP techniques. This criticism of mine hinges on the monotonic increase of learning time with the number of synapses in a neural net, and evaporates if one could prove that learning time stays invariant with the size of the network - an unlikely event. Indeed, Stephen Judd (1987) gives a proof that in general supervised training in connectionist networks is NP-complete, thus learning time goes up exponentially with the number of the synapses (gates, or nodes) in a network. He shows, that even for very restricted networks, teaching(loading) time to set the connectivity of the gates requires polynomial time. So, my criticism against connectionist neural networks seems to be correct (based on the learning(loading) time being a polynomial or exponential function of 10^{15} gates, thus orders of magnitude larger than the age of our Universe, where the unit of each learning step is "one tick of the clock of mutation" for a given species). For a deeper critique, the reader may turn to Pylyshyn (1984), and Fodor and Pylyshyn (1988).

With these brief remarks I just wanted to give the flavor of topics I raised and illustrated in my articles referred above and tried to hint at the kind of interactions physiological psychology can provide to the field of machine vision.

Bibliography

[1] Bergen, J.R. and Julesz.B. (1983). Parallel versus serial processing in rapid pattern discrimination. Nature 303, 696-698. /check this

[2] Dove, H.W., 1841, "U"ber Stereoskopie," Ann. Phys. series 2 110, 494- 98.

[3] Fender, D. and B. Julesz, 1967, "Extension of Panum's fusional area in binocularly stabilized vision," Jour. Opt. Soc. Am. 57(6), 819-30.

[4] Fodor, J.A. and Z.W. Pylyshyn, 1988, "Connectionism and cognitive architecture: A critical analysis," in Connections and Symbols, edited by S. Pinker and J. Mehler (The MIT Press, Cambridge, MA), p. 3-71.

[5] Helmholtz, H. von, 1896, Handbuch der Physiologischen Optik. Dritter Abschnitt, Zweite Auflage (Voss, Hamburg). [English translation: Helmholtz's Treatise on Physiological Optics by J.P.C. Southall, 1924, (The Optical Soc. Am.), republished by Dover Publications, 1962.]

[6] Judd, S., 1987, "Learning in networks is hard," IEEE First International Conference on Neural Networks, Vol.II, 685-692.

[7] Julesz, B., 1990 (in press), "Early vision is bottom-up, except for focal attention", in Cold Spring Harbor Symposia on Quantitative Biology–The Brain, May 30–June 6, Cold Spring Harbor, Vol. 55.

[8] Julesz, B., 1991a, (in press), "Some strategic questions in visual perception", in Proceedings of 13th European Conference on Visual Perception (ECVP), Paris, France, Sept. 4–7, 1990, Representations of Vision: Trends and Tacit Assumptions in Vision Research, edited by A. Gorea (Cambridge University Press).

[9] Julesz, B., 1991b, (in press), "Early vision and focal attention", Reviews of Modern Physics.

[10] Julesz, B., 1991c, (in press), "Consciousness and focal attention", Behavioral and Brain Sciences.

[11] Kröse, B.J.A. and B. Julesz, 1989, "The control and speed of shifts of attention," Vision Res. 29(11), 1607-1619.

[12] Nakayama, K. and M. Mackeben, 1989, "Sustained and transient components of focal visual attention," Vision Res. 29, 1631-164.

[13] Posner, M.I., 1978, "Orienting of attention," Quart. J. of Experimental Psychology 32, 3-25.

[14] Pylyshyn, Z.W., 1984, Computation and Cognition. Toward a Foundation of Cognitive Science (The MIT press, Cambridge, MA).

[15] Rumelhart, D.E. and J.L. McClelland, 1986, Parallel Distributed Processing: Explorations in the microstructure of cognition (The MIT Press, Cambridge, MA).

[16] Saarinen, J. and Julesz, B., 1991 (in press), "The speed of attentional shifts in the visual field", Proceedings of the National Academy of Sciences.

[17] Sagi, D. and B. Julesz, 1986, "Enhanced detection in the aperture of focal attention during simple discrimination tasks," Nature 321, 693-695.

[18] Sternberg, S., 1966, "High speed scanning in human memory", Science 153, 652-654.

[19] Treisman, A. and G. Gelade, 1980, "A feature-integration theory of attention," Cognitive Psychology 12, 97-136.

[20] Weichselgartner, E. and G. Sperling, 1987, "Dynamics of automatic and controlled visual attention," Science 238, 778-779.

[21] Wolfe, J.M. and K.R. Cave, 1990, "Deploying visual attention:The guided search model," in AI and the eye edited by A. Blake and T. Troscianco (J. Wiley, New York), pp. 79-103.

Towards Hierarchical Matched Filtering

Robert Hecht-Nielsen
HNC, Inc.
and
University of California, San Diego

1 Introduction

Traditionally, matched filtering has been used in application areas such as communications, radar, and sonar for detecting a specific waveform in a time series signal. In this paper we examine a new type of matched filter which is optimized for spatiotemporal pattern classification. Banks of these matched filters can be used as high-performance classifiers for spatiotemporal patterns. Unfortunately, the direct implementation of such matched filter banks for large problems (such as large-vocabulary continuous speech recognition), while attractive, is not practical. The focus of this paper is on a method for exploiting the inherent statistical redundancy of typical spatiotemporal pattern sets to allow more efficient implementations of such matched filter banks. In particular, this paper proposes a hierarchical neural network approach to this implementation problem. Before beginning the discussion of generalized matched filtering, some definitions are presented.

For the purposes of this paper a *spatiotemporal pattern* will be taken to be a bounded, continuous function $\mathbf{x} : R \longrightarrow R^n$ of compact interval support from the real numbers (i.e., time) to n-dimensional Euclidean space. Compact interval support implies that the value of the function is the zero vector except in a single closed and bounded interval of time $[a, b]$. Thus, a spatiotemporal pattern is simply a trajectory or path in n-dimensional space, parameterized by time. The set of all such spatiotemporal patterns will be denoted by $P[R, R^n]$.

In spatiotemporal pattern recognition, the typical goal is to provide classifications for relatively brief spatiotemporal patterns (such as words embedded in a continuous speech stream). For simplicity, we will assume that each such brief spatiotemporal pattern belongs to one of M *classes*. For example, in the problem of recognizing words in continuous speech, the input to the system might be a space–time pattern consisting of the time-varying power spectrum of the voltage output of a microphone monitoring the speech of a single speaker. The classes in this instance are the words in the vocabulary. As each word utterance has been completely entered into the speech classifier system, the system is expected to emit a number between 1 and M, corresponding to the vocabulary number of the word that was spoken. We shall assume that we are dealing with an uncued classification problem without interference and obscuration (i.e., a problem for which there is no significant background noise and only one pattern is present at any time; but for which the patterns appear at unknown times and may abut one another).

Spatiotemporal pattern classification has an issue associated with it that does not pertain to spatial pattern classification — namely, *spatiotemporal warping*. The term spatiotemporal warping refers to the action of a transformation $T : \mathcal{S} \subset P[R, R^n] \longrightarrow P[R, R^n]$ that maps each spatiotemporal pattern in a subset $\mathcal{S}$ of the set of all possible spatiotemporal patterns $P[R, R^n]$ to another spatiotemporal pattern in $P[R, R^n]$. Such spatiotemporal warping transformations can take many forms. One common example is the *time warp*. A time warp takes a pattern $\mathbf{x}(t)$ and transforms it into a pattern $\mathbf{x}(\theta(t))$, where θ is a strictly monotonically increasing smooth scalar function of time. Time warping has the effect of speeding up or slowing down the movement of the pattern $\mathbf{x}$ along its trajectory in R^n and of translating it forward or backward in time.

Another example of a spatiotemporal warp is the change that occurs to the sound power spectrum of a phonograph record when the same record is played at different speeds. In this instance, the spatiotemporal warp transformation is not a simple time warp, because the entire path followed by the spatiotemporal pattern is changed (each sound power feature is changed to a higher or lower frequency channel). Notice that the power spectrum spatiotemporal warping transformation associated with speeding up or slowing down a phonograph record is different from the transformation associated with speaking faster or slower. When we speak faster or slower, our vocal pitch changes very little, and therefore essentially the same sounds are emitted as in normal speech, only in a faster or slower sequence than normal. Thus, the sound power spectrum spatiotemporal warping transformation associated with speaking faster or slower is essentially a simple time warp.[1] Finally, notice that if we were considering the time-series sound signal itself as our spatiotemporal pattern (instead of its power spectrum), these situations would be reversed (speeding or slowing a record would be a time warp, and speaking faster or slower would not be).

In general, spatiotemporal pattern classifiers are required to be insensitive to a general class of spatiotemporal warping transformations. However, in the case where only spatiotemporal warping transformations that are close to the identity transform need to be accommodated, the spatiotemporal pattern can simply be viewed as a fixed path or curve in n-dimensional space. By dividing the time duration of the pattern into small enough units, we can view the pattern as a sequence of N closely spaced discrete points in n-dimensional space. Alternatively, such a pattern could then be viewed as a single point in an nN-dimensional space. Therefore, at least in principle, a spatiotemporal pattern of finite duration that is not subjected to significant spatiotemporal warping transformations can simply be treated as a spatial pattern. Alternatively, spatiotemporally warped versions of the same pattern can be viewed as *different* spatial patterns (which happen to belong to the same class). If a *time window* of a fixed number N of spatial samples is employed, the total pattern time duration can sometimes be ignored (that is, we can deal exclusively with successive time vignettes — each of which is classified individually as a

---

[1] It may be that really good sets of speech features will undergo a simple time warp transformation as speech is sped up or slowed down. However, some of the features currently used in speech recognition (such as cepstral features) do not have this property. This may be a possible area for improvement.

spatial pattern). This is the approach used by Waibel, et al in their *time–delay neural network* [8,9].

We now define the generalized matched filter. Following this, it is shown how a bank of such matched filters can be used as a classifier for general spatiotemporal patterns that is insensitive to spatiotemporal warping transformations of a given class.

2   Matched Filtering

One well-known method of pattern recognition is *template matching* or *nearest neighbor classification* [2,3], in which unknown patterns are simply compared with known examples (using an appropriate distance measurement procedure) to find the closest matching examples. Given a sufficiently rich set of example patterns, such classifiers can be shown to be near-optimal. However, for practical problems, classifiers with a sufficiently large number of example patterns are often impractical.

In this section a generalization of the classical matched filter will be presented. This generalized matched filter provides us with a means for measuring the 'distance' between the best fitting segment of a fixed example pattern and the most recent segment of an unknown pattern (with the time duration of the comparison interval determined by a fixed time windowing function μ). In the next section we will use this matched filter distance measurement to define a nearest neighbor classifier for spatiotemporal patterns.

Given two spatiotemporal patterns, $\mathbf{u}(t)$ and $\mathbf{v}(t)$, a natural way to define a space–time distance measurement for them is simply to integrate the square of the Euclidean distance $|\mathbf{u}(t) - \mathbf{v}(t)|^2$ between $\mathbf{u}$ and $\mathbf{v}$ over time. Formally, the distance measurement D corresponding to this scheme is given by

$$D(\mathbf{u}, \mathbf{v}) = \int_{-\infty}^{\infty} \ |\mathbf{u}(t) - \mathbf{v}(t)| \quad dt. \tag{1}$$

It is easy to show that this distance measurement function is a metric on $P[R, R^n]$. Thus, D has the following properties:

(**I**) $D(\mathbf{u}, \mathbf{v}) = 0$ if and only if $\mathbf{u} = \mathbf{v}$.
(**II**) $D(\mathbf{u}, \mathbf{v}) = D(\mathbf{v}, \mathbf{u})$.
(**III**) $D(\mathbf{u}, \mathbf{v}) \le D(\mathbf{u}, \mathbf{w}) + D(\mathbf{w}, \mathbf{v})$.   (2)
(**IV**) $D(\mathbf{u}, \mathbf{v}) \ge 0$.

Although this metric is mathematically neat and tidy, from a technological perspective the metric D leaves a lot to be desired. For example, let us imagine that spatiotemporal pattern $\mathbf{u}$ is exactly the same as spatiotemporal pattern $\mathbf{v}$, except that it is slightly displaced in time (that is, $\mathbf{u}(t) = \mathbf{v}(t - c)$). For most practical applications, we would want the distance between these two spatiotemporal patterns to be considered to be 0. Unfortunately, the metric D will assign a distance that could be quite large. In another situation $\mathbf{u}$ might be a time-warped version of the speech signal $\mathbf{v}$. Again, in such an instance, the metric D might well produce a distance that is quite large. In summary, there are many situations in which the metric D is not satisfactory. However, if we were to apply an appropriate *corrective* spatiotemporal warping transformation to one of the two patterns being compared, then D might serve quite adequately as a distance measurement. This is the basic idea behind the generalized matched filter.

The concept is that we want to create a distance measurement that is invariant, or at least insensitive, to the distortion of patterns by some preselected class $\mathcal{C}$ of spatiotemporal warping transformations. For example, if we wished to be insensitive to small time warps, we might define the class $\mathcal{C}$ to consist of transformations of the form $\mathbf{u}(t) \longrightarrow \mathbf{u}(\theta(t))$, where $0.5 \le d\theta/dt \le 2.0$. Of course, $\mathcal{C}$ might consist of much more complicated transformations.

Given the desire to have a distance measurement for a fixed reference pattern $\mathbf{v}$ that is invariant with respect to a class $\mathcal{C}$ of spatiotemporal warping transformations, and which only operates locally in time, a natural choice would be

$$H_{\mathbf{v}}(\mathbf{u}, t) \equiv \inf_{T \in \mathcal{C}} \int_{-\infty}^{\infty} \mu(\tau - t) \mid \mathbf{u}(\tau) - T\mathbf{v}(\tau) \mid d\tau, \qquad (3)$$

where μ is a non–negative smooth function with $\mu(\tau) \geq 0$ for $\tau \in (-a, 0)$ (where a is a non–negative constant) and $\mu(\tau) = 0$ otherwise, and where $\mathcal{C}$ is a defined set of spatiotemporal warping transformations. The function μ is called a *time windowing function*. It serves the purpose of focusing the attention of the distance measurement on the time interval $[t - a, t]$. H can be interpreted as the distance between the spatiotemporal pattern $\mathbf{u}$ over the time interval $[t - a, t]$, and the best matching warped portion (of duration $[t - a, t]$) of $\mathbf{v}$. $H_{\mathbf{v}}(\mathbf{u}, t)$ is called the *generalized multidimensional matched filter* (or simply *matched filter*, since we shall not use the traditional version in the sequel) for input spatiotemporal pattern $\mathbf{u}$, tuned to spatiotemporal pattern $\mathbf{v}$, over spatiotemporal warp class $\mathcal{C}$.

Notice that since H is based upon a distance measurement that it is not a linear structure. Thus, the pattern intensity (vector magnitude) matters. This simply means that absolute pattern intensity (e.g., absolute sound power level in speech and absolute image intensity in imagery) needs to be normalized, or preprocessed in some other way (see [7] for examples some of useful preprocessing steps). Alternatively, such normalizing transformations can be included in the set $\mathcal{C}$.

Note that the output of the generalized matched filter is zero if the match is perfect, as opposed to the usual matched filter, for which the ratio of filter output to input pattern power is maximized if the match is perfect.

Naturally, not all of the properties of the traditional linear matched filter are preserved in this new definition (linearity, for example, is lost). However, the property of being a good detector for the pattern $\mathbf{v}$ in noise often *is* preserved (depending on the set $\mathcal{C}$). To see why, notice that, if we insert a noisy signal $\mathbf{u} + \mathbf{n}$ in place of $\mathbf{u}$ (where $\mathbf{n}$ is some arbitrary, integrable, noise signal), then since $|\mathbf{u} + \mathbf{n} - T\mathbf{v}| \leq |\mathbf{u} - T\mathbf{v}| + |\mathbf{n}|$, we get

$$\begin{aligned} H_{\mathbf{v}}(\mathbf{u} + \mathbf{n}, t) \ &\leq H_{\mathbf{v}}(\mathbf{u}, t) + \inf_{T \in \mathcal{C}} \ \int_{-\infty}^{\infty} \mu(\tau - t) \ | \ \mathbf{n}(\tau) \ | \ d\tau \\ &= H_{\mathbf{v}}(\mathbf{u}, t) + \int_{-\infty}^{\infty} \mu(\tau - t) \ | \ \mathbf{n}(\tau) \ | \ d\tau \\ &= H_{\mathbf{v}}(\mathbf{u}, t) + \mathcal{N}, \end{aligned}$$

$$(4)$$

where $\mathcal{N}$ is the integrated "power" of the noise process **n** weighted by the window function μ over the time interval $[t - a, t]$. Thus, it is clear that additive noise power, combined with the input signal to the filter, will contaminate the matched filtering process in a directly additive and average-power-linear way, which is essentially as well as we can, in general, hope to do. The beauty of this linear noise-power addition bound result is that it holds despite the fact that $H_{\mathbf{v}}$ is highly nonlinear.

In the next section we use the generalized multidimensional matched filter to define a general type of spatiotemporal pattern classifier called the *nearest matched filter classifier.*

3   The Nearest Matched Filter Classifier

One way of building a pattern classifier for spatiotemporal patterns is to gather many examples of patterns belonging to each of the M classes into which each unknown input pattern is to be placed. An unknown spatiotemporal pattern can then be compared with these examples at each time t, by means of matched filters based upon the example patterns, to determine (via a classification decision policy) whether a pattern belonging to any one of the M classes has just finished arriving or not. This is the *nearest matched filter classifier.*

To make the notation concrete, let us define such a *training set* of patterns to be the set $P = \{(\mathbf{v}_1, \beta_1), (\mathbf{v}_2, \beta_2), ..., (\mathbf{v}_N, \beta_N)\}$, where $\beta_k \in \{1, 2, ..., M\}$ is the number of the class to which example pattern $\mathbf{v}_k$ belongs. The input signal, **u**, is fed to all of these matched filters in parallel (the matched filters use weighting functions that are *balanced* so that their responses are comparable). The output of the classifier at time t is a class number β determined by putting the outputs of all N matched filters into a decision policy function. For example, if we wanted to use a simple 1-nearest neighbor policy we would emit, at each time t, the class number β_i associated with the reference pattern $\mathbf{v}_i$ having the smallest matched filter output $H_{\mathbf{v}_i}(\mathbf{u}, t)$; unless the value of the smallest matched filter output exceeded a fixed threshold, in which case we would provide a class number output of 0 – meaning that the input signal does not currently match any example pattern well. Clearly, the pattern class output typically will not be smooth (it will jump abruptly from one class number to another as the winning classifier of the competition process changes). The generalized multidimensional matched filter and the nearest matched filter classifier (along with a neural network implementation of the classifier for time warps) were introduced in 1982 [6]. For further information and discussion of these concepts see [4].

The nearest matched filter classifier can be defined for a variety of spatiotemporal warping transformations. However, common choices might be time warping or pitch change transformations. Time warping would be useful, for example, for speech recognition, where the changes in how words are pronounced are typically of a time–warp nature. Pitch change transformations (such as those that occur when we speed up or slow down a phonograph record) would be useful for recognizing vehicles by their sounds, since much of the sound of a vehicle is from its engine, transmission, and wheels, which produce sounds at pitches that are directly dependent on road speed and gear selection. In every case, the use of an appropriate class of transformations will ensure that each reference pattern can serve as a model for a wide class of similar, but transformed, patterns. This effective pattern reuse greatly reduces the number of reference patterns that must be used.

Finally, the theoretical classification performance of the nearest matched filter classifier has been established for the case where $\mathcal{C}$ is the set of time translations [5]. In this case, assuming that the training set is sufficiently comprehensive (and employing a 1-nearest neighbor classification decision policy), the classifier error rate will satisfy the Cover and Hart inequality [1]

$$R^* \leq R \leq R^* \left(2 - \frac{M}{M-1} R^*\right),\tag{5}$$

where R^* is the error rate of the Bayes classifier.

The nearest matched filter classifier has one problem, and two advantages. The problem is that we may need an enormous training set; this requirement may make the direct implementation of such a classifier impossibly large and computationally burdensome (since all N

of the $H_{\mathbf{v}_k}(\mathbf{u}, t)$ integrals must be computed in parallel). The advantages are that the classifier is capable of near-Bayesian performance (at least for some classes of spatiotemporal warping transformations), and that the individual matched filters are insensitive to noise. This latter advantage is particularly important if all of the matched filters are using the same weighting function (as opposed to weighting functions that merely have the same time integral), since Equation 4 shows that all of the matched filters will then react approximately the same to additive noise. Thus, since the decision process is typically largely a relative comparison of the matched filter outputs, the classifier output will be somewhat insensitive to additive noise. The combination of guaranteed high classification accuracy (given our ability and willingness to implement a sufficient training set) and additive noise insensitivity make the nearest matched filter classifier an interesting candidate for solving spatiotemporal classification problems.

Finally, because the windowing function limits the consideration of the incoming spatiotemporal pattern to the time interval $[t-a, t]$, the nearest matched filter classifier can carry out only the first local-in-time stage of spatiotemporal pattern recognition. For many problems, local-in-time classification is not sufficient. Often, to do a good job of classification, we must exploit context information that we can obtain only by considering longer periods of time. One way to do this would be to devise a classification decision policy function that could exploit a priori syntax and context information. Because such a postprocessing operation is often essential if adequate performance is to be achieved, the nearest matched filter classifier should really be thought of as just a front end for a complete classifier. We now consider the problem of implementing a nearest matched filter classifier in a hierarchical neural network structure.

3.1 Nearest Matched Filter Classifier Implementation

In [4] a neural network for approximately implementing the nearest matched filter classifier for the class of time warp spatiotemporal warping transformations is described. This network has the disadvantage that it requires one sub-network for each example pattern in the training set. Thus, the size of the network grows linearly with the size of the training set.

For many problems, such as continuous speech recognition, the patterns in the training set will be highly redundant. In other words, these patterns will have many sub-patterns (phonemes, for example) in common – usually at several different time duration levels. Thus, from a statistical perspective, a direct implementation of such a nearest matched filter classifier will be highly inefficient, since each matched filter will contain units that are tuned to essentially the same short-term patterns that a multitude of other units are also tuned to. Consolidating these units would decrease the size of such an implementation enormously – perhaps making such systems practical. This section presents an outline of a scheme for accomplishing this consolidation by means of a new hierarchical design.

Figure 1 shows a design for a self-organizing spatiotemporal feature detector layer. This layer learns short time sequences of patterns in a way that makes it insensitive to small time warps. Perhaps the best way to describe the function of this layer is to begin with a description of how it is trained. Then its function during normal operation will be described.

During both training and normal operation of the hierarchical neural network classifier we assume that the spatiotemporal patterns are entered into the hierarchy at the bottom as sequences of vector inputs in discrete time. The sample rate is greater than the Nyquist rate for the fastest varying component of the pattern. Further, we assume that the individual patterns to be classified have durations that are all approximately the same (this condition is not necessary, but relaxing it adds complications that will be avoided in this paper). The patterns are assumed to arrive in a random order described by a fixed probability density. The only spatiotemporal warping transformations are assumed to be mild time warps. Given these assumptions, we now consider the training of layer m of the hierarchy. We assume that all of the previous layers have already been trained and their weights have been frozen.

The first step in training layer m is to train the spatial weight vectors $\mathbf{w}_{m1}$, $\mathbf{w}_{m2}$, ..., $\mathbf{w}_{mN}$. These are trained using Kohonen learning

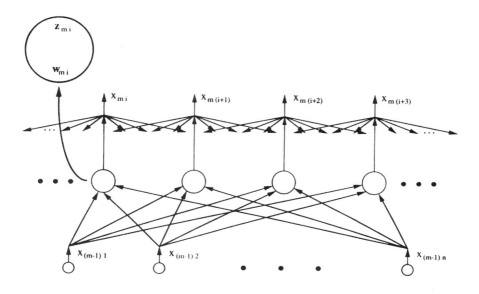

Figure 1: Schematic for a self-organizing spatiotemporal feature detector layer. The inputs to layer m are the time-varying signals $x_{(m-1)1}, x_{(m-1)2}, \ldots, x_{(m-1)n}$, which come from either the previous layer $(m - 1)$, or directly from the spatiotemporal pattern source in the outside world. The layer functions both as a spatial matching layer with spatial input weight vectors $\mathbf{w}_{m1}, \mathbf{w}_{m2}, \ldots, \mathbf{w}_{mN}$ and as a temporal sequence matching layer with temporal connection input weight vectors $\mathbf{z}_{m1}, \mathbf{z}_{m2}, \ldots, \mathbf{z}_{mN}$. The constellation of units that are highly active at any one time (units become active when they receive both strong spatial input and strong temporal input) form a spatial code that describes (often uniquely) the sequence of $\mathbf{x}_{(m-1)}(t)$ inputs over the last short time interval. These layers are arranged in a hierarchy, with each subsequent layer having a response time constant twice as long as the previous layer. At the proper level in the hierarchy (the level with an appropriately long response time constant) the activity constellation present after a complete spatiotemporal pattern to be classified has been entered will be a distinctive spatial code for that pattern. A separate mapping network can map this spatial code into pattern class and confidence level outputs.

with conscience (see [4] for details), with each successive training trial utilizing the next discrete time sample of input $\mathbf{x}_{(m-1)}(t)$ from the previous layer as the training vector. The α learning rate constant starts off at a value near 1.0 and decreases to 0 in accordance with a cooling schedule.

After this training process converges, the $\mathbf{w}_{mi}$ vectors will be distributed in $\mathbf{x}_{(m-1)}$ space such that each time sample $\mathbf{x}_{(m-1)}(t)$ of the input to layer m is equally likely to be closest (measured using Euclidean distance) to each of the $\mathbf{w}_{mi}$ weight vectors. At this point these spatial weight vectors are frozen and the training of the $\mathbf{z}_{mi}$ temporal weight vectors begins.

Before temporal weight training begins, the processing elements are modified. Unlike during spatial weight training, where the processing elements simply responded at each discrete time to the distance from the current input at that time to the unit's spatial weight vector, now the reaction to inputs will have a temporal behavior. Specifically, each processing element will now be governed by equations such as

$$x_{mi}(t) = \alpha \left(-c\, x_{mi}(t-1) + d\, U\left(\psi - |\mathbf{w}_{li} - \mathbf{x}_{m-1}(t)|\right)\right), \quad (6)$$

$$0 \leq x_{mi}(t) \leq 1,$$

$$U(\zeta) \;=\; \begin{cases} 1 & \text{if } \zeta > 0 \\ 0 & \text{if } \zeta \leq 0, \end{cases} \quad (7)$$

and

$$\alpha_{li}(\xi) \;=\; \begin{cases} \xi & \text{if } \xi \geq 0 \\ \phi\,\xi & \text{if } \xi < 0, \end{cases} \quad (8)$$

and where $\mathbf{w}_{mi}$ is the spatial weight vector of unit i of layer m, and c, d, ψ, and ϕ are positive constants, with $c, \phi < 1$.

These equations ensure that each unit is activated only if the input vector $\mathbf{x}_{(m-1)}(t)$ is sufficiently close to the spatial weight vector $\mathbf{w}_{mi}$ of that unit. The *attack function* α is used to ensure that the "spin up" of each unit is faster than than the "spin down" (see Section 6.1 of [4] for details).

Given equations of the above sort, each processing element within ψ range of the input vector $\mathbf{x}_{(m-1)}(t)$ will become activated. The constants are chosen so that this activation always hard limits at 1 within a few time units after the input vector enters the ψ sphere surrounding its weight vector. After the input vector leaves this sphere the activity of the processing element slowly decays, in accordance with Equation 6. Note that by setting the value of ψ correctly it will be possible to ensure that an approximately constant fraction of the units are always active – obviating the need for the development (as yet unachieved) of a "local" competition mechanism.

Given the above unit behaviors, a steady stream of input patterns is then entered into the system and the temporal weights z_{mij} (which are all initially zero) are modified by means of the Kosko/Klopf learning law (see Section 3.6 of [4] for details). This establishes temporal weights in accordance with commonly encountered sequences of activation of the units.

Following equilibration of the temporal weights, these weights are frozen (if desired, to improve later performance, the weights can first be "sharpened" via a sigmoidal transformation before freezing). The layer is now ready to be prepared for use. To do this, yet another transfer function is introduced.

Following the freezing of the weights of the unit, the transfer functions employed during operational use of the layer are inserted into the units. This transfer function has a form such as

$$x_{mi}(t) = \alpha\Big(- c\, x_{mi}(t-1) + $$
$$d\, U\left(\psi - |\mathbf{w}_{li} - \mathbf{x}_{m-1}(t)|\right)\left[\theta + \sum_{j \neq i} z_{mij}\, x_{mj}\right]\Big),$$

$$0 \leq x_{mi}(t) \leq 1.$$

The behavior of this transfer function is now briefly described. First, for activation of unit i of layer m to occur, the input vector $\mathbf{x}_{(m-1)}(t)$ from the previous layer must be passing through the sphere of radius ψ surrounding the unit's spatial weight vector $\mathbf{w}_{mi}$. Second, the activation level reached (if not hard limited at 1.0) will depend on the sum of the quantity θ and the temporal input intensity $\sum_{j \neq i} z_{mij} \, x_{mj}$. To achieve full activation, the temporal input intensity must be quite large (this ensures that during training unit i was frequently active following the layer m units currently supplying it highly weighted input). The offset $\theta > 0$ is used to ensure that units that lie at the start of learned spatiotemporal sequences will become at least modestly active, even though they do not have any predecessor units helping to get them activated. In the end, this scheme (and other variants) provides a spatial pattern of activity that represents a history of the trajectory of the input $\mathbf{x}_{(m-1)}(t)$ over the last brief interval of time. However, unlike the trace of an electron beam on a cathode ray tube with a long-persistence monitor, the history recorded by this network layer is in terms of a set of spatiotemporal segments burned into the network during training. If the input pattern deviates too much from one of these trajectory segments the layer will not respond much at all.

From the above observation it is clear that this spatiotemporal layer is, in fact, acting as a generalized matched filter bank over a brief interval of time, with each activity constellation representing a pattern trajectory segment learned during training. The transfer function used precludes constellations from becoming highly active unless this is so (unless, of course, the layer has been overloaded). Note that if overloading occurs the layer can simply be made larger and the ψ constant can be lowered. This allows the use of larger numbers of (more spatially discriminating) units to learn the spatiotemporal subtrajectories. Note that this layer will be insensitive to modest time warps, due to the gradual activation and deactivation behavior of the operational transfer functions.

4 Conclusions

This paper has reviewed the definition of a new matched filter for spatiotemporal patterns and introduced a hierarchical layered neural network designed to efficiently implement a bank of such matched filters for the purpose of achieving spatiotemporal pattern recognition that is insensitive to small time warps. In order to derive the desired classification information a mapping network must be employed that will transform the spatial constellations of activity at the highest layers into a class number and a confidence level.

The self-organizing layer defined here has only limited redundancy of spatial pattern representation (in contrast to the Spatiotemporal Pattern Recognizer network presented in Section 6.1 of [4], which has enormous redundancy). Each subsequent layer in the hierarchy has a time constant $1/c$ that is twice as long as the layer below. This "temporal compression" property ensures that the activity constellations at higher and higher layers act as codes for longer and longer sequences of spatiotemporal pattern. It is conjectured that if the layers are not overloaded and if the spatiotemporal patterns are sufficiently distinct, that these constellation codes will be unique. Further, in general, if the input pattern does not resemble a pattern presented during training then none of the layers will respond significantly.

The architecture presented here moves us one step closer towards efficient implementation of large matched filter banks for spatiotemporal pattern classification.

Bibliography

[1] Cover, T.M. and Hart, P.E., "Nearest neighbor pattern classification", *IEEE Trans. on Infor. Th.*, **IT-13** 21–27, January 1967.

[2] Devijver, P. A., and Kittler, J., **Pattern Recognition: A Statistical Approach**, Prentice–Hall, Englewood Cliffs NJ, 1982.

[3] Duda, R. O., and Hart, P. E., **Pattern Classification and Scene Analysis**, Wiley, New York, 1973.

[4] Hecht-Nielsen, R., **Neurocomputing**, Addison-Wesley, Reading, MA, 1990.

[5] Hecht-Nielsen, R., "Nearest matched filter classification of spatiotemporal patterns", *Applied Optics*, **26** (10), 1892–1899, 1987.

[6] Hecht-Nielsen, R., "Neural Analog Processing", *Proc. SPIE*, **360**, 180–189, 1982.

[7] Grossberg, S. [Ed.], **Neural Networks and Natural Intelligence**, MIT Press, Cambridge MA, 1988.

[8] Waibel, A., "Modular construction of time-delay neural networks for speech recognition", *Neural Computation*, **1**, 39–46, Spring 1989.

[9] Waibel, A., Hanazawa, T., Hinton, G., Shikano, K., and Lang, K., "Phoneme recognition: Neural networks vs. hidden Markov models", *Proc. ICASSP*, **S3.3**, 107–110, April 1988.

Some Variations on Training of Recurrent Networks

Gary M. Kuhn and Norman P. Herzberg
Center for Communications Research – IDA

1 Introduction

We describe some variations on training of multi-layered recurrent networks which overcome the need for an externally-supplied target function, avoid back-propagation of error derivatives in time, reduce training time, and enhance generalization.

Applied to a speech recognition problem, these variations resulted in as low a number of training iterations and as high a performance, as those reported for cross-entropy trained, hidden Markov models. However, we find that our recurrent networks have *not* provided a large performance improvement over a competing *non*-recurrent network with a similar number of weights.

2 The Task

Following [1,2,3] we have $N = 768$ speech signals X_n, selected samples of which we have concatenated into one long signal. Each X_n belongs to one of $K = 4$ classes. Each class represents one of the English letter names"b","d","e" or "v". We parameterize the speech at each $10ms$ time-frame $t = 1, \ldots, T$ of the concatenated signal, yielding vector observations $x(t)$, $T = 18347$. The parameterization is based on locally normalized filter-bank channel energies $e_i(t)$, $i = 1, \ldots, 16$.

We also have N labels $m_n = (s_n, e_n, a_n)$ which indicate the start sample s_n, the end sample e_n, and the letter name a_n for each X_n. The X_n have different durations. Letter name a_n is spoken once *somewhere* between time samples s_n and e_n.

We set up a network with sigmoid units and one hidden layer. We want to train the network to accept each $x(t)$ in turn as input, and for each input, to produce a K-dimensioned vector $o(t)$ as output. We want output unit k to turn on only while a pattern from class k is present at the input.

We believe that the response of the network to the current input should be a function of earlier inputs. We want the network to learn how to weight the current input relative to earlier inputs. We use a network architecture that can accomplish this learning. One version introduces time delays from lower layers to higher layers.[2,4] The other introduces time delays from one layer to *any* other, making the network potentially "recurrent".[3,5]

We now describe variations on network training which have led to solutions to the following problems: (1) how to overcome the need for an externally-supplied target function, (2) how to train the recurrent network without back-propagating the derivatives of error in time, and (3) how to reduce training time and enhance generalization.

3   Derive the Targets from an Input "Event" Parameter

This section presents an idea reported in [3]. We add a new speech parameter, a *temporal difference operator*, $r(t)$, defined over a time window of width $2\Delta t$ and filter-bank frequency channels $i = 1, \ldots, 16$, by

$$r(t) = \frac{\alpha}{16\Delta t} \sum_{\tau, i} max\left[0, e_i(t + \tau) - e_i(t + \tau - \Delta t)\right],$$

where $\tau = 0, \ldots, \Delta t - 1$, and $\Delta t = 10$ time frames. We use $\alpha = 2$, and clip at 1.

$r(t)$ is a shape-dependent energy increase indicator, which turns on at those time frames where the vowel turns on. $r(t)$ can be thought of as an "event" signal: when it turns on, *something* is happening.

The *target function* is based on $r(t)$. Let lag g be the (positive) number of time frames from the appearance of a value of $r(t)$ at the network input to its desired appearance on the output of output unit a_n. Then for each time frame t from s_n through e_n,

$$targ_{a_n}(t) = r(t - g),$$

and

$$targ_k(t) = 0, \ k \neq a_n.$$

During time frames s_n to $s_n + g - 1$, the target values are zero if $n = 1$, or are based on values of $r(t)$ in the preceding X_n if $n > 1$.

The main point is that the network should learn to indicate *which* event happened by reproducing input parameter $r(t)$ with a lag of g time frames on output unit a_n. To do so, it can use all of the input parameters, including $r(t)$.

4 Forward Propagate the Derivatives of the Potentials

This section presents an idea reported in several places. See [3,5-10] and the review [11].

To train network weight matrix W, we minimize E, the squared difference between observed and target outputs summed over all output units and time frames. Let weight w, from unit a to unit b with delay d, be denoted w_{abd}. We need equations for the gradient of E with respect to each weight w_{abd}.

Let $p(t)$ represent the weighted sum, or "potential" into a unit at time t. We factor the derivative of the error at output unit k with respect to weight w_{abd} as

$$\frac{\partial E_k}{\partial w_{abd}} = \sum_t \frac{\partial E_k(t)}{\partial p_k(t)} \frac{\partial p_k(t)}{\partial w_{abd}}.$$

Note that in a multi-layer *recurrent* network, the error at time t depends on potentials at all earlier times, except for those potentials in lower layers of the network that are so recent that they have not yet affected the error-producing outputs of the network.

Two training variations for the recurrent network come immediately to mind. We might store all unit outputs on a forward pass and back-propagate the error derivative to $t = 1$, accumulating the negative derivative of the error with respect to the potential of unit k, at all time frames from T back to each t.[5] Or, on the forward pass, at each t we might compute all unit outputs and then propagate the error derivative back only to time frame $t - \tau$, yielding a *truncated* approximation to the gradient.[5]

Wouldn't it be nice if we could propagate the derivative of the unit potential *forward*, and multiply by the current error derivative at the same time as the network error is generated. Then we could avoid any backward pass.

This is, of course, possible. Carrying out the differentiation, we obtain a *forward recursion* at any unit c,

$$\frac{\partial p_c(t)}{\partial w_{abd}} = \sum_{x,l} \left(w_{xcl} \frac{\partial o_x(t - l)}{\partial p_x(t - l)} \frac{\partial p_x(t - l)}{\partial w_{abd}} \right.$$

$$\left. + \begin{cases} o_x(t - l), & \text{if } (x, c, l) = (a, b, d); \\ 0, & \text{otherwise} \end{cases} \right). \tag{1}$$

From (1) we see that the difference between a feed-forward network and a recurrent network is that for the recurrent network, the derivative of a unit's potential can have other terms than just the output of the unit on the input end of the connection.

The forward recursion has the *disadvantage* that the number of partials to carry forward can get large. The number of partials can be controlled by limiting feed-back to so-called "context" units [12, 13], or by limiting the number of feedback connections, *e.g.* by using only self-loops.

For the recurrent networks which we report on here, feed-back was limited to self-loops, either on output units, or on the hidden units, and back-propagation in time was avoided using forward propagation of the derivative of the unit potentials.

5 Try Adaptive Training

To reduce training time and enhance generalization, we consider variations on (1) weight initialization, (2) frequency of weight updates, (3) adaptation of the step size, (4) adaptation of the search direction, (5) gradient evaluation during events, and (6) assignment of examples to training and cross-validation data subsets. A third and entirely separate dataset is, of course, kept for testing.

5.1 Initialization

Random initialization of the weights may produce a network which *cannot* be trained. One remedy is to *adjust* the initial weights, as follows. Evaluate E and $\partial E/\partial W$ over a small but representative number of training examples. Then, for each w_{abd}, see whether the sign of w_{abd} is the same as the sign of $\partial E/\partial w_{abd}$. If so, flip the sign of w_{abd} and re-evaluate E. If the new E is better than the previous E, keep the sign change and set E to the new E. Continue for all weights.

Applied to just 4 balanced sets of training examples, this weight adjustment takes no more time than a couple of training iterations, increases the probability that the network will be trainable, and reduces E by about a factor of 2.

5.2 Frequency of Weight Updates

In the early stages of training, a rough estimate of $\partial E/\partial W$ can be used to point the weight changes quickly in a good, if not a perfect, direction. One schedule for producing increasingly refined estimates of $\partial E/\partial W$ is the following [14]. On each iteration i through the training examples, set the size of the balanced block of examples over which $\partial E/\partial W$ is calculated and after which W is updated, to iK.

Unfortunately, for our examples, small blocks at the initial values of i produce large fluctuations in E. Also, we want to avoid increasing block size if training can continue faster at the current size.

As a result, we propose a modified schedule. Let the initial block size be the same as the number of examples over which W was initialized, and divide the training examples into training and cross-validation *sub*sets. Here, we use a ratio of 4 to 1.

Then on each iteration, evaluate $\partial E / \partial W$ and update W on each block in the *training* subset. At the end of the iteration, evaluate E_v, the error on the *cross-validation* subset. Keep the current block size until the number of increases in E_v at the current block size equals n_{Ev}. Then, if possible, increase the number of balanced sets of examples per block by 1. We set $n_{Ev} = 2$, to tolerate one uptick but no oscillation.

5.3   Adaptation of the Step Size

Having computed *some* weight-change direction Z on the current block, we search along Z for the best weight matrix $\hat{W}$ satisfying

$$\hat{W} = W + s\eta Z,$$

with $\eta = .005$. We try the following sequence of values for s. Initially, s is set to the smallest s accepted over the last $\ell = 6$ blocks. Then $E_{\hat{W}}$ is computed. Then $s \leftarrow \varphi^x s$, where $\varphi = 1.61$, and x is either $+1$ if $E_{\hat{W}}$ is an improvement or -1 if not. We accept s when $E_{\hat{W}}$ gets worse *and* either $s \leq 1$, or at least three values have been tried for s.

If three values have been tried, the accepted s is moved under the minimum of a quadratic fitted to the last three (s, E) pairs. Finally, W is updated using the accepted s.

5.4   Adaptation of the Search Direction

Rather than use ΔW ($= -\partial E / \partial W$ on the current block) with a heuristic momentum factor, the authors of [15] allowed search direction Z to be given by the conjugate gradient [16]

$$Z \leftarrow \Delta W + \gamma Z$$

with γ computed from the Polak-Ribiere formula

$$\gamma = (\Delta W - \Delta W_p) \cdot \Delta W / (\Delta W_p \cdot \Delta W_p).$$

We find that even if the previous negative gradient, ΔW_p, is computed on a different block, E falls much faster with a computed γ than with a constant value for γ.

5.5 Gradient Evaluation during Events

Even though the target function is defined for all t, a threshold ρ can be established so that $\partial E / \partial W$ is evaluated only when $r(t - g) \geq \rho$ signals an event. This provides some speed-up and allows the network to learn completely from event data. $\partial P / \partial W$ is still computed at each t. Here, we experiment with $\rho = 0.25$.

5.6 Randomized Training and Cross-Validation Subsets

The network tends to overtrain, *i.e.*, to pass from an initial stage during which E_t (the error on the training subset) and E_v are both reduced, to a second stage during which only E_t is reduced. Also, we have barely enough examples to train the weights. We want a way to control overtraining while keeping *all* examples not in the test set *available* for the training subset.

We propose the following procedure. On each iteration, re-assign the training examples *randomly* to the training or cross-validation subsets. The ratio of their sizes is still 4 to 1.

With random re-assignment to the subsets, the instantaneous errors E_t and E_v now track each other closely. More importantly, neither error falls so far that it becomes a bad predictor of error on the *test* dataset. Do they fall as far as possible consistent with good prediction of error on the test dataset? We do not know.

6 Simulation Results

Figure 1 shows the value of several quantities as a function of training iteration. Quantities 1 and 2 are E_t and E_v, the training and cross-validation training errors. Quantity 3 is proportional to the number

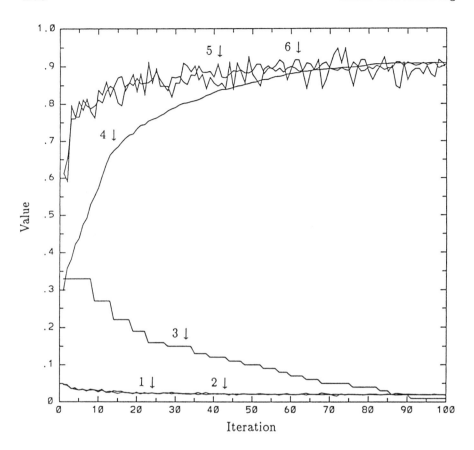

Figure 1: Plot of several quantities as a function of training iteration:

1. Training error E_t

2. Cross-validation error E_v

3. Number of blocks in training subset, divided by 100

4. Root mean square of the weights

5. Fraction of training examples correctly recognized

6. Fraction of cross-validation examples correctly recognized

of blocks in the training subset. Quantity 4 is the root mean square of the weights, which seems to have stopped growing by iteration 100. Quantities 5 and 6 are the fraction of training and cross-validation examples correctly recognized. Because the training subset is much larger, quantity 5 looks less noisy.

A recognition score is defined for the network response to concatenated presentation of those X_n kept in a test dataset.[3] The score $E_{u|n}$ for each letter name u on each X_n is the sum over time frames in X_n, of the squared difference between observed and expected network outputs, under the hypothesis that X_n is an occurrance of letter name u. The expected outputs are the same as the target values that would have been used if X_n were a training example of letter name u. The network "recognizes" X_n if $\operatorname{argmin}_u E_{u|n}$ is a_n. We now redefine $E_{u|n}$ over frames where $r(t - g) \geq \rho$.

In [3], the letter-name discrimination task is attacked using a network with one hidden layer, 4 time delays from the input units to each of 8 hidden units, and 3 time delays from the hidden units to the output units. Delays to the hidden units are 1 time-frame apart. Delays to the output units are 2 time-frames apart.

A version of that network *without* self-loops on the output units was trained on 372 X_n for 1000 training iterations, and recognized 83.6% of 396 test X_n. Adding self-loops on the output units late in training produced a network that recognized 84.6% of the test X_n.

The same non-recurrent network now trains on 672 X_n in only 100 iterations, and each iteration takes half as much time. After 100 iterations of training the non-recurrent network recognizes 88.5% of 128 test X_n. Adding self-loops on the output units and training for another 10 iterations produces a recurrent network that recognizes 89.6% of the test X_n.

In an additional simulation, a single delay was used from hidden to output units, the number of hidden units was increased to 9, and self-loops were used only on the hidden units. For this network, the total number of weights was nearly identical to the number in the network with multiple hidden-to-output delays but no recurrence. Recognition results for this additional network only reached 86.5% after 100 iterations.

The number of iterations needed to train our best recurrent network is now similar to the number needed to train hidden Markov models to cross-entropy criteria.[17] Also, the performance of our best recurrent network, 89.6%, is now as good as the 89% estimated for cross-entropy trained, hidden Markov models.[1,2]

A recently reported "scanning" feedforward time-delay neural network has apparently obtained connected recognition performance of 90.9% on this dataset.[18] Unfortunately, the recurrent, the hidden Markov, and the scanning system all perform significantly below the human level of 95%. The goal remains to reach the human level of performance, which is even 97% on our full database of 9-letter names: "*b, c, d, e, g, p, t, v*" and "*z*".

7 Conclusions

The network training variations described above reduced the number of training iterations by a factor of 10, reduced training time by a factor of 20, and contributed to a reduction in recognition errors by 33%.

Applied to a speech recognition problem, these variations resulted in as low a number of training iterations and as high a performance, as those reported for cross-entropy trained, hidden Markov models. However, we find that our recurrent networks have *not* provided a large performance improvement over a competing *non*-recurrent network with a similar number of weights.

8 Acknowledgements

This is an expanded version of paper TP6.1 given at the 24th annual Conference on Information Sciences and Systems, Princeton University, March 22, 1990. The authors thank L. Bottou, P. Brown, P. Haffner, B. Ladendorf, K. Lang, E. Ojamaa and R. Watrous for help with various aspects of this work.

Bibliography

[1] Brown, P.F. *The acoustic-modeling problem in automatic speech recognition,* IBM Computer Science Tech. Report RC 12750, p. 1–119, 1987.

[2] Lang, K.J. and G. Hinton. *The development of the Time-Delay Neural Network Architecture for speech recognition,* Tech. Report CMU-CS-88-152, Carnegie-Mellon University, p. 1–30, 1988.

[3] Kuhn, G., R.L. Watrous and B. Ladendorf. *Connected recognition with a recurrent network,* Speech Communication, Vol. 9, p. 41–49, 1990.

[4] Waibel, A., T. Hanazawa, G. Hinton, K. Shikano and K. Lang. *Phoneme Recognition using time-delay neural networks,* IEEE Trans. ASSP, Vol 37, p. 328–339, 1989.

[5] Watrous, R.L., B. Ladendorf and G. Kuhn. *Complete gradient optimization of a recurrent network applied to /b/, /d/, /g/ discrimination,* J. Acoust. Soc. Amer., Vol. 87, p. 1301–1309, 1990.

[6] Kuhn, G. *A first look at phonetic discrimination using a connectionist network with recurrent links,* CCRP - IDA SCIMP Working Paper No. 4/87, p. 1–41, 1987.

[7] Robinson, A.J., F. Fallside. *Static and dynamic error propagation networks with application to speech coding,* in D.Z. Anderson (ed.), Neural Information Processing Systems, New York, Amer. Inst. Physics, p. 632–641, 1987.

[8] Gori, M., Y. Bengio and R. De Mori. *BPS: A learning algorithm for capturing the dynamic nature of speech,* Proc. Intl. Joint Conf. on Neural Networks, Washington, D.C., Vol. II, p. 417–423, 1989.

[9] Gherrity, M. *A learning algorithm for analog, fully recurrent neural networks,* Proc. Intl. Joint Conf. on Neural Networks, Washington, D.C., Vol. I, p. 643–644, 1989.

[10] Williams, R.J., and D. Zipser. *A learning algorithm for continually running fully recurrent neural networks,* Neural Computation, Vol. 1, p. 270–280, 1989.

[11] Pearlmutter, B. *Two new learning procedures for recurrent networks,* Neural Network Review, Vol. 3, p. 99–101, 1990.

[12] Elman, J. *Finding structure in time,* CRL Tech. Report 8801, Univ. of California at San Diego, p. 1–29, 1988.

[13] Zipser, D. *A subgrouping strategy that reduces complexity and speeds up learning in recurrent networks,* ICS Tech. Report 8902, Univ. of California at San Diego, p. 1–5, 1989.

[14] Haffner, P., A. Waibel, H. Sawai and K. Shikano. *Fast backpropagation learning methods for large phonemic neural networks,* Proc. Eurospeech '89, Vol. II, p. 553–556, 1989.

[15] Webb, A., D. Lowe and M. Bedworth. *A comparison of nonlinear optimisation strategies for feed-forward adaptive layered networks,* Royal Signals and Radar Establishment memorandum 4157, Malvern, England, p. 1–33, 1988.

[16] Vapnik, V. *Estimation of Dependencies Based on Empirical Data,* Addendum A, §2. Springer-Verlag, 1982.

[17] Gopalakrishnan, J.S., D. Kanevsky, A. Nadas, D. Nahamoo, M.A. Picheny. *Decoder selection based on cross-entropies,* Proc. IEEE Intl. Conf. on Acoustics, Speech and Signal Processing, New York, Vol. I, p. 20–23, 1988.

[18] Lang, K.J., A.H. Waibel, and G.E.Hinton. *A Time-Delay Neural Network Architecture for Isolated Word Recognition,* Neural Networks, Vol. 3, p. 23–43, 1990.

Generalized Perceptron Networks with Nonlinear Discriminant Functions[1]

S. Y. Kung
K. Diamantaras
W.D. Mao
J.S. Taur

Princeton University
Princeton, NJ 08544

1 Introduction

The objective of this chapter is to provide a systematic exploration of the nonliner perceptron-type networks. For supervised training, the training patterns must be provided in terms of input/output pattern pairs. They are denoted as $[\mathcal{X}, \mathcal{Y}] = \{[\mathbf{x}_1, \mathbf{y}_1], [\mathbf{x}_2, \mathbf{y}_2], \ldots, [\mathbf{x}_M, \mathbf{y}_M]\}$, where M is the number of training pairs.

When applying (both single and multiple layer) supervised neural networks to real applications, two types of basic problem formulations may be adopted:

- *competition-based formulation:*

  Under this formulation, it is not necessary to have the exact values of teachers as direct reference. Instead, the teacher only provide information whether a correct classification is achieved for every training pattern. In other words, the training set $\mathcal{Y}$ will be simply a set of integers labeling the correct class corresponding to each input pattern, i.e. $\mathcal{Y} = \{y_i \in I^1\}$. *The objective of the training is*

[1]This research was supported in part by AFOSR Grant 89-0501.

to determine the weights which successfully separate different clusters of patterns and ensure the correct node wins the competition against the rest of the nodes.

- *approximation-based formulation:*

  Under this formulation, it is assumed that the (exact) values of teachers are available as direct reference. The teacher of the training set $\mathcal{Y}$ will be real-valued N-dimensional vector, i.e. $\mathbf{y}_i = \in R^N$. In other words, corresponding to a specific input pattern each of the N output nodes is assigned a desired value. (This is in a sharp contrast to the competition-based formulation.) *The objective of the training is to determine the optimal weights which minimize the (least-square) error distance between the teacher's value and the actual response.*

Both formulations lead to very similar mathematical techniques in the actual computations for training. For example, gradients of discriminant functions and back-propagation recursions are useful for both approaches. The main difference is that the approximation formulation can take advantage of having teachers as direct reference while the competition formulation does not need such information.

One can convert a competition formulation into an approximation formulation: Let $y^c = i$ and $\mathbf{y}^a$ denote the teacher values for the competition and approximation formulations respectively. If $y^c = i$, then $\mathbf{y}^a = [-1, -1, \ldots, 1, \ldots, -1]^T$, a vector with all elements being -1 except the ith element which is 1.

1.1   Linear vs Nonlinear Discriminant Functions

Linear Separability by Decision Hyperplanes

Most popular neural models, such as perceptron, ADALINE, and back-propagation nets, are based on "hyperplane" separated decision regions. Namely, the classification depends on the values of (linear) hyperplane functions $f(\sum_i^P w_i x_i + \theta)$ in P-dimensional space.

Patterns divided into a number of groups are called linearly separable if there is a set of hyperplanes which separate each group from the others.

As an example, let us consider the vector space divided into two separate regions by the hyperplane

$$\sum_{j}^{P} w_j x_j + \theta = 0.$$

For the notational simplicity, it is more convenient (and without loss of generality) to regard θ just as another one of the weights (say $\theta = w_{P+1}$). The hyperplane decision equation can be written as follows

$$\mathbf{w}^T \mathbf{z} = 0$$

where we denote $\mathbf{w} = [w_1 \ w_2 \ldots w_P \ \theta]^T$ and $\mathbf{z} = [x_1 \ x_2 \ldots x_P \ 1]^T$, i.e. z is the augmented pattern $\mathbf{x}$. As an example, consider a two-input perceptron with bias θ equal to zero. Then the separating hyperplane is defined by

$$w_1 x_1 + w_2 x_2 = 0.$$

Every pattern lying on the positive side of this hyperplane will give an output activation 1 and all other patterns will give an output activation 0.

Nonlinear Separability (or Linear Nonseparability)

A set of pattern vectors are called "linearly nonseparable" (or simply "nonlinearly separable") if they are not linearly separable.

An example of a linearly nonseparable function (XOR-like) with two inputs can be shown below:

$$
\begin{aligned}
(1, \ 1) \ &\longrightarrow \ 1 \\
(1, \ -1) \ &\longrightarrow \ -1 \\
(-1, \ -1) \ &\longrightarrow \ 1 \\
(-1, \ 1) \ &\longrightarrow \ -1
\end{aligned}
\tag{1}
$$

Nonlinear functions of the inputs applied to the single neuron can yield nonlinear decision boundaries, for example consider the function:

$$y = w_0 + x_1 w_1 + x_1^2 w_{11} + x_1 x_2 w_{12} + x_2^2 w_{22} + x_2 w_z = 0. \tag{2}$$

The nonlinearly separable function illustrated in Eq. 1 can be realized by this configuration with proper choice of the weights. The usage of such nonlinearity can be generalized for more inputs than two and for higher degree polynomial functions of the inputs.

A recent study showed that some other types of functions could also be very appealing, especially where the "locality" of patterns plays a vital role. In this case a "hypersphere"-based classification function (i.e. $f(\sum_i^P (w_i - x_i)^2)$) becomes useful. This offers an effective tool to combat linearly nonseparable clustering.

2   Approximation Based Approach

In this section, two types of approximation based neural nets for nonlinear separable problems will be studied. The first type is single layer networks, where nonlinear discriminant functions are adopted to cope with nonlinear separability. The other type is multiple layer networks, where the discriminant functions can be linear or nonlinear. It is preferably linear from numerical performance perspective and the nonlinear separability can be effectively handled by the nonlinear neuron activation functions (e.g. sigmoid functions). One typical example is the BP learning algorithm, where the basis functions for the approximation are restricted to be in a linear form $f(\sum_j w_{ij}x_j + \theta_i)$.

2.1   Overview

To effectively seek a solution which minimizes the error function, we need to determine (1) the updating directions, (2) the learning step sizes and (3) the type of method (adaptive vs. block).

Determination of the updating directions

The first important decision is the choice of the direction of updating. Two popular and computationally efficient methods are described below:

- *First order methods: e.g. gradient descent.* At any point, the direction of the adaptation step is the opposite of the gradient of the error-function E. More elaborately we have

$$\mathbf{w}^{new} = \mathbf{w} + \Delta\mathbf{w} \tag{3}$$
$$= \mathbf{w} - \eta E_w \tag{4}$$

- *Second order methods: e.g. conjugate gradient.* A more sophisticated approach is to involve a second-order or momentum term in determining the direction of updating. For example, a conjugate gradient vector $\mathbf{d}$ is defined by a proper combination of the gradient and the previous updating vector. Mathematically,

$$\mathbf{w}^{new} = \mathbf{w} + \Delta\mathbf{w} \tag{5}$$
$$= \mathbf{w} - \eta\mathbf{d} \tag{6}$$
$$\mathbf{d}^{new} = E_w - \beta\mathbf{d} \tag{7}$$

Determination of the learning step sizes

The above rules only specify the direction of the updating move. It is equally desirable to be able to specify the step size of the updating step η, since it would directly affect the training speed. Two approaches are considered:

- *Pre-assigned step sizes* One way is simply to make η very small so to guarantee that the system never jeopardizes the numerical stability. This often results in very slow training. Another way is to start with an initially large η and decrease it gradually. The initial convergency will be rough but fast, while gradually the convergency will become slower but finer;

- *Adaptively adjusted step sizes* Similar to the Kaczmarz's projection method in which the size of the move is adjusted to best fit each pair of incoming input-output training patterns.

Data-adaptive vs. Block Methods

The optimization methods can also be categorized by their on-line or off-line processing modes. In the data-adaptive approaches the assumption is that the data come in a sequential manner and the current updating step is decided only by using the current datum. The previous data are used for updating the internal parameters of the model and they are not "remembered" by the system.

The block methods, on the other hand, work on a given block of data which are explicitly stored in the memory and are collectively used to calculate the updating step. Therefore, the updating step is taken only after all the data in the block are presented to the system. In contrast, in the data-adaptive methods, updating is performed upon each presentation of a new datum.

It is understood that the block methods should be more robust than the adaptive ones, mainly because they can average the information from all the input patterns unlike the data-adaptive methods which are more vulnerable to the noisy information of each individual pattern. This is true for simple cases where the error surface is quadratic [1] as well as for more complex cases.

The order of a method also affects its robustness. First order methods can perform reasonably well in the adaptive case, while for second order methods this will be more difficult. This is so because the second order term is noisier than the first one and its use can degrade the robustness. Therefore, second order methods, like conjugate gradient, are most often implemented in the block mode.

In order to differentiate between data-adaptive and block methods we introduce the concept of iterations vs. sweeps. An iteration is a presentation of a single datum to the system, while a sweep is the presentation of a whole block of data to it. The data-adaptive methods update the weights at the iteration level as opposed to the block methods which update them after one sweep. Two different time indices are used for these different time scales (usually m for iterations and k for sweeps) in order to avoid confusion. We can say further that the concept of iterations is not even defined for the data-adaptive mode of operation and similarly neither is the concept of sweeps for the block mode. But in order to compare the adaptive methods with the block ones we need to use the same time scale (i.e. index) for both. To remedy the situation the same block of data used for the block methods can be used for the adaptive ones by simply repeating it in a periodical fashion. In this way we can define the concept of sweeps for the adaptive mode of operation, and this can be the basis of a fair comparison between the modes.

2.2 Single Layer Network With Nonlinear Network Function

Suppose that we have a single layer network with a fixed but arbitrary function $f(\mathbf{x}, \mathbf{w})$ incorporated in its units. The function has a set of parameters described collectively by the vector $\mathbf{w}$ which may or may not be thought of as synaptic weights multiplying the input patterns. In the following we use the notation h_z to denote the partial derivative of the function h with respect to z. If h is a scalar and z is a vector then it is the same as the gradient of h, ∇h, with respect to z. If both h and z are vectors then h_z is a matrix with entries $a_{ij} = \dfrac{\partial h_i}{\partial z_j}$. Similarly, h_{zz} will denote the second derivative of h with respect to z.

A commonly used criterion function is the sum-of-squared-error criterion

$$E = \sum_{m=1}^{M} \mathcal{E}^{(m)} \tag{8}$$

$$\mathcal{E}^{(m)} = \frac{1}{2}\left(t^{(m)} - f(\mathbf{x}^{(m)}, \mathbf{w}^{(m)})\right)^2 \tag{9}$$

where $t^{(m)}$ are the desired values at the output unit for each pattern $\mathbf{x}^{(m)}$ in the input, i.e. they are the teacher values for the approximation. Notice that the above formulation only describes the single-output case. It is understood that if there are N output units in a single-layer net we can simply treat them separately, as if we had N distinct single-output nets. (The weights of one unit do not, in any way, affect the activations of the other units.) Therefore, we shall only focus our discussion on the single-output case. Some simple mathematics leads to

$$\Delta\mathbf{w}^{(m)} = -\eta\mathcal{E}_w^{(m)}$$
$$= \eta\left(t^{(m)} - f(\mathbf{x}^{(m)}, \mathbf{w}^{(m)})\right)f_w(\mathbf{x}^{(m)}, \mathbf{w}^{(m)}) \tag{10}$$

If we use here the gradient projection approach, the condition that needs to be satisfied by the step size $(\eta^{(m)})$ is that $\mathbf{w}^{(m+1)}$ is such that

$$t^{(m)} \approx f(\mathbf{x}^{(m)}, \mathbf{w}^{(m+1)}) \approx f(\mathbf{x}^{(m)}, \mathbf{w}^{(m)}) + \{f_w(\mathbf{x}^{(m)}, \mathbf{w}^{(m)})\}^T(\mathbf{w}^{(m+1)} - \mathbf{w}^{(m)})$$
$$(11)$$

where an approximation by a first order Taylor series expansion around $\mathbf{w}^{(m)}$ is used.

Substituting Eq. 10 in to the above, we have

$$t^{(m)} - f(\mathbf{x}^{(m)}, \mathbf{w}^{(m+1)}) \approx \eta^{(m)} \left(t^{(m)} - f(\mathbf{x}^{(m)}, \mathbf{w}^{(m)})\right) \|f_w(\mathbf{x}^{(m)}, \mathbf{w}^{(m)})\|^2\right)$$
$$(12)$$

This leads to the following choice of learning rate

$$\eta^{(m)} = \frac{1}{\|f_w(\mathbf{x}^{(m)}, \mathbf{w}^{(m)})\|^2} \qquad (13)$$

As we discussed above it is not wise to use this value for η throughout the training phase but rather it is advisable to decrease it gradually in order to achieve finer convergence. Thus the learning rate η will take the final form

$$\eta^{(m)} = \frac{\lambda^{(m)}}{\|f_w(\mathbf{x}^{(m)}, \mathbf{w}^{(m)})\|^2}. \qquad (14)$$

where $0 < \lambda^{(m)} \le 1$.

Example 2.1 Now we are ready to show that Kaczmarz linear projection method [3] is a special case of the above. Indeed, if

$$f(\mathbf{x}, \mathbf{w}) = \mathbf{w}^T\mathbf{x}$$

then

$$f_w(\mathbf{x}^{(m)}, \mathbf{w}^{(m)}) = \mathbf{x}^{(m)}$$

therefore the learning rule becomes

$$\mathbf{w}^{(m+1)} = \mathbf{w}^{(m)} + \eta(t^{(m)} - \mathbf{w}^{(m)T}\mathbf{x}^{(m)})\mathbf{x}^{(m)} \qquad (15)$$

and the learning rate formula gives

$$\eta^{(m)} = \frac{\lambda^{(m)}}{\|\mathbf{x}^{(m)}\|^2}. \qquad (16)$$

as in [3].

Example 2.2 Assume that the connection function is linear and the activation function is sigmoid. Then

$$f(\mathbf{x}, \mathbf{w}) = f(\mathbf{w}^T \mathbf{x})$$

where

$$f(u) = \frac{1}{1 + e^{-u}}.$$

We have

$$f_w(\mathbf{w}^T \mathbf{x}) = f_u(\mathbf{w}^T \mathbf{x}) \mathbf{x}$$

therefore the learning rate formula (setting $\lambda = 1$) becomes

$$\eta^{(m)} = \frac{1}{(f_u(\mathbf{w}^T \mathbf{x}))^2 \|\mathbf{x}^{(m)}\|^2}. \tag{17}$$

A constant learning rate may be adopted by using the *expectation value* of the above ($E\{\eta\}$). If we treat each $\{x_i^{(m)}\}$ as a random variable with equal probability (50%) of being either 0 or 1, then the expectation value $E\{\|\mathbf{x}^{(m)}\|^2\}$ is

$$(P + 1)\, \mathrm{E}\{(x_i^{(m)})^2\} = \frac{P + 1}{2}.$$

Since f is a sigmoid function we have

$$f_u(u) = f(u)\,(1 - f(u))$$

where $0 \le f(u) \le 1$. The expectation value of $f_u(u)$ can be approximately estimated as $\frac{1}{6}$, if we assume $f(u)$ is uniformly distributed between 0 and 1.

Now the expectation value of the optimal learning rate $E\{\eta\}$ can be derived:

$$E\{\eta\} = E\{f_u\}^{-2}\, E\{\|\mathbf{x}\|^{-2}\} = 36\, E\{\|\mathbf{x}\|^{-2}\} \approx \frac{72}{P + 1}. \tag{18}$$

In the simulations reported in [4], this optimal learning rate can achieve a fast learning rate but yet not so fast as to incur instability in the iterations.

2.3   Projection Methods for Multi-Layer Networks

In the following we are going to discuss the gradient descent approach for multi-layer perceptrons. We will concentrate on the case where the nonlinear function incorporated in the neurons is of the form $\phi(\mathbf{w}^T\mathbf{x})$. We will also try later to extend the results to the more general case where the nonlinear function is of the form $\phi(\mathbf{w}, \mathbf{x})$.

Many-Layer Networks: the Chain Rule

In the most general case the network has L layers, each layer having its own nonlinear function and its own set of weights associated with it. Let $f^{(l)}$ denote the nonlinear function incorporated in the units of layer l, and let $\mathbf{W}(l)$ denote the matrix of weights feeding layer l. Let $\mathbf{w}_i(l)$ denote the i-th column of this matrix, and let N_l denote the number of columns, or equivalently, the number of neurons in layer l. The activation vector of the neurons at layer l will be denoted by

$$\mathbf{a}(l) = \left[a_1(l), \ldots, a_{N_l}(l)\right]^T, \quad l = 1 \ldots L,$$

These activation vectors are defined recursively through the activations of the previous layer as follows

$$a_i(1) = f^{(1)}(\{\mathbf{w}_i(1)\}^T\mathbf{x}) \tag{19}$$

$$a_i(l) = f^{(l)}(\{\mathbf{w}_i(l)\}^T\mathbf{a}(l-1)), \quad l = 2, \ldots, L. \tag{20}$$

The output of the network is the vector $\mathbf{a}(L)$ (since we allow more than one output units) and the sum-of-square-error criterion becomes

$$E = \sum_{m=1}^{M} \mathcal{E}^{(m)} \tag{21}$$

$$\mathcal{E}^{(m)} = \frac{1}{2}\sum_{i=1}^{N_L}\left\{t_i^{(m)} - a_i^{(m)}(L)\right\}^2. \tag{22}$$

Using again the data-adaptive gradient descent we have

$$\Delta\mathbf{w}_i^{(m)}(l) = -\eta\mathcal{E}_{w_i(l)}^{(m)}$$

$$= -\eta \{\mathbf{a}^{(m)}(l)\}_{w_i(l)} \mathcal{E}^{(m)}_{\mathbf{a}(l)}$$

$$= -\eta \{a_i^{(m)}(l)\}_{w_i(l)} \mathcal{E}^{(m)}_{a_i(l)} \quad \text{for all } l = 1, \ldots, L.$$

Defining

$$\delta_i(l) = -\mathcal{E}_{a_i(l)}$$

and

$$u_i(l) = \mathbf{w}_i(l)^T \mathbf{a}(l-1)$$

for each neuron i in layer l, the updating step becomes the classical Back-Propagation rule [7]

$$\Delta \mathbf{w}_i^{(m)}(l) = \eta \delta_i^{(m)}(l) f_w^{(l)}(\mathbf{w}_i^{(m)}(l)^T \mathbf{a}^{(m)}(l-1)) \tag{23}$$

$$= \eta \delta_i^{(m)}(l) f_u^{(l)}(u_i^{(m)}) \mathbf{a}^{(m)}(l-1), \quad l = 1, \ldots, L. \tag{24}$$

Furthermore, $\delta_i^{(m)}(l)$ can be defined recursively as follows

$$\delta_i^{(m)}(L) = \{t_i^{(m)} - a_i^{(m)}(L)\}, \quad \text{for the output layer } L \tag{25}$$

$$\delta_i^{(m)}(l) = \sum_{k=1}^{N_{l+1}} \delta_k^{(m)}(l+1) w_{ki}^{(m)}(l) f_u^{(l+1)}(u_k^{(m)}(l+1)),$$

$$\text{for all layers } l = L-1, \ldots, 1 \tag{26}$$

The Energy Projection Method

A first approach for the estimation of the optimal η in the BP algorithm can be described by the following requirement:

$$\mathcal{E}^{(m)'} \leq \epsilon \tag{27}$$

where ϵ denotes the tolerance which could be pre-assigned or estimated on the fly. For simplicity we shall put $\epsilon \approx 0$, i.e.

$$\mathcal{E}^{(m)'} \approx 0. \tag{28}$$

The familiar first order Taylor expansion can be used again to give

$$\mathcal{E}^{(m)'} \approx 0 \approx \mathcal{E}^{(m)} + \mathcal{E}^{(m)^T}_{\tilde{w}} \Delta \tilde{\mathbf{w}}^{(m)}. \tag{29}$$

Since

$$\Delta \tilde{\mathbf{w}}^{(m)} = -\eta \mathcal{E}_{\tilde{w}}^{(m)},$$

from Eq. 29 it follows that

$$\mathcal{E}^{(m)} = \eta \|\mathcal{E}_{\tilde{w}}^{(m)}\|^2$$

therefore, η is estimated by

$$\eta = \frac{\mathcal{E}^{(m)}}{\|\mathcal{E}_{\tilde{w}}^{(m)}\|^2} \tag{30}$$

Some discussion is in order here. The requirement of Eq. 27 can be potentially too greedy (namely leading too large η), since it cannot be guaranteed that $\mathcal{E}^{(m)'}$ to be reduced to 0 (or even approximately 0) along the direction of the current gradient. But this greediness can be offset by using a scaling factor $\lambda < 1$ to scale down the learning step η:

$$\eta = \frac{\lambda \mathcal{E}^{(m)}}{\|\mathcal{E}_{\tilde{w}}^{(m)}\|^2} \tag{31}$$

The estimate of λ will depend on the number of outputs ($\lambda \approx 1/\sqrt{N}$. Its derivation is simpler after we first introduce the least-square projection below.

The Least Squares Projection Method

Another (more sophisticated) approach for estimating η which tries to overcome the difficulties of the previous method, is to establish a least-squares optimality criterion to be minimized

$$\text{minimize } \mathcal{E}^{(m)'} = \frac{1}{2} \sum_{i=1}^{N_L} \left\{ t_i^{(m)} - a_i^{(m)'}(L) \right\}^2. \tag{32}$$

where $a_i^{(m)'}(L)$ is the activation of the output unit i under the same input pattern $\mathbf{x}^{(m)}$ but after the weights are updated.

In order to simplify the analysis we define the total set of weights in the network by the (long) vector $\tilde{\mathbf{w}}$. Then the activations of the output units are just functions of $\tilde{\mathbf{w}}$. The first order Taylor expansion of $a_i^{(m)'}(L)$ yields

$$a_i^{(m)'}(L) = a_i^{(m)}(L) + \{a_i^{(m)}(L)\}_{\tilde{w}}^T \Delta \tilde{\mathbf{w}}^{(m)} \qquad (33)$$

Furthermore, since we follow a gradient updating rule we have

$$\Delta \tilde{\mathbf{w}}^{(m)} = -\eta \mathcal{E}_{\tilde{w}}^{(m)} \qquad (34)$$

Plugging the above into Eq. 33 we get

$$a_i^{(m)'}(L) = a_i^{(m)}(L) - \eta \{a_i^{(m)}(L)\}_{\tilde{w}}^T \mathcal{E}_{\tilde{w}}^{(m)} \qquad (35)$$

We will define

$$c_i^{(m)} = \{a_i^{(m)}(L)\}_{\tilde{w}}^T \mathcal{E}_{\tilde{w}}^{(m)}$$

therefore, we will have

$$a_i^{(m)'}(L) = a_i^{(m)}(L) + \eta c_i^{(m)} \qquad (36)$$

The least-squares solution of the criterion (Eq. 32) leads then to the following choice of the learning rate

$$\eta^{(m)} = \frac{\sum_i (t_i^{(m)} - a_i^{(m)}(L)) c_i^{(m)}}{\sum_i \{c_i^{(m)}\}^2} \qquad (37)$$

The value c_i can be back-propagated in a similar fashion as the error δ. The straightforward computation of c_i would require $\mathcal{O}(N^3)$ operation where N is the size of the network. However it the one-rank property of the layered net is exploited it can reduce the computation into $\mathcal{O}(N^2)$ operations. The procedure is detailed below:
We define

$$\xi_{ik}(l) = \{a_i(L)\}_{a_k(l)}, \quad i = 1, \ldots, N_L, \ k = 1, \ldots, N_l.$$

Note that ξ can be computed in a BP-type recursion:

$$\xi_{ik}^{(m)}(L) = \begin{cases} 1, & \text{if } i = k \\ 0, & \text{if } i \neq k \end{cases} \text{ for the output layer } L \tag{38}$$

$$\xi_{ik}^{(m)}(l) = \sum_{j=1}^{N_{l+1}} \xi_{ij}^{(m)}(l+1)w_{jk}^{(m)}(l)f_u^{(l+1)}(u_k^{(m+1)}(l+1)),$$
$$\text{for all layers } l = L-1, \ldots, 1 \tag{39}$$

hence

$$\begin{aligned}
c_i^{(m)} &= \{\mathcal{E}^{(m)}\}_{w_i(L)}^T \{a_i^{(m)}(L)\}_{w_i(L)} + \cdots \\
&\quad + \sum_{k=1}^{N_1} \{\mathcal{E}^{(m)}\}_{w_k(1)}^T \{a_i^{(m)}(L)\}_{w_k(1)} \\
&= \{\xi_{ii}^{(m)}(L)f_u^{(L)}(u_i^{(m)}(L))\mathbf{a}^{(m)}(L-1)\}^T \\
&\quad \{\delta_i^{(m)}(L)f_u^{(L)}(u_i^{(m)}(L))\mathbf{a}^{(m)}(L-1)\} + \cdots \\
&\quad + \eta \sum_{k=1}^{N_1} \{\xi_{ik}^{(m)}(1)f_u^{(1)}(u_k^{(m)}(1))\mathbf{x}^{(m)}\}^T \\
&\quad \{\delta_k^{(m)}(1)f_u^{(1)}(u_k^{(m)}(1))\mathbf{x}^{(m)}\} \tag{40} \\
&= \xi_{ii}^{(m)}(L)\delta_i^{(m)}(L)\{f_u^{(L)}(u_i^{(m)}(L))\}^2 \|\mathbf{a}^{(m)}(L-1)\|^2 + \cdots \\
&\quad + \eta \sum_{k=1}^{N_1} \xi_{ik}^{(m)}(1)\delta_k^{(m)}(1)\{f_u^{(1)}(u_k^{(m)}(1))\}^2 \|\mathbf{x}^{(m)}\|^2. \tag{41}
\end{aligned}$$

Theoretical Comparison Between Two Projection Methods

The specific optimality criterion adopted by the least-squares projection is perhaps more realistic than the energy projection. Indeed, the criterion used in energy projection is too greedy. However, if there is only a single output, then the energy projection and the the least-squares projection yield exactly the same result. A rough analysis, making a very bold assumption that all the involved terms are random and uncorrelated, leads us to conclude that the step size in Eq. 30 is estimated to be $\sqrt{N}$ times that of Eq. 37. Therefore, in an effort to better equalize the energy projection with the least-square projection, we propose to use $\lambda \approx \dfrac{1}{\sqrt{N}}$, and Eq. 31 becomes:

$$\eta = \frac{\mathcal{E}^{(m)}}{\sqrt{N}\|\mathcal{E}_{\tilde{w}}^{(m)}\|^2}$$

which is what used in all our subsequent simulations.

The advantage of the energy projection approach over the least-squares projection, is its computational efficiency, since it doesn't need to compute the extra back-propagated signal ξ (it implies computational savings of one order of magnitude for three- or higher-layer networks). More precisely, for the two layers case the energy method requires $\mathcal{O}(N^2)$ operations as does the conventional BP, where (N is the number of input units which for simplicity is assumed to be equal to the number of hidden as well as output units; in this way N is giving in a sense the "size" of the network). The least squares method requires $\mathcal{O}(7N^2)$ operations instead. For the three or more layers case, the energy projection method and the conventional BP method have again the same computational costs per sweep, ($\mathcal{O}(7N^2)$ operations - for the three layers networks). For the three or more layers case, the least-squares method would incur $\mathcal{O}(N^3)$ operations per sweep and thus it becomes computationally less attractive. The numerical comparisons between various types of BP algorithms will be discussed later in this section.

2.4 Conjugate Gradient Methods for Multi-Layer Networks

The conjugate-gradient algorithm has become increasingly popular for training the BP network. The conjugate-gradient algorithm can search the minimum of a multivariate function faster than the (conventional) gradient-descent procedure for BP networks. The memory usage is on the same order as the number of weights. The conjugate-gradient technique get arounds the problems of determining several critical parameters, e.g. learning-rate for the gradient type methods, making it much easier to use. [6]

In this section, we shall discuss the conjugate gradient method [5] [6] for training multi-layer neural nets. We will perform a comparison study between this and the previous learning algorithms in a later section. We are going to assume throughout the discussion that the method is used in block-mode as explain in a previous section.

The Conjugate Gradient Algorithm

Let us define the energy (or error) function E for the multilayer net in the same way as in the previous sections

$$E = \frac{1}{2} \sum_{m=1}^{M} \sum_{i=1}^{N_L} \left(t_i^{(m)} - a_i^{(m)}(L) \right)^2 \tag{42}$$

Let us further expand the energy at sweep $k+1$ in a second order Taylor expansion with respect to the energy at sweep k:

$$E^{(k+1)} = E^{(k)} + \{E_{\tilde{w}}^{(k)}\}^T \Delta \tilde{\mathbf{w}}_k + \{\Delta \tilde{\mathbf{w}}_k\}^T E_{\tilde{w}\tilde{w}}^{(k)} \Delta \tilde{\mathbf{w}}_k. \tag{43}$$

where, as before, $\tilde{\mathbf{w}}$ is a (long) vector containing all the weights of the network.

Now the weight-updating is not merely a move along the gradient direction but it is instead, the combination of the gradient with some additional momentum term which carries information about the previous updating step:

$$\Delta \mathbf{w}_k = \eta_k \mathbf{d}_k \tag{44}$$

where

$$\mathbf{d}_k = -E_w^{(k)} + \beta_k \mathbf{d}_{k-1}. \tag{45}$$

The conjugate gradient algorithm for minimizing E is as follows:

- **Step 1:** Start from any initial point $\tilde{\mathbf{w}}_0$.
  Compute $\mathbf{d}_0 = -E_{\tilde{w}}^{(0)}$.

- **Step 2:** At each step k do the following iteration loop:

Update the $\tilde{\mathbf{w}}$ vector: Pick η so as to minimize the energy at the next step (Eq. 43). Substituting $\Delta\tilde{\mathbf{w}}$ in Eq. 43 we get

$$E^{(k+1)} = E^{(k)} + \eta_k \{E_{\tilde{w}}^{(k)}\}^T \mathbf{d}_k + \eta_k^2 \mathbf{d}_k^T E_{\tilde{w}\tilde{w}}^{(k)} \mathbf{d}_k \qquad (46)$$

and the minimizing value for η is

$$\eta_k = -\frac{\{E_{\tilde{w}}^{(k)}\}^T \mathbf{d}_k}{\mathbf{d}_k^T E_{\tilde{w}\tilde{w}}^{(k)} \mathbf{d}_k} \qquad (47)$$

Finally, the updating move is

$$\tilde{\mathbf{w}}_{k+1} = \tilde{\mathbf{w}}_k + \eta_k \mathbf{d}_k \qquad (48)$$

Compute $E_{\tilde{w}}^{(k+1)}$.

Update the direction vector d: Pick β_k so as to minimize $\mathbf{d}_k^T E_{\tilde{w}\tilde{w}}^{(k)} \mathbf{d}_k$. We have

$$\begin{aligned} \mathbf{d}_k^T E_{\tilde{w}\tilde{w}}^{(k)} \mathbf{d}_k &= (-E_{\tilde{w}}^{(k)} + \beta_k \mathbf{d}_{k-1})^T E_{\tilde{w}\tilde{w}}^{(k)} (-E_{\tilde{w}}^{(k)} + \beta_k \mathbf{d}_{k-1}) \\ &= \{E_{\tilde{w}}^{(k)}\}^T E_{\tilde{w}\tilde{w}}^{(k)} E_{\tilde{w}}^{(k)} - 2\beta_k \{E_{\tilde{w}}^{(k)}\}^T E_{\tilde{w}\tilde{w}}^{(k)} \mathbf{d}_{k-1} \\ &\quad + \beta_k^2 \mathbf{d}_{k-1}^T E_{\tilde{w}\tilde{w}}^{(k)} \mathbf{d}_{k-1}. \end{aligned} \qquad (49)$$

Then

$$\beta_k = \frac{\{E_{\tilde{w}}^{(k)}\}^T E_{\tilde{w}\tilde{w}}^{(k)} \mathbf{d}_{k-1}}{\mathbf{d}_{k-1}^T E_{\tilde{w}\tilde{w}}^{(k)} \mathbf{d}_{k-1}} \qquad (50)$$

and the update of the vector d is

$$\mathbf{d}_{k+1} = -E_{\tilde{w}}^{(k+1)} + \beta_k \mathbf{d}_k \qquad (51)$$

It is argued that quadratic approximation can be effectively used in general functions especially near the solution area [5] [6].

2.5 Numerical and Simulation Comparisons

Comparison of Two Projection Methods We have implemented the two projection techniques previously proposed. We shall provide a comparison between the two methods. Then we shall compare them with the conjugate gradient method. Finally, a comparison with with the conventional BP method (with optimal fixed η) will be provided.

The model consists of a two layers of linear combination networks with sigmoid neuron activation functions. Our key experiment in on a five-on-five problem, i.e. a classification problem with five classes of five dimensional patterns. Each of the five classes had a *center* randomly chosen inside the hypercube $[0, 1]^5$ and a different *spread* for each dimension chosen randomly (both for each class and for each dimension of the class) between two limits a and b. We ran many experiments for different values of these limits and the three experiments reported here are the most typical. The choice of a and b for these are: experiment 1: $[a, b] = [0.03, 0.15]$, experiment 2: $[a, b] = [0.1, 0.4]$ and experiment 3: $[a, b] = [0.2, 0.7]$. The total number of patterns was 500, i.e 100 for each class. We had 5 input, 5 hidden and 5 output neurons in our net. The teacher value was 1 for the output neuron i iff the input pattern belonged to class i, and 0 otherwise. In all the experiments below the value for λ was 1 for the least-squares projection, and $1/\sqrt{5}$ for the energy projection method. The results of the experiments are depicted in Figures 1 and 2.

The two methods proposed in the previous sections, namely, the least-squares projection and the energy projection methods for estimating η were compared on the five class problem described above. Our first observation is that both the least-squares projection and the energy projection methods are "jumpy". A plausible explanation for the "jumpiness" of both the projection methods is that they are aggressive, trying to accomplish as much as possible with each newly available pattern thus incurring the risk of overadjustment. If the jumpiness condition becomes serious, it could push the neuron values into saturation, where they could be trapped because the gradient would be very close to zero. Based on the above analysis and the actual simulations, we have concluded that a reasonable ceiling of the learning step η is critical for successful numerical performance, Otherwise, there is a risk of pushing neurons into saturation and getting them trapped there if the ceiling is set to be too high. In fact, in one experiment (Figure 3), the least-squares projection failed to converge with ceiling 100 but it did converge

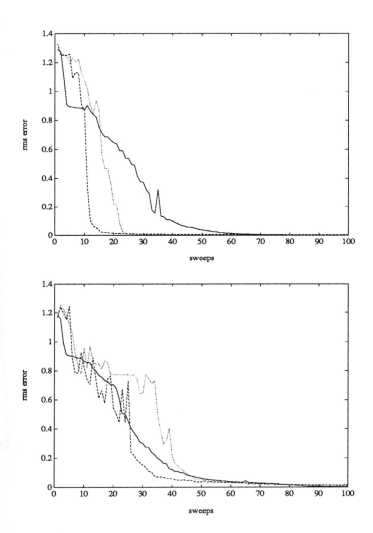

Figure 1: Results of experiments 1 (top) and 2 (bottom) for the five class problem. We compare the conjugate-gradient method (solid line), with BP with least-squares projection (dashed line) and BP with energy projection (dotted line).

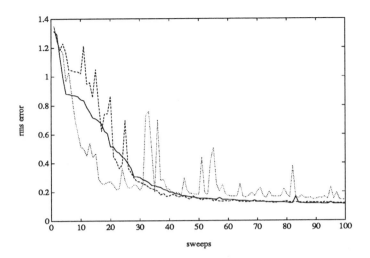

Figure 2: Result of experiment 3 for the five class problem. We show
the error for the conjugate-gradient method (solid line), the BP method
with least-squares projection (dashed line) and the BP method with
energy projection (dotted line).

when the ceiling was reset to 50. (It is intersting to note that for the
same experiment, the least-square method indeed converged whith the
ceiling 100 but λ reduced to 0.5.) Nevertheless, if the ceiling is reasonably low the saturation can be effectively avoided and yet it does not
noticeably affect the convergence speeds. For all the other results in
Figures 1 and 2, a (relatively high) ceiling of η was adopted ($\eta \leq 100$)
for both the projection methods.

An interesting fact about the energy projection curves is that, in the
more difficult cases, the method can be "jumpy" even when the error has
reached bottom. That is explained by the "greediness" of the energy
approach which pushes to suppress the error to zero even when it is
not achievable. It implies the need of smaller λ or a nonzero tolerance
ϵ when the going gets tough. On the other hand, the least-squares
projection method, seems to be jumpier at the beginning but become
better behaved when it reaches steady state.

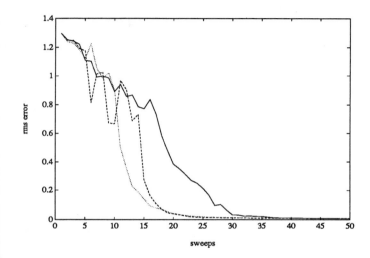

Figure 3: Yet another 5-class experiment. The energy projection method (solid line) converged with ceiling 100 and $\lambda = 1/5^{\frac{1}{2}}$. The least-squares projection method did not converge for ceiling 100 and $\lambda = 1$, it did converge with ceiling 50 and $\lambda = 1$ (dashed line), and with ceiling 100 and $\lambda = 0.5$ (dotted line).

Projection Method vs. Conjugate-Gradient Method For comparison we have implemented the conjugate-gradient method, which operates in block mode as opposed to the data-adaptive mode of projection and traditional BP techniques. The results are shown in Figures 1 and 2. We have observed that the error curve for the conjugate gradient method is much smoother than both the projection methods. One possible reason is that the conjugate gradient method is not as aggressive as projection method. On the other hand, this should not be really surprising because the conjugate-gradient method is implemented as a block method. We have previously contended that the block method has a clear advantage of smoothness because it averages over the entire set of data.

In terms of numbers of sweeps for convergency, the (least-squares and energy) projection methods and the conjugate gradient method appear to be in the same range and no clear advantage can be claimed by any method. While we are not able to compare the computation costs between the projection method and conjugate-gradient method, we suspect they again fall into the same range.

Projection Method vs. Traditional BP Method To compare the relative performance between the (least-squares and energy) projection methods and the traditional BP with "optimal" fixed η, simulations are performed on the five-on-five and exclusive-or problems (Figures 4) and 5). It is important to bear in mind that the best fixed η is not available to us beforehand and it is determined *only* after extensive simulations. The simulations show that the projection approach has similar performance with respect to the traditional BP method with the best fixed η. But this suggests an important advantage enjoyed by the projection methods, since, as mentioned above, the best η for BP is usually unknown. However, the role of the ceiling is again critical for the projection methods in these simulations. Here a "reasonable" ceiling is something around 20. (A ceiling of 100 would lead to saturation.) It seems that the more demanding the problem the smaller the ceiling must be in order to avoid saturation.

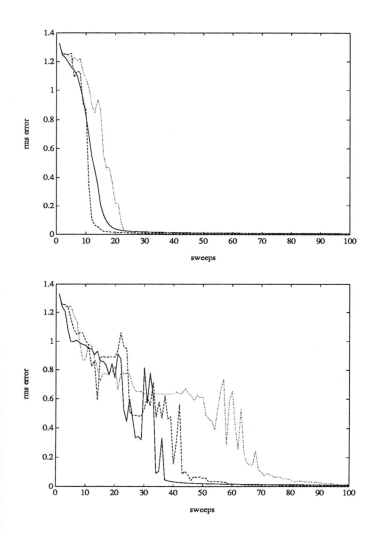

Figure 4: The 5 class problem again with parameters [0.03,0.15] (top) and [0.1,0.3] (bottom). The best plain BP (solid line) has $\eta = 6$ both for the left and the right experiment. and it is compared with the least-squares projection (dashed line) and the energy projection method (dotted line).

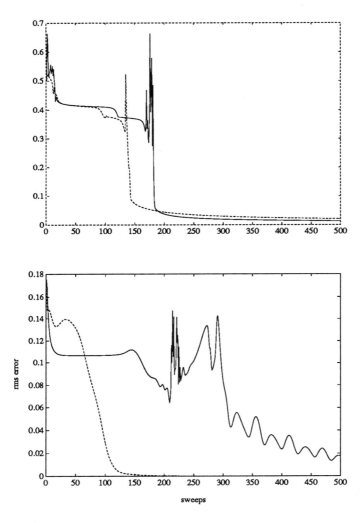

Figure 5: The two-input XOR problem (top) and three-input XOR problem (bottom). The best plain BP (solid line) has $\eta = 19$ on the left, and $\eta = 11$ on the right experiment. The least-squares projection and the energy projection methods give exactly the same curve (dashed line).

3 Competition based approach

3.1 Generalized Perceptron Network (Binary Classification Case)

Given a discriminant function: $K(\mathbf{x}, \mathbf{w})$, this generalized perceptron model can be described by the following formula:

$$u = K(\mathbf{x}, \mathbf{w}) = \tilde{K}(\mathbf{x}, \tilde{\mathbf{w}}) + \theta \tag{52}$$

and the output of the network is:

$$y = \begin{cases} 1, & u > 0 \\ 0, & u \leq 0 \end{cases} \tag{53}$$

where $\mathbf{x}$ is the input value, and y is the output activation.
$K(\mathbf{x}, \mathbf{w})$ is assumed to be analytical for all finite $\mathbf{x}$ and $\mathbf{w}$, therefore $\mathbf{K}_w(\mathbf{x}^{(m)}, \mathbf{w}^{(m)})$ and $\mathbf{K}_{ww}(\mathbf{x}^{(m)}, \mathbf{w}^{(m)})$ are bounded. Given a training set $S = \{\mathbf{x}^{(1)}, \ldots, \mathbf{x}^{(M)}\}$ where $\mathbf{x} \in R^N$, and each element either belongs to a class Ω or not, the class Ω is said to be K-separable from the rest of the world, with respect to set S, iff there exists a vector $\mathbf{w}$ such that: $\mathbf{x}$ belongs to Ω if and only if $K(\mathbf{x}, \mathbf{w}) > 0$.
The Generalized Perceptron learning algorithm is supervised, namely there exists a teacher signal $t^{(m)}$ for each output $y^{(m)}$ corresponding to each input $\mathbf{x}^{(m)}$. The algorithm is described below.
At the m-th iteration, the m-th training pattern $\mathbf{x}^{(m)}$ is presented and the algorithm performs the following iteration:

$$\Delta \mathbf{w}^{(m)} = \eta(t^{(m)} - y^{(m)}) \mathbf{K}_w(\mathbf{x}^{(m)}, \mathbf{w}^{(m)}) \tag{54}$$

where the learning rate η is positive, and $\mathbf{K}_w$ is the first order gradient vector for $K(\mathbf{x}, \mathbf{w})$ with respect to $\mathbf{w}$, i.e.

$$\mathbf{K}_w(\mathbf{x}, \mathbf{w}) = \left[\frac{\partial}{\partial w_1} K(\mathbf{x}, \mathbf{w}), \ldots, \frac{\partial}{\partial w_N} K(\mathbf{x}, \mathbf{w}), \frac{\partial}{\partial \theta} K(\mathbf{x}, \mathbf{w}) \right]^T \tag{55}$$

Note that the weights are updated by adding or subtracting a (fixed or varying) increment of the pattern only if it is misclassified. There is no updating if the pattern is classified correctly. The M training patterns are assumed to be presented in a cyclic order in many sweeps, using the same updating rule at each step.

Examples:

Case I: Gaussian Function

If

$$K(\mathbf{x}, \mathbf{w}) = e^{-\frac{\|\mathbf{x}-\mathbf{w}\|^2}{2}} \tag{56}$$

then the corresponding learning equation is:

$$\mathbf{w}^{(m+1)} = \mathbf{w}^{(m)} - \eta K(\mathbf{x}, \mathbf{w})(\mathbf{x} - \mathbf{w}) \tag{57}$$

Theorem 3.1 (Convergence of Generalized Perceptron Network)
Assume that the training set S are K-separable by $K(\mathbf{x}, \mathbf{w})$, and η is a small positive number. Then the generalized perceptron algorithm converges to a correct solution in a finite number of iterations.

Proof: Assume that $\mathbf{w}^*$ is any solution vector, i.e. for any training pattern $\mathbf{x}$:

$K(\mathbf{x}, \mathbf{w}^*) > 0$, for $\mathbf{x}$ in class Ω;
$K(\mathbf{x}, \mathbf{w}^*) < 0$, for $\mathbf{x}$ not in class Ω;

Since we assume the learning rate η is very small, it is valid to use an approximation by a second-order Taylor's expansion:

$$
\begin{aligned}
K(\mathbf{x}, \mathbf{w}^{(m+1)}) =\ & K(\mathbf{x}, \mathbf{w}^{(m)}) \\
& + \Delta\mathbf{w}^{(m)^T}\mathbf{K}_w(\mathbf{x}, \mathbf{w}^{(m)}) \\
& + \frac{1}{2}\Delta\mathbf{w}^{(m)^T}\mathbf{K}_{ww}(\mathbf{x}, \mathbf{w}^{(m)})\Delta\mathbf{w}^{(m)} \\
& + \text{ third or higher order terms}
\end{aligned}
$$

Substituting Equation 54 into the above equation, we have:

$$
\begin{aligned}
K(\mathbf{x}, \mathbf{w}^{(m+1)}) =\ & K(\mathbf{x}, \mathbf{w}^{(m)}) + \eta(t^{(m)} - y^{(m)})\|\mathbf{K}_w(\mathbf{x}, \mathbf{w}^{(m)})\|^2 \\
& + \frac{1}{2}\eta^2\mathbf{K}_w(\mathbf{x}, \mathbf{w}^{(m)})^T\mathbf{K}_{ww}(\mathbf{x}, \mathbf{w}^{(m)})\mathbf{K}_w(\mathbf{x}, \mathbf{w}^{(m)}) \\
& + \text{ third or higher order terms}
\end{aligned}
$$

We observe that, in case of misclassification, the (binary) values of $t^{(m)}$ and $y^{(m)}$ are different (either 1/0 or 0/1) so

$$(t^{(m)} - y^{(m)})^2 = 1 \tag{58}$$

Furthermore,

$$(t^{(m)} - y^{(m)})K(\mathbf{x}, \mathbf{w}^{(m)}) = -|K(\mathbf{x}, \mathbf{w}^{(m)})| \leq 0 \tag{59}$$

$$(t^{(m)} - y^{(m)})K(\mathbf{x}, \mathbf{w}^*) = |K(\mathbf{x}, \mathbf{w}^{(m)})| \geq 0 \tag{60}$$

It follows that

$$
\begin{aligned}
&[K(\mathbf{x}, \mathbf{w}^{(m+1)}) - K(\mathbf{x}, \mathbf{w}^*)]^2 \\
&= \Big[K(\mathbf{x}, \mathbf{w}^{(m)}) - K(\mathbf{x}, \mathbf{w}^*) + \eta(t^{(m)} - y^{(m)})\|\mathbf{K}_w(\mathbf{x}, \mathbf{w}^{(m)})\|^2 \\
&\quad + \frac{1}{2}\eta^2 \mathbf{K}_w(\mathbf{x}, \mathbf{w}^{(m)})^T \mathbf{K}_{ww}(\mathbf{x}, \mathbf{w}^{(m)})\mathbf{K}_w(\mathbf{x}, \mathbf{w}^{(m)})\Big]^2 \\
&= [K(\mathbf{x}, \mathbf{w}^{(m)}) - K(\mathbf{x}, \mathbf{w}^*)]^2 \\
&\quad + 2\eta(t^{(m)} - y^{(m)})[K(\mathbf{x}, \mathbf{w}^{(m)}) - K(\mathbf{x}, \mathbf{w}^*)]\|\mathbf{K}_w(\mathbf{x}, \mathbf{w}^{(m)})\|^2 \\
&\quad + \eta^2\Big\{\|\mathbf{K}_w(\mathbf{x}, \mathbf{w}^{(m)})\|^4 \\
&\quad + \mathbf{K}_w(\mathbf{x}, \mathbf{w}^{(m)})^T \mathbf{K}_{ww}(\mathbf{x}, \mathbf{w}^{(m)})\mathbf{K}_w(\mathbf{x}, \mathbf{w}^{(m)})[K(\mathbf{x}, \mathbf{w}^{(m)}) - K(\mathbf{x}, \mathbf{w}^*)]\Big\} \\
&\quad + \text{third or higher order terms} \\
&= [K(\mathbf{x}, \mathbf{w}^{(m)}) - K(\mathbf{x}, \mathbf{w}^*)]^2 \\
&\quad - 2\eta\big(|K(\mathbf{x}, \mathbf{w}^{(m)})| + |K(\mathbf{x}, \mathbf{w}^*)|\big)\|\mathbf{K}_w(\mathbf{x}, \mathbf{w}^{(m)})\|^2 \\
&\quad + \eta^2\Big\{\|\mathbf{K}_w(\mathbf{x}, \mathbf{w}^{(m)})\|^4 \\
&\quad + \mathbf{K}_w(\mathbf{x}, \mathbf{w}^{(m)})^T \mathbf{K}_{ww}(\mathbf{x}, \mathbf{w}^{(m)})\mathbf{K}_w(\mathbf{x}, \mathbf{w}^{(m)})[K(\mathbf{x}, \mathbf{w}^{(m)}) - K(\mathbf{x}, \mathbf{w}^*)]\Big\} \\
&\quad + \text{third or higher order terms}
\end{aligned}
$$

There always exists a small and positive η so that the first-order term will dominate the second-order (and positive) term and make the squared-error

$$[K(\mathbf{x}, \mathbf{w}^{(m+1)}) - K(\mathbf{x}, \mathbf{w}^*)]^2$$

decrease by a finite amount in each updating. Since the squared-error cannot become negative, the iterations must terminate within a finite number of corrections. If there is no required updating during an entire sweep, it implies that a correct solution is already obtained and the algorithm should terminate. This proves the generalized perceptron network will converge in finite number of iterations.

To provide a coarse bound for the learning rate η, we note that as long as η is chosen so that

$$\eta \Big\{ \Big| \|\mathbf{K}_w(\mathbf{x}, \mathbf{w}^{(m)})\|^4$$
$$+ \mathbf{K}_w(\mathbf{x}, \mathbf{w}^{(m)})^T \mathbf{K}_{ww}(\mathbf{x}, \mathbf{w}^{(m)}) \mathbf{K}_w(\mathbf{x}, \mathbf{w}^{(m)}) [K(\mathbf{x}, \mathbf{w}^{(m)}) - K(\mathbf{x}, \mathbf{w}^*)] \Big| \Big\}$$

is less than

$$\Big(|K(\mathbf{x}, \mathbf{w}^{(m)})| + |K(\mathbf{x}, \mathbf{w}^*)| \Big) \|\mathbf{K}_w(\mathbf{x}, \mathbf{w}^{(m)})\|^2,$$

then in each iteration the squared-error decreases by at least the following amount

$$\eta(|K(\mathbf{x}, \mathbf{w}^{(m)})| + |K(\mathbf{x}, \mathbf{w}^*)|) \|\mathbf{K}_w(\mathbf{x}, \mathbf{w}^{(m)})\|^2 \qquad (61)$$

The decrement will be nonzero, since we have the following:

- For all training patterns $\mathbf{x}$, $|K(\mathbf{x}, \mathbf{w}^*)| > 0$ (this is the condition for K-separability.)

- For all $\mathbf{x}$ and $\mathbf{w}$,

$$\|\mathbf{K}_w(\mathbf{x}, \mathbf{w})\|^2 = \sum_i \|\frac{\partial}{\partial w_i} K(\mathbf{x}, \mathbf{w})\|^2 + \|\frac{\partial}{\partial \theta} K(\mathbf{x}, \mathbf{w})\|^2$$

$$\geq \|\frac{\partial}{\partial \theta} K(\mathbf{x}, \mathbf{w})\|^2 = 1 > 0$$

Corollary: Without using an adaptive threshold θ, then we need an additional assumption that $\|\mathbf{K}_w(\mathbf{x}, \mathbf{w})\|^2 > 0$, so that the theorem will remain valid. (This assumption is in practicality valid barring rare exceptions.)

Example 3.1 The example of a linearly nonseparable function (XOR-like) described in the previous section can be solved by using a hypersphere-like discriminant function:

$$u = w_1(x_1 - w_2)^2 + w_3(x_2 - w_4)^2 - w_5.$$

$$y = 1 \;\; if \;\; u > 0, \;\; otherwise \;\; y = 0$$

In this example, the center of the ellipse (w_2, w_4) is fixed to $(0,0)$. The initial values of the weights are set as

$$[w_1, w_3, w_5] = [0.4, -0.7, -2]$$

Using the updating rule described above, the network converges in one sweep to a a correct solution:

$$[w_1, w_3, w_5] = [1.4, 0.3, -1]$$

3.2 Generalized Perceptron Network (Multiple Classification Case)

We are given a training set $S = \{\mathbf{x}^{(1)}, \ldots, \mathbf{x}^{(M)}\}$ where $\mathbf{x}^{(m)} \in R^N$, and each element belongs to one of the C classes: $\Omega_1, \ldots, \Omega_C$. Correspondingly, there are C discriminant functions: $K(\mathbf{x}, \mathbf{w}_i) \;\; for \;\; i = 1, \ldots, C$. The classes are said to be K-separable with respect to set S iff there exists a set of $\mathbf{w}_k^*, k = 1, \ldots, C$ such that for each $\mathbf{x} \in \Omega_i$, $K(\mathbf{x}^{(m)}, \mathbf{w}_i^*) > K(\mathbf{x}^{(m)}, \mathbf{w}_j^*)$, for $i = 1, \ldots, C$, $j = 1, \ldots, C$, $and \;\; j \neq i$.

Suppose $\mathbf{x}^{(m)}$ belongs to class Ω_i. Then the learning algorithm performs the following iteration:

(1) If $K(\mathbf{x}^{(m)}, \mathbf{w}_i^{(m)}) > K(\mathbf{x}^{(m)}, \mathbf{w}_j^{(m)})$

for all $j \neq i$, i.e. $\mathbf{x}^{(m)}$ is classified into the correct class, then:

$$\mathbf{w}_k^{(m+1)} = \mathbf{w}_k^{(m)} \;\; for \;\; all \;\; k = 1, \ldots, C \qquad (62)$$

(2) If $K(\mathbf{x}^{(m)}, \mathbf{w}_i^{(m)}) < K(\mathbf{x}^{(m)}, \mathbf{w}_j^{(m)})$

for some $j \neq i$, i.e. $\mathbf{x}^{(m)}$ is misclassified, then for i and all such j:

$$\mathbf{w}_i^{(m+1)} = \mathbf{w}_i^{(m)} + \eta \mathbf{K}_w(\mathbf{x}^{(m)}, \mathbf{w}_i^{(m)}) \tag{63}$$

$$\mathbf{w}_j^{(m+1)} = \mathbf{w}_j^{(m)} - \eta \mathbf{K}_w(\mathbf{x}^{(m)}, \mathbf{w}_j^{(m)}) \tag{64}$$

where $\mathbf{K}_w$ is defined by Equation 55.

And $\mathbf{w}_k^{(m+1)} = \mathbf{w}_k^{(m)}$ for all $k \neq i$ and $k \neq j$.

Theorem 3.2 (Convergence of Generalized Perceptron Network) (Multiple-Class Case) *Assume that the set S are K-separable by $K(\mathbf{x}, \mathbf{w}_i)$ for $i = 1, \dots, L$. If η is a small positive number. Then the above learning algorithm converges to a correct solution in a finite number of iterations.*

Proof:
We adopt a generalized Kesler construction[2] which converts the multiclass problem into a two-class problem. We construct a new single nonlinear discriminant function for a binary classification problem, $\hat{K}(\pi, \mathbf{W})$, where $\mathbf{W} = [\mathbf{w}_1^T, \mathbf{w}_2^T, \dots, \mathbf{w}_C^T]^T$, and π denotes a new training input pattern defined below:
Without loss of generality, it is assumed that $x \in \omega_i$:

- Define $\pi_{ij} \equiv [\sigma_j(x), x]$, for all $1 \leq j \leq C$, except $j = i$.

- Define
$$\sigma_j \equiv [\sigma_{j1}, \sigma_{j2}, \cdots, \sigma_{jC}]$$

  where

  $$\sigma_{jk}(x) = \begin{cases} 1, & k = i \\ -1, & k = j \\ 0, otherwise \end{cases} \tag{65}$$

  for all $k = 1, \cdots, C$.

- In short, for each of the M original training patterns(x), we generate $(C - 1)$ training patterns denoted π_{ij}.

	Training set	Testing set	Total set
no. of misclassifications	9	23	32
error percentage	1.17%	6.97%	2.99%

Table 1: Simulation results of the generalized perceptron network for texture classification problem

Since there are M original patterns, so a set of $M \times (C - 1)$ new training patterns can be generated. Let π be any element of this set, we can now define

$$\hat{K}(\pi, \mathbf{W}) = \sum_k \sigma_{jk}(x) K(\mathbf{x}, \mathbf{w}_k) \tag{66}$$

where $\sigma_{jk}(x)$ is defined above.

Example 3.2 To study the performance of the multiple-class generalized perceptron network to texture analysis using coocurrence matrices, we use 11 Brodatz textures (texture numbers 84, 57, 77, 33, 28, 49, 68, 16, 103, 3 and 34). For each texture, 100 64×64 blocks are randomly chosen. The coocurrence matrices are computed and averaged into 4×4 matrices. After this, the rows are stacked into a column vector which is used as sample data. 70 of the samples are used as training set and 30 of the samples are used as testing set.

$$K(\mathbf{x}, \mathbf{w}_i) = \sum_{j=1}^{11} w_j (x_j - w_{cj})^2 + \theta_i$$

is chosen as the discriminant function.
To give an indication of convergency speed, the training curve is shown in Figure 7. The classification performance is summarized in Table 3.2

Comparison between Competition and approximation approaches
This comparison can only be carried out with respect to classification

Figure 6: Sample textures used in the classification experiment.

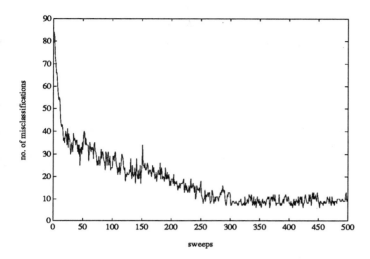

Figure 7: Training curves for texture classification experiment (number of misclassifications vs. sweep number)

problems, where both competition and approximation based approaches are applicable. In the approximation approach, suitable learning rates may be adopted to achieve faster convergence than a fixed learning rate approach. In contrast, the learning rate for the competition approach should be kept small enough to guarantee the convergence of the weights. However, only those patterns which are misclassified are involved in the training of the network. As the number of misclassifications decreases, the amount of training computation also decreases proportionally. The approximation method does not enjoy this advantage. Another drawback of approximation method is that the proper values of teachers are usually unavailable. A bad set of teacher values may result in poor performance in terms of convergence speed and final mean square-error or classification errors. The information needed for the competition approach is not as strict as that for the approximation approach. As long as the correct neuron wins, the exact values of the outputs are not important. So the competition approach is more flexible.

As an example of numerical comparison, both competition and approximation approaches are applied to the classification of texture data (cf. Fig. 6). The approximation method is very slow and the mean square error remains very large after 500 sweeps. For this application, the competition approach performs much better than the approximation method.(cf. Fig 7)

It is important to note that, however, there are many other (non-classification-type) applications, e.g. curve fitting and regularization problems, where the competition-based formulation is simply not applicable. For such applications, only the approximation-based formulation may be adopted.

4 Concluding Remarks

Approximation-type and competition-type approaches for nonlinear separable problems have been studied. Convergence proof and some numerical considerations are discussed. Simulations for artificial and real data are performed and the results for the various proposed methods are reported and compared. The simulations so far point to the following observations: the simulation results are satisfactory with regard to the speed of the gradient-projection for single- and multi-layer networks using nonlinear discriminant functions. In terms of performance, the single-layer case is not as good as the multi-layer one, but we should keep in mind that a single-layer net has less parameters, hence less flexibility than a multi-layer net. The projection method for a two-layer perceptron network has satisfactory performance for the artificial data. It seems that the gradient-projection and conjugate-gradient methods have similar computation time and error performance. However, the block method is smoother than the data-adaptive method. In terms of real texture classification problem, only the competition-based approach has yielded a satisfactory result both in computation time and performance. However, it should be noted that these results only indicate some interesting directions for future and more thorough investigations. At this stage, it would be unwise to come to any definitive conclusion.

Bibliography

[1] B. Widrow and S. D. Stearns, *Adaptive Signal Processing*, Prentice Hall, Englewood Cliffs, NJ, 1986.

[2] R. O. Duda and P. E. Hart, *Pattern Classification and Scene Analysis*, Wiley, N.Y., 1973.

[3] S. Kaczmarz, Angenäherte Auflösung von Systemen Linearer Gleichungen, Bull. Int. Acad. Polon. Sci. (Series A), 355–357, 1937.

[4] S. Y. Kung and J. N. Hwang, *An Algebraic Projection Analysis for Optimal Hidden Units Size and Learning Rate in Back-Propagation Learning*, in IEEE, Int'l Conf. on Neural Networks, ICNN'88, San Diego, pages Vol.1: 363–370, July 1988.

[5] D. G. Luenberger, *Linear and Nonlinear Programming*, Addison-Wesley Publishing Co., 1984.

[6] M. J. D. Powell, *Restart Procedure for the Conjugate Gradient Method*, Mathematical Programming, 12:241–254, April 1977.

[7] D. E. Rumelhart, J. L. McClelland, and the PDP Research Group, *Parallel Distributed Processing (PDP): Exploration in the Microstructure of Cognition (Vol. 1)*, MIT Press, Cambridge, Massachusetts, 1986.

Neural Tree Networks

Ananth Sankar and Richard J. Mammone
CAIP Center and Dept. of Electrical Engineering
Rutgers University
Piscataway, NJ 08855-1390

1   Introduction

Pattern classification is a fairly mature subject and there have been
many books written on this field [8, 30, 28, 9]. The supervised pattern classification problem can be stated as: Given a set of training
feature vectors, X_i, each with an associated class label Y_i, find a retrieval system that will produce the correct label , Y_i for any feature
vector, X_i The retrieval system is determined by using a training
algorithm. In recent years there has been increased interest in the
use of neural networks as pattern classifiers and associative memories [24, 11, 12, 16, 15, 17, 33, 5, 6]. Feedforward neural networks,
in particular, have emerged as one of the most successful neural network architectures. The basic building block for feedforward neural
networks is a neuron which calculates a non-linear function of the
weighted sum of its inputs. Thus the neuron can be specified by
its weights and the non-linear activation function. In a feedforward
neural network these neurons are arranged in layers such that the
outputs of one layer are connected to the inputs of the next layer.
The input feature vector is fed to the first layer of neurons whose
outputs become the inputs for the second layer of neurons and so
on and finally the output of the last layer is the output of the network. The last layer is called the output layer and all other layers
are called hidden layers. An n-layer network is one that has $n - 1$
hidden layers and one output layer. The weights of such systems are
typically found by supervised training algorithms that use a training
set of labeled feature vectors. The problem of training a feedforward

network is NP-complete [14] and therefore one must look for good heuristic solutions. Currently the most popular heuristic is backpropagation [24, 32, 19], which is essentially a gradient descent method over an error surface. For networks with hidden layers, this error surface is non-quadratic, and creates problems with local minima. In addition, the exact number of hidden neurons and the connectivity between layers must be specified before learning can begin. In practice, however, one cannot guarantee that backpropagation will find the correct weights for a given number of neurons and a particular training set. The most common solution to this problem is to choose the number of hidden neurons by trial and error.

Decision trees provide another popular approach to pattern classification   [4, 20, 21, 10, 27]. The structure of a decision tree is recursive in that each node of a decision tree has a set of child nodes, each of which is also a decision tree. The terminal nodes have no child nodes and are called leaf nodes. It has been shown that constructing a decision tree with the shortest length to solve a given classification task is NP-complete [13]. Thus all existing algorithms to grow decision trees are heuristic methods. The essential idea in these algorithms is to solve the problem by using a divide and conquer approach. The root of the tree partitions the feature space into subsets, assigning each subset to a child node. This partitioning is also called splitting. The usual way to split the feature space is to generate a list of possible splits and then search through this list to find the best split [4]. This splitting process is continued until each terminal or leaf node corresponds to one class. Different ways of generating the search space of partitions and evaluating the "goodness" of a split lead to different decision tree algorithms like CART [4] and ID3 [21]. These algorithms require an exhaustive search through a list of arbitrarily generated splits. This search process is computationally inefficient. In addition, since the list of possible splits is generated in an adhoc manner, the solution may not be close to the optimal solution. Most decision tree algorithms use splits which result in regions whose boundaries are perpendicular to the feature space axes. This is a severe limitation in cases where the problem is linearly separable but the decision hyperplane is not perpendicular to a feature axis since many perpendicular splits would be needed to approximate the hyperplane. CART [4] allows for non-perpendicular splits but this, too, involves an exhaustive search technique.

In this paper we introduce a new neural network architecture which is a combination of feedforward neural networks and decision trees. The architecture is called a Neural Tree Network (NTN). The NTN architecture is a tree with a single layer neural net at each of its nodes. The new architecture is grown during the learning process rather than specified a priori as in feedforward neural networks. We show that the NTN architecture offers a substantial implementation advantage over feedforward neural networks. A new learning algorithm which grows the NTN is also described. The new learning algorithm is based on the method of gradient descent and does not require an exhaustive search as previously used in training algorithms for decision trees. The splits are not restricted to be perpendicular to the feature space axes and the new algorithm is guaranteed to converge to a solution. Simulation results show that the new algorithm is faster than backpropagation and produces smaller trees than conventional decision trees.

This paper extends the results of our earlier work on two class problems [1] to the multi-class case. The paper is organized as follows. Section 2 discusses the new neural net architecture. In section 3, we describe the new algorithm that grows the NTN. In the discussion of the new architecture and algorithm, we concentrate on the two class problem for the sake of simplicity. In section 4, we extend the new method to multi-class pattern recognition problems. Section 5 shows simulation results and compares the new algorithm to backpropagation and decision trees and section 6 gives the summary and conclusions.

2 The New Architecture

In this section the new architecture is described for the two class case. This leads to a binary tree structure. The more general multi-class case is discussed in the next section. The NTN uses a tree architecture which implements a sequential linear decision making strategy. Each node at every level of the NTN corresponds to an exclusive subset of the training data and the leaf nodes of the NTN completely partition the training set.

Each internal tree node consists of a single neuron which can represent two classes while the leaf nodes are used to make decisions as to class membership. Thus the internal nodes route the data to the appropriate leaf node which then classifies the data.

We now consider the number of nodes used in a NTN and a feedforward neural network. Cover [7] has shown that the probability of finding a linearly separable dichotomy of $2d$ points in d-dimensional space approaches 1 when d is large. The NTN partitions the original training set of N feature vectors recursively so that the number of training vectors for each NTN node becomes smaller as we go down the NTN from the root to the leaves. From Cover's result [7] it is clear that if the number of training vectors in an internal NTN node is $2d$ or less, then that NTN node can correctly classify the vectors and thus will have two child nodes that are both leaves. A balanced NTN requires $\frac{N}{2d}$ such nodes to classify all the N training vectors. Thus the number of leaf nodes is $\frac{N}{d}$ and the number of internal nodes is $\frac{N}{d} - 1$. However, the leaf nodes do not contain processing units as do the internal nodes. Thus the number of processing nodes is $\frac{N}{d} - 1$. A feedforward neural network with $\frac{N}{d}$ hidden nodes can represent any two class problem [2] and therefore both the NTN and the feedforward neural net require the same number of nodes to exactly represent the training data. A feedforward neural network fires all $\frac{N}{d}$ nodes in parallel during retrieval and also needs an extra time unit for the output unit to fire. Thus the total processing time taken is two time units. The balanced NTN, however, fires $log_2 \frac{N}{d}$ nodes in sequence. Therefore the time taken for retrieval is $log_2 \frac{N}{d}$. The NTN , however, can be implemented with a single processor and a look up table that stores the weights of all $\frac{N}{d}$ nodes. This implementation is shown in figure 1. Depending upon the output of the processor, the next weight vector is loaded from the look up table. To realize a feedforward neural net, all $\frac{N}{d}$ nodes must be physically implemented. Therefore there is a trade-off between retrieval speed and cost of implementation. If implementation efficiency is mea-

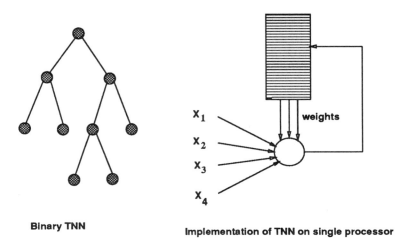

Binary TNN

Implementation of TNN on single processor

Figure 1: Implementation of NTN by single processor

sured as the product of retrieval time and number of processors, the NTN offers a substantial advantage in that its implementation efficiency is $log_2 \frac{N}{d}$ as compared to $2\frac{N}{d}$ for feedforward neural networks. The above analysis gives the number of neurons required for the exact representation of the training set. For good generalization, this number must be much smaller [3]. Computer simulations to date indicate that, given the same number of nodes, the NTN achieves similar generalization to feedforward networks.

The recursive structure of the NTN suggests a recursive learning algorithm. In the next section a new recursive learning algorithm is presented.

3   The Learning Algorithm

The learning algorithm operates on each NTN node. In the description of the algorithm, we consider an arbitrary node t of the NTN that processes a subset S_t of the training data. If S_t contains only one class, then the node becomes a leaf node and is labeled by the appropriate class label. If S_t contains two classes, then a single neuron is used to find a hyperplane that separates the feature vectors into two subsets. These subsets of training data are processed by each of two child nodes using the same algorithm.

Since the case where S_t has only one class is trivial, we concentrate on the case when the number of classes is two. In this case a neuron is used to process S_t. The neuron computes a non-linear function of the dot product of its inputs and its weights. The output of the neuron is given by:

$$y = \frac{1}{1 + e^{\sum_i w_i x_i}} \tag{1}$$

where x_i is the ith input to the neuron and w_i is the weight from input i to the neuron.

One may view the training process as placing a hyperplane so as to separate as many data points as possible and so get the minimum number of errors. The standard gradient descent techniques used to train feedforward neural networks minimize the L2 norm of the errors which is, however, sensitive to a few statistical outliers, i.e. a few misclassifications. This results in poor solutions if the problem is not linearly separable [1, 26]. The L1 norm is more robust than the L2 norm in that the effect of outliers is diminished. Therefore minimizing the L1 norm results in a better partition of a non-linearly separable training set [1, 26]. The use of the L1 norm has also been found to result in faster learning [25]. In the new algorithm, each neuron is trained by using a gradient descent technique to minimize the L1 norm of the errors. The L1 error when pattern j is presented to the network is defined by:

$$E_j = \mid o_j - y_j \mid \tag{2}$$

where o_j is the required output for the neuron when training pattern j is presented and y_j is the actual output of the neuron.

The weights of the neuron are updated only if its output and target do not agree. The update rule for the neuron when pattern j is presented to the network is given by:

$$w_k^{n+1} = w_k^n - \eta \frac{\partial E_j}{\partial w_k} \tag{3}$$

where η is a gain term which is taken to lie between 0 and 1 and k ranges over the input space dimensions.

Substituting the derivative of the L1 error in equation 3, we get

$$w_k^{n+1} = w_k^n - \eta y_j (1 - y_j) sgn(o_j - y_j) x_k \qquad (4)$$

The gradient descent algorithm requires that the error function, E_j, be differentiable at all points. The L1 norm does not have a derivative at the origin but this does not affect the algorithm since no updates are made when the output agrees with the target.

After the output error has converged, a check is made to see if the error is less than a predetermined threshold. If the error is less than the threshold then the neuron separates the classes in S_t and the tree growing process is stopped. If not, a hyperplane is formed by the above algorithm which partitions the training set into two subsets. Each subset is assigned to a child node and the algorithm is then used recursively on each child node. If the hyperplane does not split the training data, then the neuron is retrained with the two feature vectors from opposite classes that produce the maximum error. This procedure guarantees that the neuron will split the training set. We summarize the training algorithm in the following pseudo code:

INPUT A NTN node t, training examples $\{\mathbf{X_k}, Y_k\}$ and the number of classes, $N_{C,t}$. $\mathbf{X_k}$ is a real valued feature vector of dimension m. Y_k is a binary valued class label.

OUTPUT A Neural Tree Network with a single neuron at each internal NTN node. The weights for the neurons at these NTN nodes are calculated by the algorithm and the leaf nodes are labeled by the appropriate class.

ALGORITHM

If $N_{C,t} = 1$

Then :

    1. Label the node by the appropriate class

2. STOP

Else :

1. Set up a neuron at the tree node
2. Use the L1 norm update rule to train the neuron until the error has converged
3. **If** the neuron splits the training data
   Then :

   (a) Grow 2 child nodes

   (b) Use the neuron to split the training data into the two child nodes

   (c) Calculate the number of classes , $N_{C,i}$, for each child node i

   (d) Repeat the algorithm for each child node

   Else :

   (a) Find the two training examples of opposite output value that result in maximum error

   (b) Retrain the neuron with these two training examples

   (c) Repeat the same process as above for growing child nodes and repeat the algorithm for each child node

We now describe how the Neural Tree Network classifies a test feature vector. The feature vector enters the NTN at its root. The neuron at each node is used to route the feature vector to one of the child nodes. Classification is done at the leaf nodes of the NTN. The pseudo-code for the classifying algorithm is given below:

INPUT A feature vector, X_k and a node t in the tree neural network.

OUTPUT The class label Y_k classifying the feature vector.

ALGORITHM

If the node is a leaf

Then : Classify the feature vector by the label of the tree node.

Else : Use the neuron at the NTN node to route the feature vector to a child node. Repeat the above algorithm for the child node.

4 Generalization to Multi-Class Problems

In this section we show how the above method can be generalized to the multi-class problem. We first define linear separability for the multi-class case. We show that a distinction must be made between geometric separability and the "separability" of the mapping induced by labeling the classes of a given geometric situation in different ways.

Linear separability for two class problems is well defined. A two class problem is said to be linearly separable if there exists a hyperplane such that the two classes lie on opposite sides of the hyperplane. The separating hyperplane for such a problem can be found easily by using a number of algorithms such as the perceptron algorithm [23]. Also since there are only two classes, labeling is trivial; one class is labeled by 1 and the other by 0. The resulting mapping can be learned by a single neuron.

When the number of classes is greater than two, the concept of linear separability becomes more complicated. For the general p-class problem Ullmann defines several kinds of separability such as one/many, one/one and many/many separability [30]. For the purposes of this paper we shall define geometrical linear separability (GLS) as follows:

Definition 1 *A p-class problem with features from q-dimensional space is said to be geometrically linearly separable iff $q-1$-dimensional hyperplanes can be drawn in such a way that, for all $i = 1 \ldots p$, every member of class i lies within the same region defined by these hyperplanes and no member of class $j \neq i$ lies within that region.*

This definition of separability takes into consideration only the geometry of the problem. We stress that even if a problem is geometrically linearly separable by the above definition, the labeling scheme used may render the resulting mapping unseparable by a single layer neural network. Geometric linear separability only implies the separability of at least one labeling of the classes such that the resulting mapping from feature space to label space is learnable by a single layer neural network. We define such a mapping as a linearly separable mapping (LSM). Figure 2 shows a linearly separable geometry in feature space and two labeling schemes–one is linearly separable and the other is not. Thus both problems are GLS but only the second labeling is LSM. It is clear that the number of hyperplanes needed to separate p classes is m, where $log_2 p \leq m \leq p$. If $m = p$, then one could use the standard binary basis vectors to label the classes. This encoding scheme is called the local encoding scheme. If $m = log_2 p$, then all possible bit combinations of the m-bit string must be used as class labels. This is called the distributed encoding scheme. Presently little is known about the optimal selection of label length, m. It is usually determined arbitrarily. We have used a local encoding scheme in the results reported in section 5.

We now extend the NTN algorithm to the multi-class case. Suppose that NTN node t operates on a subregion R_t of the original feature space. Let the subset of the original training set corresponding to R_t be S_t. Also let p be the number of classes in S_t. We use p neurons at node t and a local encoding scheme to label the classes, so that each neuron corresponds to a different class. After training the neural network, a feature vector is classified by the neuron that has the maximum output value. Thus feature vector $\mathbf{X}$ is classified as class i if

$$f(\mathbf{W_i}.\mathbf{X}) > f(\mathbf{W_j}.\mathbf{X}) \quad \forall j \neq i \qquad (5)$$

where $\mathbf{W_i}$ is the weight vector for neuron i.

The splitting rule used here is to assign all feature vectors that are classified as class i to child node $i, 1 \leq i \leq p$. This splitting rule divides R_t into p convex regions $R_{t,i}, i = 1 \ldots p$. This convexity is proved by the argument below:

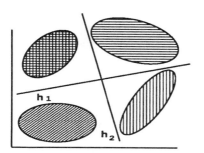

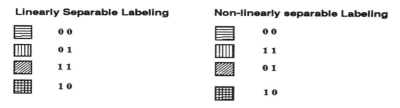

Figure 2: Linear and Non-linearly separable labelings of the same problem

Suppose that $\mathbf{X_1}$ and $\mathbf{X_2}$ belong to $R_{t,i}$. From the above splitting rule

$$f(\mathbf{W_i}.\mathbf{X_1}) > f(\mathbf{W_j}.\mathbf{X_1}) \quad \forall j \neq i \tag{6}$$

$$f(\mathbf{W_i}.\mathbf{X_2}) > f(\mathbf{W_j}.\mathbf{X_2}) \quad \forall j \neq i \tag{7}$$

Since f is monotonically increasing, this gives

$$\mathbf{W_i}.\mathbf{X_1} > \mathbf{W_j}.\mathbf{X_1} \quad \forall j \neq i \tag{8}$$

$$\mathbf{W_i}.\mathbf{X_2} > \mathbf{W_j}.\mathbf{X_2} \quad \forall j \neq i \tag{9}$$

Consider the point $\mathbf{X}$

$$\mathbf{X} = \lambda \mathbf{X_1} + (1 - \lambda)\mathbf{X_2} \quad 0 \leq \lambda \leq 1$$

From equations 8 and 9

$$\lambda \mathbf{W_i}.\mathbf{X_1} > \lambda \mathbf{W_j}.\mathbf{X_1} \quad \forall j \neq i \qquad (10)$$

$$(1 - \lambda)\mathbf{W_i}.\mathbf{X_2} > (1 - \lambda)\mathbf{W_j}.\mathbf{X_2} \quad \forall j \neq i \qquad (11)$$

Thus

$$\mathbf{W_i}.\mathbf{X} > \mathbf{W_j}.\mathbf{X} \quad \forall j \neq i$$

From this and the fact that f is monotonically increasing,

$$f(\mathbf{W_i}.\mathbf{X}) > f(\mathbf{W_j}.\mathbf{X}) \quad \forall j \neq i$$

Thus if $\mathbf{X_1}$ and $\mathbf{X_2}$ belong to $R_{t,i}$, then $\mathbf{X} = \lambda\mathbf{X_1} + (1 - \lambda)\mathbf{X_2}$ also belongs to $R_{t,i}$ and hence $R_{t,i}$ is convex.

Thus NTN node t has at most p child nodes, each operating on a convex subregion of the original feature space. If $m < p$ neurons are used then the number of child nodes could be very large. This is seen by the following argument. If m neurons are used at NTN node t such that $log_2 p \leq m < p$, then a non-local encoding scheme must be used to label the classes. In other words each neuron does not correspond to a different class and so classification cannot be done on the basis of the neuron that has maximum output. The m hyperplanes corresponding to the neurons form regions in the feature space. A simple splitting rule that can be used is to assign all feature vectors in a particular region to the same child node. If the input feature space dimension is d then the maximum number of regions that can be formed by m hyperplanes is

$$\sum_{i=0}^{d} \binom{m}{i} = \Omega(d^m)$$

This is easily derived using a recursion given in [18]. This also gives an upper bound for the number of child nodes. If m is large then the number of child nodes could be large. From our simulations we find that this splitting rule results in very wide NTN structures. As already mentioned, using p neurons and a local encoding scheme results in at most p child nodes as compared to $\Omega(d^m)$ child nodes when $m < p$ neurons are used.

a	b	c	d	$(a \vee b) \oplus (c \wedge d)$
0	0	0	0	0
0	0	0	1	0
0	0	1	0	0
0	0	1	1	1
0	1	0	0	1
0	1	0	1	1
0	1	1	0	1
0	1	1	1	0
1	0	0	0	1
1	0	0	1	1
1	0	1	0	1
1	0	1	1	0
1	1	0	0	1
1	1	0	1	1
1	1	1	0	1
1	1	1	1	0

Table 1: Truth Table for $(a \vee b) \oplus (c \wedge d)$

5 Simulation Results

In this section we present simulation results which demonstrate the performance of the new algorithm on two non-linearly separable boolean functions and a speaker independent vowel recognition task. The two boolean functions are the standard XOR function and the following 4 input boolean function.

$(a \vee b) \oplus (c \wedge d)$

The truth table for this function is shown in table 1. For both these functions the number of classes is two. We use a single neuron at each NTN node and consequently label the two classes as '0' and '1'.

Figure 3 shows the NTN grown for the XOR problem and also

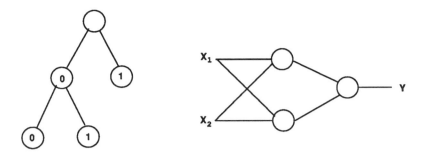

TNN   **Feedforward Neural Network**

Figure 3: NTN and Feedforward structure for XOR

Algorithm	Number of epochs	Number of weight updates
NTN	30	315
Backpropagation	256	9216

Table 2: Number of learning epochs to solve XOR

the feedforward neural network that solves the problem. As can be seen the NTN uses only two nodes whereas the feedforward neural network needs three nodes. Table 2 tabulates the number of epochs taken by the NTN algorithm and backpropagation to learn the XOR problem. It should be noted that each NTN epoch is less costly than each backpropagation epoch for the following reasons:

1. In backpropagation, each epoch trains all the nodes in the network. In the NTN each epoch trains only one node in the network.

2. In the NTN, as we traverse the tree from the root to the leaf nodes, the number of training patterns becomes less and hence each epoch of training has fewer training patterns presented to the network

Algorithm	Number of epochs	Number of weight updates
NTN	77	4350
Backpropagation	715	217360

Table 3: Number of learning epochs to solve $(a \lor b) \oplus (c \land d)$

For the above reasons, we also show the number of weight updates for both algorithms. From the table, it is clear that the NTN is much faster than backpropagation.

Figure 4 shows the feedforward network with three hidden units that solves the second boolean function and also the trees which were grown using the NTN algorithm, ID3 and perceptron trees. Perceptron trees are a combination of ID3 and perceptrons [31]. The approach is to use an ID3 splitting rule if the problem is not linearly separable and a perceptron if it is linearly separable. Thus a perceptron tree is a tree where the leaf nodes are perceptrons and the internal nodes are ID3 nodes. The new NTN algorithm uses 3 nodes as compared to 8 nodes for ID3 and 5 nodes for perceptron trees.

Table 3 compares the new training algorithm with backpropagation in terms of the number of epochs and the number of weight updates needed to learn the problem. For backpropagation, we used a network with one hidden layer containing 3 hidden units. Thus there were a total of 4 nodes in the feedforward network. As can be seen from the table, the new algorithm trained much faster than backpropagation.

It is interesting to note the following relation between NTN's and feedforward neural networks. Consider the two class case corresponding to a binary NTN structure. The leaf nodes are labeled '1' and '0' corresponding to the two classes. Each internal NTN node corresponds to a boolean variable. This variable is a '1' or a '0', depending on which child node the feature vector is routed to. A NTN essentially implements a disjunct of conjuncts. Each path from the root of the NTN to a leaf node labeled by '1' corresponds to a conjunct. Thus the NTN implements the disjunct of the paths from the root to the leaves that are labeled '1'. If this boolean func-

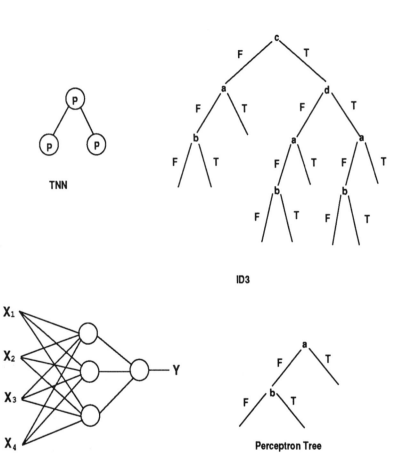

Figure 4: Trees and feedforward network for $(a \vee b) \oplus (c \wedge d)$

Initialization type	XOR	$(a \vee b) \oplus (c \wedge d)$
Random initialization	256	715
Initialization using NTN weights	79	91

Table 4: Effect of different initializations

tion (the disjunct of conjuncts implemented by the NTN) is linearly separable then the NTN can be mapped onto a feedforward neural network with one hidden layer in the following way. Each NTN node corresponds to a hidden unit in the neural network and the output node of the neural network implements the boolean function (which is linearly separable). The weights of the hidden units are initialized by the NTN nodes. The output node weights are initialized to small random numbers. The training time for this neural network is greatly decreased due to the fact that the hidden unit weights have been set correctly by using the NTN. This method also directly gives the number of hidden nodes that is required in the feedforward neural network as opposed to finding the number of hidden nodes by trial and error. Table 4 shows the average number of epochs to train a neural network for the XOR problem and the boolean problem, $(a \vee b) \oplus (c \wedge d)$. The first row shows the number of epochs when all the weights were randomly initialized and the second row shows the number of epochs when the hidden unit weights were initialized using the NTN. We must also include the number of epochs which the NTN took to train. The table takes this into consideration. Again, note that each NTN epoch is less costly than each neural neural net epoch, so the increase in learning rate is actually better than the table indicates.

The NTN was also tried on a speaker independent vowel recognition task. A training set of 528 feature vectors representing 11 vowel sounds are to be classified. These features are obtained from 4 male and 4 female speakers, each saying each vowel 6 times. The experiment used an independent testing set of 462 features obtained from another 4 male and 3 female speakers each saying each vowel 6 times. The features are 10 log area parameters calculated using six 512 sample Hamming windowed segments from the steady part of the vowel. Details of this data set can be obtained from [22]. Experiments have been performed to evaluate the performance of various feedforward neural networks with different numbers of hidden units and different types of nodes [22]. The performance of CART [4] on this task has been reported in [29]. These results are given in table 5. The NTN algorithm was used to grow a NTN using the training data of 528 training samples. A modified version of the pruning algorithm given in [4] was used to prune the NTN. The performance of the NTN on the test set is shown in table 5. The table shows that the NTN performs much better than CART but is similar in performance to a feedforward neural network with radial basis function nodes or guassian nodes. The NTN, however, grows the correct number of neurons while learning as opposed to feedforward neural networks where one must know the number of hidden neurons before learning can begin. As shown in the table 5, if the number of hidden units is not chosen properly, the performance is quite poor. The new NTN algorithm also trains much faster than backpropagation on this task.

6   Summary and Conclusion

We have introduced a new neural network architecture which combines decision trees and feedforward neural networks. This architecture offers an attractive implementation trade-off over conventional feedforward neural nets. The new learning algorithm grows the network as opposed to backpropagation where the network architecture has to specified before learning can begin. The new algorithm forms splits of the training data using a gradient descent technique and does not have to resort to exhaustive search techniques as used in ID3 and CART. We have presented simulation results which show that the new method grows smaller trees than conventional decision tree approaches and also trains faster than backpropagation.

Classifier	Number of hidden units	Percent correct
Single-layer perceptron	–	33
Multi-layer perceptron	88	51
Multi-layer perceptron	22	45
Multi-layer perceptron	11	44
Radial Basis Function	528	53
Radial Basis Function	88	48
Guassian Node Network	528	55
Guassian Node Network	88	53
Guassian Node Network	22	54
Guassian Node Network	11	47
Square Node Network	88	55
Square Node Network	22	51
Square Node Network	11	50
Nearest Neighbor	–	56
CART	–	44
NTN	–	54

Table 5: Results on Speaker Independent Vowel Recognition

Bibliography

[1] A.Sankar and R.J. Mammone. A Fast Learning Algorithm for Tree Neural Networks. In *Proceedings of the 1990 Conference on Information Sciences and Systems*, pages 638–642, March 1990.

[2] E.B. Baum. On the capabilities of multilayer perceptrons. *Journal of Complexity*, 4(3):193–215, September 1988.

[3] E.B. Baum. What Size Net Gives Valid Generalization? *Neural Computation*, 1(1):151–160, 1989.

[4] L. Breiman, J.H. Friedman, R.A. Olshen, and C.J. Stone. *Classification and Regression Trees*. Wadsworth international group, Belmont,CA, 1984.

[5] G.A. Carpenter and S. Grossberg. Neural Dynamics of Category Learning and Recognition: Attention, Memory Consolidation and Amnesia. *Brain Structure, Learning and Memory*, 1986.

[6] M.A. Cohen and S. Grossberg. Absolute Stability of Global Pattern Formation and Parallel Memory Storage by Competitive Neural Networks. *IEEE Transactions on Systems, Man and Cybernetics*, SMC-13(5):815–826, 1983.

[7] Thomas M. Cover. Geometrical and statistical properties of systems of linear inequalities with applications in pattern recognition. *IEEE Transactions on Electronic Computers*, 1965.

[8] R.O. Duda and P.E. Hart. *Pattern Classification and Scene Analysis*. John Wiley & sons, 1973.

[9] K.S. Fu. *Syntactic Pattern Recognition and Applications*. Prentice Hall, 1982.

[10] C.R.P. Hartmann, P.K. Varshney, K.G. Mehrotra, and C.L. Gerberich. Application of Information Theory to the Construction of Efficient Decision Trees. *IEEE Transactions on Information Theory*, IT-28:565–577, July 1982.

[11] J.J. Hopfield. Neural Networks and Pysical Systems with Emergent Collective Computational Abilities. *Proceedings of the National Academy of Science*, 79:2554–2558, April 1982.

[12] J.J. Hopfield. Neurons with Graded Response have Collective Computational Properties like those of Two State Neurons. *Proceedings of the National Academy of Science*, 81:3088–3092, May 1984.

[13] L. Hyafil and R.L. Rivest. Constructing Optimal Decision Trees is NP-Complete. *Information Processing Letters*, 5(1):15–17, 1976.

[14] Stephen Judd. Learning in networks is hard. In *Proceedings of the IEEE First International Conference on Neural Networks*, volume 2, pages 685–692, June 1987.

[15] T. Kohonen. Self Organized Formation of Topologically Correct Feature Maps. *Biological Cybernetics*, 43:59–69, 1982.

[16] T. Kohonen. *Self Organization and Associative Memory*. Springer Verlag, 1984.

[17] T. Kohonen. The Neural Phonetic Typewriter. *Computer*, pages 1–2, 1988.

[18] S. Muroga. *Threshold logic and its applications*, pages 271–272. Wiley, 1971.

[19] D.B. Parker. Learning Logic. Technical Report TR-47, MIT, Center for computational research in economics and management science, 1985.

[20] J.R. Quinlan. *Learning Efficient Classification Procedures and their Applications to Chess End Games*. Tioga Publishing Company, Palo Alto, 1983. In R.S. Michalski, J.G. Carbonell and T.M. Mitchell,(Eds), Machine Learning: An artificial intelligence approach.

[21] J.R. Quinlan. Induction of Decision Trees. *Machine Learning*, 1:81–106, 1986.

[22] A.J. Robinson. *Dynamic Error Propagation networks*. PhD thesis, CAmbridge University Engineering Department, 1989.

[23] F. Rosenblatt. *Principles of Neurodynamics*. Spartan, New York, 1962.

[24] D.E. Rumelhart and J.L. McClelland. *Parallel Distributed Processing*. MIT Cambridge Press, 1986.

[25] A. Sankar and R.J. Mammone. A new fast learning algorithm for feedforward neural networks using the l1 norm of the error. Technical Report TR-115, Rutgers University, 1990.

[26] A. Sankar and R.J. Mammone. Tree structured neural networks. Technical Report TR-122, Rutgers University, 1990.

[27] I.K. Sethi and B. Chaterjee. Efficient decision tree design for discrete variable pattern recognition problems. *Pattern Recognition*, 9:197–206, 1978.

[28] J.T. Tou and R.C. Gonzalez. *Pattern Recognition Principles*. Addison-Wesley, 1974.

[29] Ah Chung Tsoi and R.A. Pearson. Comparison of three classification techniques, cart, c4.5, and multi-layer perceptrons. Presented at NIPS 1990.

[30] J.R. Ullmann. *Pattern Recognition Techniques*. Crane, Russak & Co., 1973.

[31] P.E. Utgoff. Perceptron trees: A case study in hybrid concept representation. In *Proceedings of the seventh national conference on artificial intelligence*, St. Paul, MN, 1988. Morgan-Kaufman.

[32] P. Werbos. *Beyond Regression: New tools for prediction and analysis in the behavioral sciences*. PhD thesis, Harvard University, 1974.

[33] B. Widrow and S.D. Stearns. *Adaptive Signal Processing*. Prentice-Hall, New Jersey, 1985.

Capabilities and Training of Feedforward Nets

Eduardo D. Sontag
Rutgers University

1 Introduction

This paper surveys recent work by the author on learning and representational capabilities of feedforward nets. The learning results show that, among two possible variants of the so-called backpropagation training method for sigmoidal nets, both of which variants are used in practice, one is a better generalization of the older perceptron training algorithm than the other. The representation results show that nets consisting of sigmoidal neurons have at least twice the representational capabilities of nets that use classical threshold neurons, at least when this increase is quantified in terms of classification power. On the other hand, threshold nets are shown to be more useful when approximating implicit functions, as illustrated with an application to a typical control problem.

1.1 Classification Problems

One typical application of neural nets is in binary classification problems. During a training or supervised learning stage, examples and counterexamples, labeled *true* and *false* respectively, are presented, and parameters are adjusted so as to make the network's numerical output consistent with the desired labels. (Various conventions can be used: for instance, a positive output may be understood as *true* and a negative one as *false*.) Later, during actual operation, the output given by the net when a new input is presented will be taken as the network's guess at a classification.

One set of issues to be addressed when implementing the above ideas deals with the algorithms used for the adjustment of parameters during the training stage. Typically, a *cost* function is proposed, that measures the discrepancy between the desired output and the output of a net having a given set of parameters. One then attempts to minimize this cost, over the space of all parameters, to arrive at a network that best matches the given training data. This last step involves a hard nonlinear minimization problem, and several variants of gradient descent have been proposed to solve it; in fact, the use of sigmoidal activation functions –as opposed to simpler thresholds– is to a great extent motivated by the requirement that the cost should be differentiable as a function of the parameters, so that gradient descent can be employed. There is one major exception to the use of gradient descent and sigmoids, though, and that is the case of networks having no (or equivalently from the viewpoint of representation, just one) hidden unit; in that case one can apply either linear programming techniques or the classical "perceptron learning rule," because the problem is then essentially linear. Section 2 deals with minimization problems; we show that among two possible variants of the cost functions, the gradient descent approach applied to one reduces perfectly to the older perceptron rule, while the other results in serious potential problems, including convergence to inconsistent parameters. (It would appear that in practice, both techniques are used without regard to these dangers; in fact, the "bad" variant is the one most often described in papers.)

A second and equally important set of issues deals with the architecture of the network: type of activation functions, number of units, interconnection pattern. Typically, in classification problems, one uses either "threshold" or "sigmoidal" units and these are arranged in a feedforward manner. A good rule of thumb is that the number of units (and hence of tunable parameters) should be small; otherwise the network will tend to "memorize" the training data, with no data compression or "feature extraction," and it will not be able to classify correctly inputs which had not been seen during the training stage. (This informal rule can be justified in various manners, theoretically through the use of "PAC" learning, or experimentally through the generation of random training and testing inputs based on given probability distributions.) Thus it is of interest to study the minimal number of neurons needed in order to attain a certain classification objective; Section 3 below deals with this problem. Some of the main conclusions quantify the difference between the use of sigmoidal versus threshold nets. Section 4 deals with the problem of interpolation as opposed to classification, but for sigmoidal nets one obtains similar estimates as before. Finally, Section 5 shows that multiple hidden layers increase approximation capabilities, if one is interested in approximating not just continuous functions but also inverses of such functions, as illustrated with an example from control theory.

1.2 Basic Definitions

Let N be a positive integer. A *dichotomy* (S_-, S_+) on a finite set $S \subseteq \mathbb{R}^N$ is a partition $S = S_- \bigcup S_+$ of S into two disjoint subsets. (One often expresses this as a "coloring" of S into two colors.) A function $f : \mathbb{R}^N \to \mathbb{R}$ will be said to *implement* this dichotomy if it holds that

$$f(u) > 0 \text{ for } u \in S_+ \text{ and } f(u) < 0 \text{ for } u \in S_- \ .$$

We define a "neural net" as a function of a certain type, corresponding to the idea of feedforward interconnections, via additive links, of neurons each of which has a scalar response θ. For any fixed function $\theta : \mathbb{R} \to \mathbb{R}$, we say that f is a *single hidden layer neural net with k hidden neurons of type θ and no direct input to output connections* (or just that f is a "(k, θ)-net") if there are real numbers

$$w_0, w_1, \ldots, w_k, \tau_1, \ldots, \tau_k$$

and vectors

$$v_1, \ldots, v_k \in \mathbb{R}^N$$

such that, for all $u \in \mathbb{R}^N$,

$$f(u) = w_0 + \sum_{i=1}^{k} w_i \, \theta(v_i.u - \tau_i) \tag{1}$$

where the dot indicates inner product.

For fixed θ, and under mild assumptions on θ, such neural nets can be used to approximate uniformly arbitrary continuous functions on compacts. See for instance [6], [8]. In particular, they can be used to implement arbitrary dichotomies on finite sets.

In neural net practice, one often takes θ to be the *standard sigmoid*

$$\theta(x) = \sigma(x) = \frac{1}{1 + e^{-x}}$$

or equivalently, up to translations and change of coordinates, the hyperbolic tangent $\theta(x) = \tanh(x)$. Another usual choice is the hardlimiter or *Heaviside* or *threshold* function

$$\theta(x) = \mathcal{H}(x) = \begin{cases} 0 & \text{if } x \le 0 \\ 1 & \text{if } x > 0 \end{cases}$$

which can be approximated well by $\sigma(\gamma x)$ when the "gain" γ is large. Most analysis, including studies of circuit complexity and the theory of threshold logic, has been done for $\mathcal{H}$, but as explained earlier, in practice one often uses the standard sigmoid.

2 Gradient Descent

Assume that one wishes to find a function f that implements a given dichotomy (S_-, S_+) on a set S, and f is to be chosen from a class of functions parameterized by variables $\mu = (\mu_1, \ldots, \mu_\kappa)$ (for instance, the class of all (k, θ)-nets, for fixed k and θ, parameterized by the possible weights and biases v_i, τ_i). Write for now $F(u, \mu)$ for the function $f(u)$ obtained when using the parameters μ. Thus, we wish to find a set of values for the parameters μ so that $F(u, \mu) > 0$ for $u \in S_+$ and $F(u, \mu) < 0$ for $u \in S_-$. As described in the Introduction, one approach is to set up an error function

$$E(\mu) := \sum_{u \in S} E_u(\mu)$$

where $E_u(\mu)$ measures the failure of $F(u, \mu)$ to be positive, if $u \in S_+$, or the failure of $F(u, \mu)$ to be negative, if $u \in S_+$. The question to be treated next has to do with the precise choice of these measures $E_u(\mu)$. Since the point that we are interested in discussing is already well illustrated by the particular case of $(1,\theta)$-nets, we shall restrict for the remainder of this section to $k = 1$.

As far as recognition properties are concerned, nets with $k = 1$ implement linearly separable dichotomies. More precisely, assume that θ is a nondecreasing function, and that the following property holds:

(P) $t_+ := \lim_{x \to +\infty} \theta(x)$ and $t_- := \lim_{x \to -\infty} \theta(x)$ exist, $t_- < t_+$.

Fix any real number λ in the interval (t_-, t_+). Then, the following properties are equivalent, for any given finite dichotomy (S_-, S_+):

1. There is some $(1,\theta)$-net implementing this dichotomy.

2. There exist $\bar{v} \in \mathbb{R}^N$ and $\bar{\tau} \in \mathbb{R}$ such that

$$\bar{v}.u > \bar{\tau} \text{ for } u \in S_+ \text{ and } \bar{v}.u < \bar{\tau} \text{ for } u \in S_- . \qquad (2)$$

3. There exist $v \in \mathbb{R}^N$ and $\tau \in \mathbb{R}$ such that

$$\theta(v.u - \tau) > \lambda \text{ for } u \in S_+ \text{ and } \theta(v.u - \tau) < \lambda \text{ for } u \in S_- . \qquad (3)$$

The equivalence is trivial from the definitions: Property 1 means that there are v, τ, w_0, w such that

$$w_0 + w\theta(v.u - \tau) \qquad (4)$$

has the right sign; if $w > 0$, this implies that $\theta(v.u_+ - \tau) > \theta(v.u_- - \tau)$ whenever $x_+ \in S_+$ and $x_- \in S_-$, which in turn implies (because θ is nondecreasing) that $v.x_+ > v.u_-$ for such pairs, and therefore Property 2 holds too. On the other hand, if Property 2 holds, then

$$\lim_{\gamma \to +\infty} \gamma(\bar{v}.u - \bar{\tau}) = +\infty$$

uniformly on the finite set S_+, which implies that $\theta(\gamma(\bar{v}.u - \bar{\tau})) > \lambda$ for all $u \in S_+$ if γ is large enough, and for the same reason $\theta(\gamma(\bar{v}.u - \bar{\tau})) < \lambda$ for all $u \in S_-$ for such γ, so Property 3 holds too. Finally, if this latter Property holds then the net in Equation (4) implements the dichotomy, using $w = 1$ and $w_0 = -\lambda$.

Given a dichotomy, the problem of determining if there exist a vector $\overline{v} \in \mathbb{R}^N$ and a number $\overline{\tau} \in \mathbb{R}$ such that Equation (2) holds (that is, if the sets S_+ and S_- are *linearly separable*) is a simple linear programming question, and there are very efficient methods for solving it as well as for finding explicit solutions $(\overline{v}, \overline{\tau})$. More in connection with nets, the classical *perceptron learning procedure* (see e.g. [7]) provides a recursive rule for finding one such solution provided that any exist. The perceptron rule is very simple, and it is worth recalling next, since we shall later compare it to gradient descent. We write

$$\hat{u} := (u, -1) \tag{5}$$

for each element of S, and use the notations $\hat{S}$, $\hat{S}_+$, and $\hat{S}_-$ for the points of the form $(u, -1)$ with u in S, S_+, and S_- respectively. Using these notations, the question becomes that of finding a vector

$$\nu = (\overline{v}, \overline{\tau}) \tag{6}$$

such that $\nu.\hat{u} < 0$ if $\hat{u} \in \hat{S}_+$ and this inner product is negative on $\hat{S}_-$. We first give an arbitrary starting value for ν. Now the possible elements in $\hat{S}$ are presented one after the other in an infinite sequence, with the only restriction that every element must appear infinitely often. For each element of this sequence, the corresponding inequality is tested. If the sign of the inequality is wrong, the estimate for ν is updated as follows: $\nu := \nu + \hat{u}$ if $\hat{u}$ is in $\hat{S}_+$, and $\nu := \nu - \hat{u}$ if $\hat{u}$ is in $\hat{S}_-$; if the sign was right, no change is made. It is a very old result that this procedure converges in finitely many steps to a solution ν, when starting at any initial guess for ν, if the original sets are linearly separable.

Since the existence of $v \in \mathbb{R}^N$ and $\tau \in \mathbb{R}$ such that Equation (3) holds is equivalent to the solution of the linear separability problem, it would seem useless to study directly Property 3. However, we wish to do so in order to exhibit in this simplified case some problems that may arise in the general case of hidden units ($k > 1$), which is not so easy to analyse. (We have observed the same problems experimentally, but there seems to be no easy way to give a theorem in the general case.) We deal with that Property next.

The restriction to the case $k = 1$ of the popular "backpropagation" technique for solving this problem –or at least of one often-used variant of it,– is essentially as follows. First pick two numbers α and β so that $t_- < \alpha < \lambda < \beta < t_+$. Using again the notation in Equations (5) and (6), now consider the cost

$$E(\nu) := (1/2) \sum_{\hat{u} \in \hat{S}} (\delta_{\hat{u}} - \theta(\nu.\hat{u}))^2 \qquad (7)$$

where $\delta_{\hat{u}}$ equals β if $\hat{u} \in \hat{S}_+$ and equals α otherwise. (The terminology "target values" is standard for α and β.) One now attempts to minimize E as a function of ν. If a small value results, it will follow that $\theta(\nu.\hat{u})$ will be approximately equal to α, and hence less than λ, when $\hat{u} \in \hat{S}_-$, and similarly for elements of $\hat{S}_+$, and the classification problem is solved. Unfortunately, there are local minima problems associated to this procedure; see for instance [17], [4], [11]. False (i.e., non-global) local minima can occur *even if the sets are separable*. Moreover, even if there is only one local (and hence global) minimum, the resulting solution may fail to separate (hence the title of [4]). (For a theoretical study of local minima in a more general hidden-unit case, $k > 1$, see for instance [3] and references there.)

The reason for this difficulty is very simple to understand, and is as follows: In trying to minimize E, one is trying to fit the values α and β *exactly*, when it would be sufficient for classification that $\theta(\nu.\hat{u})$ be less than α for $\hat{u}$ in $\hat{S}_-$, and bigger than β for $\hat{u}$ in $\hat{S}_+$. The precise fitting may force the parameters ν to be chosen so as to make most terms small at the cost of leaving one term large. This can be illustrated with an example. Assume that $N = 1$ and S consists of five points u_i so that u_1 and u_2 are very close to -1, u_3 and u_4 are very close to 1, and $u_5 = -0.9$. The dichotomy is given by $S_- := \{u_1, u_2\}$ and $S_+ := \{u_3, u_4, u_5\}$. Obviously these are linearly separable (pick $\bar{v} = 1, \bar{\tau} = -0.95$). We now pose the minimization problem, using the standard sigmoid $\theta = \sigma$, $\lambda := 0.5$, and target values $\alpha := 0.2$, $\beta := 0.8$. That is, we must minimize the error

$$(0.8 - \sigma(-0.9v - \tau))^2 + 2(0.8 - \sigma(v - \tau))^2 + 2(0.2 - \sigma(-v - \tau))^2$$

as a function of v and τ. There is a unique local (and global) minimum, attained at the unique values $v = 0.971$ and $\tau = -0.516$. It turns out that these parameter values do not separate: for $\hat{u} = (-0.9, 1)$, $\sigma(v.\hat{u}) = 0.411 < 0.5$. The classification of x_5 has been traded-off for a better perfect fit of the other points. Note that the cutoff between classes happens approximately at $\hat{u} = -1/2$. (Of course, redefining λ as 0.4 one could say that this solution f separates, but this redefinition can only be done a fortriori, once we know the solution. In any case, it is easy to give examples in dimension $N = 2$ in which the same pathology happens but where there is no possible redefinition of λ that helps; see the references cited earlier.) Figure 1 (function f in the plot, darker one) shows the resulting $(1, \sigma)$-net.

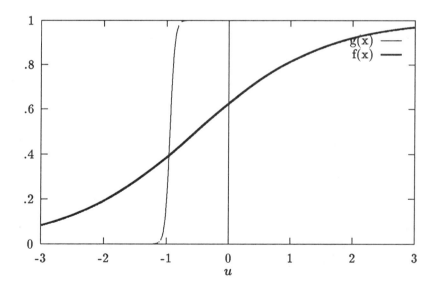

Figure 1: *Non-separating minimum*

The second plot in Figure 1, corresponding to the function

$$g(x) = \sigma(27.73x + 26.34),$$

does satisfy Property 3 (the values for -1, -0.9 and 1 are at 0.2, 0.8, and approximately 1, respectively; the cutoff with $\lambda = 0.5$ happens at $u = -0.95$). The parameters $(27.73, 26.34)$ were obtained as described below; they are *not* obtained by minimizing the above error function.

The solution to the difficulties raised by the above discussion, namely that gradient descent may give wrong results even when the data is separable, lies in not adding a penalty if $\theta(v.\hat{u})$ is already less than α and $\hat{u} \in \hat{S}_-$ (and similarly for $\hat{S}_+$). In other words, the corresponding term in Equation (7) is taken to be zero. Thus one has to minimize the new function

$$E^*(v) := (1/2) \sum_{\hat{u} \in \hat{S}} (\delta_{\hat{u}} - \theta(v.\hat{u}))^2_{\varepsilon(\hat{u})} \tag{8}$$

where we are using the notations

$$(r)^2_+ := \begin{cases} 0 & \text{if } r \leq 0 \\ r^2 & \text{if } r > 0 \end{cases}$$

and $(r)^2_- := (-r)^2_+$ for any number r, and $\varepsilon(\hat{u}) = +$ if $\hat{u} \in \hat{S}_+$ or $\varepsilon(\hat{u}) = -$ if $\hat{u} \in \hat{S}_-$.

The new error function E^* will be called, for lack of a better term, the "nonstrict" error measure corresponding to the problem at hand; note that E is differentiable (if θ is), but in general is not second-order differentiable. To motivate the use of this measure, a comparison with the perceptron procedure is useful. A discrete gradient descent step for minimizing E^* takes the form of updating each parameter v_i (where v_i denotes the ith coordinate of v) by iterating the rule:

$$v_i := v_i + \rho \hat{u}_i$$

($\hat{u}_i$ is the ith coordinate of $\hat{u}$), where

$$\rho = (\delta_{\hat{u}} - \theta(v.\hat{u}))\theta'(v.\hat{u}) \tag{9}$$

if the classification is incorrect and $\rho = 0$ otherwise. This is the precise analogue of the perceptron rule (for which ρ is always either zero or ± 1). When using E instead of E^* one would use Equation (9) always, even if the classification was correct. The function g in Figure 1 was obtained by minimizing E^* (we used a numerical technique, as a test of the method, but the solution can be obtained in closed form: just fit exactly the values at -1 and -0.9 to obtain $v = 20 \ln 4$ and $\tau = -19 \ln 4$; the value at 1 has been relaxed to about 1, which is greater than 0.8 but contributes zero error in the nonstrict error measure).

The use of E^* was first suggested in [17], who also proved a convergence result under restrictive hypotheses (which do not allow for sigmoids). In [16], we proved that there are no false local minima for E^* if the data is separable, and that the gradient descent differential equation converges in finite time to a separating solution, from a random initial state. Note that the unique minimum of E^* is zero, for separable data, and it is achieved at any separating solution. (Actually, the result proved there is considerably more general, as it deals with a wider class of optimization problems. The only difficulty in the proof has to do with the fact that ρ will tend to zero; one has to use a dynamical-systems argument involving LaSalle invariance.)

Thus we conclude that the use of a nonstrict error function provides the correct generalization of the perceptron learning rule. This provides strong evidence that one should use nonstrict error functions also in the general (hidden unit) case. In [16] we also compared the sigmoid results to known facts in pattern recognition, where nonstrict measures had also been proposed (for linear activation functions σ). This paper also showed why, *even if using the nonstrict measure*, there may be false local minima (for nonseparable data), even for $k = 1$ (no hidden units) and binary training vectors; the necessary counterexample was based on a construction in [15].

3   Representational Capabilities

One may express the classification power of a class of functions, such as those computable by neural nets with a fixed architecture and a fixed number of neurons, in terms of set shattering. In this approach, a class of functions is considered to be more powerful than another if it can be used to implement arbitrary partitions on sets of larger cardinality.

Let $\mathcal{F}$ be a class of functions from $\mathbb{R}^N$ to $\mathbb{R}$, assumed to be nontrivial, in the sense that for each point $u \in \mathbb{R}^N$ there is some $f_1 \in \mathcal{F}$ so that $f_1(u) > 0$ and some $f_2 \in \mathcal{F}$ so that $f_2(u) < 0$. This class *shatters* the set $S \subseteq R^N$ if each dichotomy on S can be implemented by some $f \in \mathcal{F}$.

As in [12], we consider for any class of functions $\mathcal{F}$ as above, the following two measures of classification power, dealing with "best" and "worst" cases respectively: $\overline{\mu}(\mathcal{F})$ denotes the largest integer $1 \leq l$ (possibly ∞) so that there is at least *some* set S of cardinality l in $\mathbb{R}^N$ which can be shattered by $\mathcal{F}$, while $\underline{\mu}(\mathcal{F})$ is the largest integer $1 \leq l$ (possibly ∞) so that *every* set of cardinality l can be shattered by $\mathcal{F}$. Note that $\underline{\mu}(\mathcal{F}) \leq \overline{\mu}(\mathcal{F})$ for every class $\mathcal{F}$. The integer $\overline{\mu}$ is the same as the *Vapnik-Chervonenkis (VC) dimension* of the class $\mathcal{F}$ (see for instance [2] for VC dimension).

Some of the results obtained in [12] are as follows. We use the notation $\underline{\mu}(k, \theta, N)$ for $\underline{\mu}(\mathcal{F})$ if $\mathcal{F}$ is the class of (k, θ)-nets in $\mathbb{R}^N$, and similarly for $\overline{\mu}$.

Theorem 1 *For each k, N, $\underline{\mu}(k, \mathcal{H}, N) = k + 1$, $\underline{\mu}(k, \sigma, N) \geq 2k$.* ∎

Theorem 2 *For each k, $2k + 1 \leq \overline{\mu}(k, \mathcal{H}, 2)$, $4k - 1 \leq \overline{\mu}(k, \sigma, 2)$.* ∎

The main conclusion from the first result is that sigmoids at least double recognition power for arbitrary sets. We conjecture that

$$\frac{\overline{\mu}(k, \sigma, N)}{\overline{\mu}(k, \mathcal{H}, N)} = 2 + O\left(\frac{1}{k}\right)$$

for all N; this is true for $N = 1$ and is strongly suggested by Theorem 2 (the first bound appears to be quite tight). Unfortunately the proof of this theorem is based on a result from [1] regarding arrangements of points in the plane, a fact which does not generalize to dimension three or higher. Other results in [12] deal with the effect of direct connections from inputs to outputs.

Finally, we also gave in [12] results valid specifically for sets of binary vectors. For example, it is a trivial consequence from the given

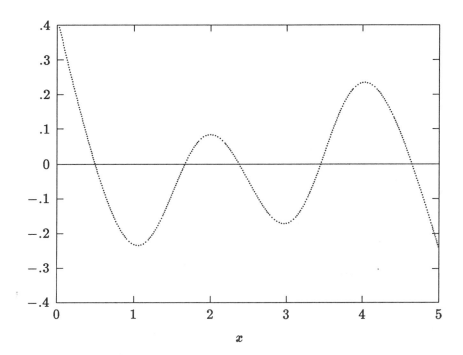

Figure 2: 5-bit parity with 3 sigmoids

results that parity on n bits can be computed with $\lceil \frac{n+1}{2} \rceil$ hidden sigmoidal units (rather than the n that –apparently, though it is still an open problem– are needed when using Heavisides). For instance,

$$f(x) := 10.4 + 2\sigma(3x - 4.5) + 2\sigma(3x - 10.5) - 20\sigma(x/5)$$

computes 5-bit parity with 3 sigmoidal neurons, $x := \sum x_i$. (See Figure 2.)

It is also shown in [12] that the function of $2n$ variables (say, with n odd),

$$\text{XOR} \left(\text{MAJ} (x_1, \dots, x_n), \text{MAJ} (y_1, \dots, y_n) \right)$$

(where $\text{MAJ} (x_1, \dots, x_n)$ is the "majority" function that equals "1" if the majority of the x_i's are one, and zero otherwise,) can be implemented by nets with a fixed number (four) of sigmoidal neurons, that is, a $(4, \sigma)$-net, independently of n, but it can be shown –personal communication by W. Maass– that it is impossible to implement such functions with $(k, \mathcal{H})$-nets, k independent of n.

4 Interpolation

Assume now that θ satisfies (P) with $t_- = -1$ and $t_+ = 1$ (this can be always assumed after rescaling) that in addition it is continuous and there is some point c such that θ is differentiable at c and $\theta'(c) \neq 0$. For instance, the standard response function tanh (or σ after rescaling) satisfies these properties. For such a θ we have:

Theorem 3 *Given any $2n + 1$ (distinct) points $x_0, \ldots, x_{2n}$ in R^N, any $\varepsilon > 0$, and any sequence of real numbers $y_0, \ldots, y_{2n}$, there exists some $(n + 1, \theta)$-net f such that $|f(x_i) - y_i| < \varepsilon$ for each i.*

Before proving this theorem, we establish an easy technical result:

Lemma 4.1 Assume given real numbers $p, q, \alpha, \beta, \varepsilon, \delta$ so that $\varepsilon > 0$, $\delta > 0$, and $\alpha < q < \beta$. Then, there exists some real numbers a, b, c, d so that, if $f(x) := d + a\theta(bx + c)$, then the following properties hold:

1. $f(p) = q$.

2. $|f(x) - \alpha| < \varepsilon$ for all $x \leq p - \delta$.

3. $|f(x) - \beta| < \varepsilon$ for all $x \geq p + \delta$.

Proof. Let $\rho > 0$ be smaller than $\beta - q$, $q - \alpha$, and ε. Consider the function
$$g(\xi) := \frac{\beta - \alpha}{2}\theta(\xi) + \frac{\beta + \alpha}{2} .$$
Note that $g(\xi)$ approaches α, β at $-\infty, +\infty$, so there is some $K > 0$ so that $|g(\xi) - \alpha| < \rho$ if $\xi \leq -K$ and $|g(\xi) - \beta| < \rho$ if $\xi \geq K$. Pick any $\gamma > 2K/\delta$ and define for this γ, $f_0(x) := g(\gamma x)$. Then,

$$|f_0(x) - \alpha| < \rho \text{ if } x \leq -\delta/2$$

and
$$|f_0(x) - \beta| < \rho \text{ if } x \geq \delta/2 \ .$$

As $f_0(\delta/2) > \beta - \rho > q$ and $f_0(-\delta/2) < \alpha + \rho < q$, by continuity of f_0 (here we use that θ is continuous) there must be some $u \in (-\delta/2, \delta/2)$ so that $f_0(u) = q$. Finally, we let

$$f(x) := f_0(x + u - p) \ .$$

Clearly this satisfies $f(p) = q$. For any $x \leq p - \delta$ it holds that $z := x + u - p \leq -\delta/2$, so $|f(x) - \alpha| = |f_0(z) - \alpha| < \rho < \varepsilon$, as desired. The property for $x \geq \delta/2$ is proved analogously. ∎

Now we prove Theorem 3. Note first that it is sufficient to prove it for $N = 1$, as one can perform the usual reduction of first finding a vector v whose inner products with the x_i's are all distinct. Now assume that we have already proved that for any two *increasing* sequences of real numbers

$$x_0 < x_1 < \ldots < x_{2n} \text{ and } z_0 < z_1 < \ldots < z_{2n} \tag{10}$$

there is some (k, θ)-net so that

$$|f(x_i) - z_i| < \varepsilon/2 \tag{11}$$

for each i. The result then follows from here. Indeed, given the original data, we may assume that the x_i are already in increasing order (reorder them, if necessary). Now pick any real d so that

$$d > \frac{y_i - y_{i+1}}{x_{i+1} - x_i}$$

for all $i = 0, \ldots, 2n - 1$. Letting $z_i := x_i d + y_i$, these are now in increasing order. Let f be so that equation (11) holds for each i. By Lemma 7.2 in [12], there are some numbers a, b, c so that

$$|a + \theta(bx_i + c) + dx_i| < \varepsilon/2$$

for each i. Then $|f(x_i) + a + \theta(bx_i + c) - y_i| < \varepsilon$, as wanted.

Thus, we must prove the result for the particular case of increasing sequences (10), which we do via an argument somewhat analogous to that used in [5] for showing the (weaker) fact that one can approximately interpolate n points using $n - 1$ neurons. We show inductively:

Given data (10) and any $\varepsilon > 0$, there exists an (n, θ)-net f so that

$$|f(x_i) - z_i| < \varepsilon \text{ for each } i = 0, \ldots, 2n \tag{12}$$

and

$$|f(x) - z_{2n}| < \varepsilon \text{ for all } x \geq x_{2n} . \tag{13}$$

For $n = 1$ this follows from Lemma 4.1, by choosing $p = x_1$, $q = z_1$, $\alpha = z_0$, $\beta = z_2$, and δ less than $x_1 - x_0$ and $x_2 - x_1$. Assume now that an $(n - 1, \theta)$-net f_1 has been obtained for $x_0, \ldots, x_{2n-2}$ and $z_0, \ldots, z_{2n-2}$, and so that

$$|f_1(x_i) - z_i| < \varepsilon/2 \text{ for each } i = 0, \ldots, 2n - 2 \tag{14}$$

and

$$|f_1(x) - z_{2n-2}| < \varepsilon/2 \text{ for all } x \geq x_{2n-2} . \tag{15}$$

Note that this last inequality holds in particular for x_{2n-1} as well as for all $x \geq x_{2n}$. Now let f_2 be as in Lemma 4.1, with δ less than $x_{2n-1} - x_{2n-2}$ and $x_{2n} - x_{2n-1}$, $\alpha = 0$, $\beta = z_{2n} - z_{2n-2}$, $q = z_{2n-1} - z_{2n-2}$, and $p = x_{2n-1}$, and so that

$$|f_2(x)| < \varepsilon/2 \text{ for all } x < x_{2n-1} - \delta \tag{16}$$

and

$$|f_2(x) - \beta| < \varepsilon/2 \text{ for all } x > x_{2n-1} + \delta . \tag{17}$$

It follows that $f := f_1 + f_2$ is as desired for the inductive step. This completes the proof of the Theorem. ∎

Thus we can approximately interpolate any $2n - 1$ points using n sigmoidal neurons. It is not hard to prove as a corollary that, for the standard sigmoid, this "approximate" interpolation property holds in the following stronger sense: for an open dense set of $2n - 1$ points, one can achieve an open dense set of values; the proof involves looking first at points with rational coordinates, and using that on such points one is dealing basically with rational functions (after a diffeomorphism), plus some theory of semialgebraic sets. We conjecture that one should be able to interpolate at $2n$ points. Note that for $n = 2$ this is easy to achieve: just choose the slope d so that some $z_i - z_{i+1}$ becomes zero and the z_i are allowed to be nonincreasing or nondecreasing. The same proof, changing the signs if necessary, gives the wanted net.

5 Inverting Functions

Until now, we dealt only with single-hidden layer nets. As remarked above, such nets are "universal" approximators, in the sense that they are dense in the space of continuous functions on any compact subset of $\mathbb{R}^n$, with uniform norm, and they are also dense in L^p, on compacts, for any finite p. These approximations hold for almost arbitrary functions θ. However, in a certain sense, which we describe next, such nets are less powerful than nets with two hidden layers. We will say that a function $f : \mathbb{R}^N \to \mathbb{R}$ is *computable by a two-hidden-layer net* if there exist l functions $f_1, \ldots, f_l$, $l \geq 0$, so that $f(u) = w_0 + \sum_{i=1}^{l} w_i \theta(f_i(u))$ for some $w_1, \ldots, w_l \in \mathbb{R}$ and the f_i's are single-hidden-layer nets.

It is proved in [14] that for each integers m, p, any continuous function $f : \mathbb{R}^m \to \mathbb{R}^p$, any compact subset $C \subseteq \mathbb{R}^p$ included in the image of f, and any $\varepsilon > 0$, there exists some function $\phi : \mathbb{R}^m \to \mathbb{R}^p$, each of whose coordinates is computable by a two-hidden-layer net, so that $\|f(\phi(u)) - u\| < \varepsilon$ for all $u \in C$. That is to say, one may always obtain approximations of (one-sided) inverses of continuous maps. (The proof is not hard, and follows closely the ideas in [9].) But it is also proved there that there are examples of functions f as above whose inverses cannot be approximated by single-hidden-layer nets. Essentially, the difficulty has to do with the fact that the universal approximation results do not hold in L^∞.

The results are applied in [14] to the following problem. Consider nonlinear control systems

$$x(t+1) \ = \ P(x(t), u(t)) \tag{18}$$

whose states evolve in $\mathbb{R}^n$, having controls $u(t)$ that take values in $\mathbb{R}^m$, and with P sufficiently smooth and satisfying $P(0,0) = 0$. We assume that the system can be *locally* stabilized with linear feedback, i.e. there is some matrix F so that the closed loop system with right-hand side $P(x(t), Fx(t))$ is locally asymptotically stable. (See for instance [13], Section 4.8, for more on the topic of nonlinear stabilizability.) The system (18) is *asymptotically controllable* if for each state x_0 there is some infinite control sequence $u(0), u(1), \ldots$ such that the corresponding solution with $x(0) = x_0$ satisfies that $x(t) \to 0$ as $t \to \infty$. This condition is obviously the weakest possible one if any type of controller is to stabilize the system. We say that $K : \mathbb{R}^n \to \mathbb{R}^m$ is a *type-1 feedback* if each coordinate of K has the form $Fx + f(x)$, where F is linear and f is a single-hidden layer net, and that it is a *type-2 feedback* if it can be written in this manner with f is computable by a two-hidden layer net. These are feedback laws that can be computed by nets with one or two hidden layers respectively, and having m output neurons and possible direct connections from inputs to outputs (these connections provide the linear term). The following is also proved in [14]:

Theorem 4 *Let $\theta = \mathcal{H}$. For each system as above, and each compact subset C of the state space, there exists some feedback law of type 2 that globally stabilizes (18) on C, that is, so that C is in the domain of asymptotically stability of $x^+ = P(x, K(x))$. On the other hand, there exist systems as above, and compact sets C, for which no possible feedback law of type 1 stabilizes C.* ∎

The positive result, in this case as well as for continuous time systems under sampling, is based on ideas from [10]. The negative result remains if $\theta = \tanh$, or if θ is one of many other functions used in neural net practice. Basically, the proof is based on the fact that single-layer nets cannot approximate inverses, but two hidden layers are sufficient. Other problems of interest, such as inverse kinematics approximation, have the same flavor.

6 Acknowledgements

This research was supported in part by Siemens Corporate Research, Princeton, NJ, and in part by the CAIP Center, Rutgers University.

Bibliography

[1] T. Asano, J. Hershberger, J. Pach, E.D. Sontag, D. Souivaine, and S. Suri, *Separating Bi-Chromatic Points by Parallel Lines*, Proceedings of the Second Canadian Conference on Computational Geometry, Ottawa, Canada, 1990, p. 46-49.

[2] E.B. Baum, *On the capabilities of multilayer perceptrons*, J.Complexity 4, 1988, p. 193-215.

[3] E.K. Blum *Approximation of Boolean functions by sigmoidal networks: Part I: XOR and other two-variable functions*, Neural Computation 1, 1989, p. 532-540.

[4] M. Brady, R. Raghavan and J. Slawny, *Backpropagation fails to separate where perceptrons succeed*, IEEE Trans. Circuits and Systems 36, 1989, p. 665-674.

[5] D. Chester, *Why two hidden layers and better than one*, Proc. Int. Joint Conf. on Neural Networks, Washington, DC, Jan. 1990, IEEE Publications, 1990, p. I.265-268.

[6] G. Cybenko, *Approximation by superpositions of a sigmoidal function*, Math. Control, Signals, and Systems 2, 1989, p. 303-314.

[7] R.O. Duda and P.E. Hart, *Pattern Classification and Scene Analysis*, Wiley, New York, 1973.

[8] K.M. Hornik, M. Stinchcombe, and H. White, *Multilayer feedforward networks are universal approximators*, Neural Networks 2, 1989, p. 359-366.

[9] E.D. Sontag, *Remarks on piecewise-linear algebra*, Pacific J.Math., 98, 1982, p. 183-201.

[10] E.D. Sontag, *Nonlinear regulation: The piecewise linear approach*, IEEE Trans. Autom. Control AC-26, 1981, p. 346-358.

[11] E.D. Sontag, *Some remarks on the backpropagation algorithm for neural net learning*, Report SYCON-88-02, *Rutgers Center for Systems and Control*, June 1988.

[12] E.D. Sontag, *Comparing sigmoids and Heavisides*, Proc. Conference Info. Sci. and Systems, Princeton, 1990, p. 654-659.

[13] E.D. Sontag, *Mathematical Control Theory: Deterministic Finite Dimensional Systems*, Springer, New York, 1990.

[14] E.D. Sontag, *Feedback Stabilization Using Two-Hidden-Layer Nets*, Report SYCON-90-11, *Rutgers Center for Systems and Control*, October 1990.

[15] E.D. Sontag and H.J. Sussmann *Backpropagation can give rise to spurious local minima even for networks without hidden layers*, Complex Systems **3**, 1989, p. 91-106.

[16] E.D. Sontag and H.J. Sussmann, *Backpropagation separates when perceptrons do*, in Proc. IEEE Int. Conf. Neural Networks, Washington, DC, June 1989, p. I-639/642.

[17] B.S. Wittner and J.S. Denker, *Strategies for teaching layered networks classification tasks*, Proc. Conf. Neural Info. Proc. Systems, Denver, 1987, Dana Anderson (Ed.), AIP Press.

A Fast Learning Algorithm for Multilayer Neural Network Based on Projection Methods

Shu-jen Yeh
Rensselaer Polytechnic Inst.

Henry Stark
Illinois Inst. of Technology

1 Introduction

Artificial neural nets shows great promise as associative memories [6, 7, 3] and pattern classifiers [2, 12, 4]. As is well known, the single layer perceptron can yield good results as pattern classifier when the classes are separable by hyperplanes but fails when this condition is not met. Thus the exclusive-or problem cannot be solved by a single layer neural net nor, for example, can the classification of classes distinguished by distance-from-the-origin [9]. On the other hand, many problems of practical interest can be solved by two-layer neural nets, including the ones cited above. To train a multi-layer neural net there exist a number of learning algorithms of which the back-propagation learning rule (BPLR) is the most popular. The BPLR is an iterative gradient search algorithm designed to minimize the mean-square error between the actual output of a multi-layer feed-forward net and the desired output. It is also well known that the BPLR shows good performance in learning but exhibits slow learning speed in many cases.

In Fig. 1 is shown , for the sake of illustration, a two-layer neural net, with $\mathbf{x}_i$ denoting the actual input, $\mathbf{y}_i^*$ the desired output and $\mathbf{y}_i$ the actual output. One way to view the slow convergence of the BPLR is to recall how it controls the network's learning. For each i, i.e., each specific training sample, the BPLR seeks to find the adjustments in the weight matrices $\mathbf{W}$ and $\mathbf{T}$ in an attempt

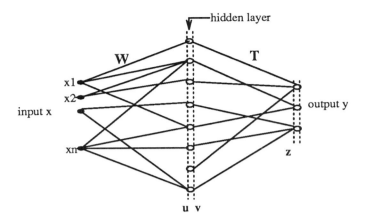

Figure 1: A two layer network. **W** and **T** are the interconnection weight matrices from input to hidden layer, and from hidden layer to output layer, respectively.

to minimize the error between $\mathbf{y}_i^*$ and $\mathbf{y}_i$. The trouble is that the adjustments made is case i may not be suitable for $i-1$ or $i+1$, etc. If the degree-of-freedom of the net (i.e., the number of nodes and interconnects) is large enough, then hopefully there will result a final pair of **W** and **T** matrices that will correctly classify most test patterns, if the training runs are numerous. By adjusting the net for each training sample without consideration of the others, the BPLR fails to develop the global strategy for the network optimization.

In this paper we attempt to develop a sequential learning rule that seeks to satisfy the multiple constraints imposed by the collection of training samples. The algorithm has its roots in the method of projections onto convex sets (POCS) [17, 14] and its extension to non-convex sets, the method of generalized projections (GP) [8].

To the best of our knowledge the first to use projection methods in neural nets study was Marks II and his co-workers; basically they related projection operators to the operations in the nets [10]. In this paper, our own use of projection methods in neural nets is quite different: we use these methods to develop iterative learning algorithms not unlike back-propagation but with different criteria;

the projection operators are used to adjust the weights in respond to the present training sample. In spirit, our work is much closer to Widrow's *minimal disturbance principle* in multilayer net learning [16] than it is to Marks' work.

In trying to develop a learning algorithm based on projection methods we ran into a number of difficulties. The first one was the non-convexity of the constraint sets imposed by individual training data $\{\mathbf{x}_i\}$. We decided to leave this as a topic for further research and applied the projectors as in the generalized projection methods.

Another problem that materialized was that the learning rule which resulted from the projection method is implicit. That is, the exact projection method formula is described by a system of coupled non-linear algebraic equations, which are difficult to solve analytically. Such a solution is somewhat impractical so one way to proceed is to make some approximations that would lead to a practical learning algorithm. The result of all these considerations is a learning rule which we called the projection-method learning rule (PMLR), although perhaps a more precise name would have been the *approximate* projection-method learning rule. As we shall see it gave good results for the learning problems considered.

The organization of this paper is as follows: in Section 2 we review briefly the projection methods. In Section 3 we derive the PMLR from first principles, and we apply it to the exclusive-or (XOR) problem and the distance-from-the-origin classification problem in Section 4. We also compare our results withe those from the BPLR for the same problems. Finally we furnish some concluding remarks in Section 5.

2   Review of Projection Methods

2.1   The Method of Projections Onto Convex Sets

POCS deals with the problem of finding an object (e.g. a signal, function, image, etc.) in a proper space that satisfies multiple constraints. When all constraint sets are convex, there exists a powerful theory in finding an object that satisfies all the constraints. Below we give a brief review of POCS.

The theory of convex projections developed by Bregman [1] and Gubin *et al.* [5] was first applied to image processing by Youla and Webb [18].

To begin with, assume that all the objects of interest are elements of a Hilbert space $\mathcal{H}$. Now consider a closed convex set $C \subset \mathcal{H}$. For any $f \in \mathcal{H}$, the projection Pf of f onto C is the element in C closest to f. If C is closed and convex, Pf exists and is uniquely determined by f and C from the minimality criterion

$$\| f - Pf \| = \min_{g \in C} \| f - g \|. \tag{1}$$

This rule, which assigns to every $f \in \mathcal{H}$ its nearest neighbor in C, defines the (in general) nonlinear projection operator $P : \mathcal{H} \to C$ without ambiguity.

The basic idea of the iterative POCS method is as follows: A known property of the unknown $f \in \mathcal{H}$ restricts f to lie in a closed convex set C_i. Thus, for m known properties there are m closed convex sets C_i, $i = 1, 2, \ldots, m$, and $f \in C_0 \doteq \cap_{i=1}^{m} C_i$. Then the problem is to find a point of C_0 given the sets C_i and the associated projection operators P_i, $i = 1, 2, \ldots m$. Based on fundamental theorems given by Opial [11] and Gubin *et al.* [5], the sequence $\{f_k\}$ generated by the recursion relation

$$f_{k+1} = P_m P_{m-1} \cdots P_1 f_k; \quad k = 0, 1, \ldots, \tag{2}$$

or more generally by

$$f_{k+1} = T_m T_{m-1} \cdots T_1 f_k; \quad k = 0, 1, \ldots \tag{3}$$

converges weakly to a point in C_0, where T_i is the relaxed projector defined as $T_i \doteq I + \mu_i(P_i - I), 0 < \mu_i < 2$. The μ_i's are relaxation parameters and can be used to accelerate the rate of convergence of the algorithm; I is the identity operator. However, determining the ideal values of the λ's is generally a difficult problem and for nonlinear convex sets they are often set to values somewhat arbitrarily between 1 and 2.

2.2 The Method of Generalized Projections

When one or more of the sets $C_1, C_2, \ldots, C_m$ are non-convex, the convergence of the algorithms given in (2) or (3) is not guaranteed, although sometimes the topology of the sets is such that convergence will almost always result (e.g. the case of two intersecting rings).

Levi and Stark [8] showed that if one or both of the sets C_1 and C_2 is nonconvex, then the algorithm (2) or (3) retains the *set-distance error reduction* (SDER) property. At any iteration, say the kth, we have

$$Z(f^{(k+1)}) \leq Z(T_1 f^{(k)}) \leq Z(f^{(k)}), \quad k = 0, 1, .. \qquad (4)$$

where the functional Z denotes the sum of the norm distances of its argument from the sets C_1 and C_2. That is, for y arbitrary in $\mathcal{H}$,

$$Z(y) \doteq \|P_1 y - y\| + \|P_2 y - y\|. \qquad (5)$$

The SDER property holds for a wide range of relaxation parameters including the value of unity [8]. The value of Z can be used to monitor the dynamics of the algorithm. Note that Z attains the value of zero if a feasible solution $\hat{f} \in C_0$ is reached. There is yet no general theory for non-convex projections regarding the condition under which the "trap" will or will not be present.

3 Derivation of the Projection Method Learning Rule

We adopt the notation used in Fig. 1 and demonstrate the derivation for two-layer (i.e. one hidden layer) network; the method is extendable to networks with more layers. Let N_{in} be the number of input nodes, N_h be the number of hidden-layer nodes, and N_{out} be the number of output nodes. The notation $(\mathbf{W}, \mathbf{T})$ refers to a two-tuple matrix pair that specifies the connection weights between layers of nodes and bias levels of neurons; that is, the adjustable bias level of a neuron is viewed as the connection weight from an additional node that has a fixed output value one. The mathematical working space is the collection of all such two-tuple matrix pairs with proper dimensions, with addition and multiplication operations being

$$(\mathbf{W}_1, \mathbf{T}_1) + (\mathbf{W}_2, \mathbf{T}_2) \doteq (\mathbf{W}_1 + \mathbf{W}_2, \mathbf{T}_1 + \mathbf{T}_2), \qquad (6)$$

$$\alpha(\mathbf{W}, \mathbf{T}) \doteq (\alpha\mathbf{W}, \alpha\mathbf{T}), \qquad (7)$$

inner product being

$$\langle (\mathbf{W}_1, \mathbf{T}_1), (\mathbf{W}_2, \mathbf{T}_2) \rangle \doteq \sum_{i,j} w_{1ij} w_{2ij} + \sum_{k,l} t_{1kl} t_{2kl}, \qquad (8)$$

and with inner-product derived norm. This space is isomorphic to the $N_h \times (N_{in} + 1) + N_{out} \times N_h$ dimensional Euclidean space, and it represents all possible variations of a two-layer network with the specific topology (i.e. number of input nodes, hidden nodes,...) and specific neuron activation functions.

The set $C_i \doteq \{(\mathbf{W}^*, \mathbf{T}^*) : \rho(\mathbf{T}^*\rho(\mathbf{W}^*\mathbf{x}_i)) = \mathbf{y}_i^*\}$ is the set of all matrix pairs $(\mathbf{W}^*, \mathbf{T}^*)$ that produce the desired output $\mathbf{y}_i^*$ when the training sample $\mathbf{x}_i$ is applied. The subscript i $(i = 1, \ldots, N_s)$ indicates the ith training sample or the constraint set imposed by that sample. We were not able to show the convexity of such sets in the present or other Hilbert space setting; however we decided to proceed with the projection method, since experiences with other problems involving nonconvex sets had shown us that the undesirable trap case did not always present itself and the projection method was worth trying even if nonconvex sets were involved.

The function $\rho(\cdot)$ is the point-wise non-linearity that characterizes the action of the neurons. Strictly speaking the neuron activation functions for the two layers need not be the same, although for simplicity, we assume they are.

In finding the projector upon C_i, we dropped the subscript i to simplify the notation. For any $(\mathbf{W}^*, \mathbf{T}^*) \in C$, we have

$$\mathbf{y}^* = \rho(\mathbf{T}^*\rho(\mathbf{W}^*\mathbf{x})), \qquad (9)$$

where $\mathbf{x}$ is an N_{in}−dimensional training vector $(x_1, \ldots, x_{N_{in}})^T$ and $\mathbf{y}^*$ is an N_{out}-dimensional vector $(y_1, \ldots, y_{N_{out}})^T$. We assume that $\rho(\cdot)$ is invertible and differentiable. Then with $\mathbf{z} \doteq \rho^{-1}(\mathbf{y})$ and $\mathbf{z}^* \doteq$

$\rho^{-1}(\mathbf{y}^*)$, the projector P is such that $P((\mathbf{W}, \mathbf{T})) = (\mathbf{W}^*, \mathbf{T}^*)$, subject to

$$\mathbf{z}^* = \mathbf{T}^* \rho(\mathbf{W}^* \mathbf{x}). \tag{10}$$

Thus the problem of finding the projection $(\mathbf{W}^*, \mathbf{T}^*)$ is a constrained minimization problem with the following Lagrangian:

$$L = \sum_{i,j}(w_{ij}^* - w_{ij})^2 + \sum_{k,i}(t_{ki}^* - t_{ki})^2 + \sum_k \lambda_k [\sum_i t_{ki}^* \rho(\sum_j w_{ij}^* x_j) - z_k^*]. \tag{11}$$

By setting

$$\frac{\partial L}{\partial w_{ij}^*} = \frac{\partial L}{\partial t_{ki}^*} = 0 \tag{12}$$

and using the constraint in Eq. (10), we obtain the following learning rule:

$$t_{ki}^* = t_{ki} + e_k v_i^*, \tag{13}$$

$$w_{ij}^* = w_{ij} + \sum_k e_k t_{ki}^* \rho'(u_i^*) x_j, \tag{14}$$

where

$$e_k \doteq \frac{z_k^* - \tilde{z}_k}{\|\mathbf{v}^*\|^2},$$

$$v_i^* \doteq \rho(\sum_j w_{ij}^* x_j),$$

$$u_i^* \doteq \sum_j w_{ij}^* x_j = \rho^{-1}(v_i^*),$$

$$\tilde{z}_k \doteq \sum_i t_{ki} v_i^*,$$

$$\|\mathbf{v}^*\|^2 \doteq \sum_i (v_i^*)^2,$$

$$\rho'(\alpha) \doteq \frac{d\rho}{d\alpha}.$$

The reader will observe that the learning rule given by Eqs. (13) and (14) is quite complex and difficult to implement, at least for software implementation. In Eq. (13) $\{t_{ki}^*\}$ depends in a non-linear way on $\{w_{ij}^*\}$ and so does $\{w_{ij}^*\}$ in Eq. (14) on $\{t_{ki}^*\}$.

An obvious simplification is to decouple $\{t^*_{ki}\}$ from $\{w^*_{ij}\}$ in Eq. (13), and linearize Eq. (14) in $\{w^*_{ij}\}$. Then what results is

$$t^*_{ki} = t_{ki} + e^{(0)}_k v^{(0)}_i, \tag{15}$$

$$w^*_{ij} = w_{ij} + \sum_k e^{(0)}_k t^*_{ki} \rho'(u^{(0)}_i) x_j, \tag{16}$$

where

$$e^{(0)}_k \doteq \frac{z^*_k - z^{(0)}_k}{\|\mathbf{v}^{(0)}\|^2},$$

$$v^{(0)}_i \doteq \rho(\sum_j w_{ij} x_j),$$

$$\|\mathbf{v}^{(0)}\|^2 \doteq \sum_i (v^{(0)}_i)^2,$$

$$u^{(0)}_i \doteq \sum_j w_{ij} x_j = \rho^{-1}(v^{(0)}_i),$$

$$z^{(0)}_k \doteq \sum_i t_{ki} v^{(0)}_i.$$

Finally, by introducing a relaxation parameter μ, Eqs. (15) and (16) can be rewritten as,

$$\triangle t^*_{ki} \doteq t^*_{ki} - t_{ki} = \mu e^{(0)}_k v^{(0)}_i, \tag{17}$$

$$\triangle w^*_{ij} \doteq w^*_{ij} - w_{ij} = \mu \sum_k e^{(0)}_k t^*_{ki} \rho'(u^{(0)}_i) x_j. \tag{18}$$

We shall call these two equations the projection method learning rule (PMLR).

For the sake of comparison, the back-propagation learning rule is listed here:

$$\triangle t^{(BP)}_{ki} = \eta \delta^{(BP)}_k v^{(0)}_i, \tag{19}$$

$$\triangle w^{(BP)}_{ij} = \eta \sum_k \delta^{(BP)}_k t_{ki} \rho'(u^{(0)}_i) x_j, \tag{20}$$

where η is a parameter like μ in the above, and $\delta_k^{(BP)}$ is defined as

$$\delta_k^{(BP)} \doteq \rho'(z_k^{(0)})[y_k^* - \rho(z_k^{(0)})]. \tag{21}$$

It is interesting to note that the PMLR and the BPLR resemble each other in the form, despite the fact that they are based on quite different principles. Both are in the form of the *generalized delta rule*. However, as we shall see in the simulation, the characteristics of their behavior are quite different, and the difference becomes more drastic as the neuron activation function gets more nonlinear. Indeed the error terms in the BPLR (and therefore the adjustment in weights) can get very small as the derivative of the nonlinear function goes to zero; on the contrary in the PMLR errors in this region are emphasized.

Let us summarize in words the essential difference, as we understand it, between the PMLR and the BPLR. In the BPLR, an attempt is made to adjust the interconnections for each training sample so as to minimize the error between the actual and desired outputs. The underlying similarity between the patterns is ignored and the *hope* is that the minimization for each pattern will result in interconnections that are effective for the ensemble.

In the PMLR, the interconnections effective for the ensemble of N_s training samples $\mathbf{x}_i$ is represented by the intersection of N_s sets. The goal is to reach a point in this intersection by an iterative algorithm that always works when the N_s sets are convex but may not work when one or more sets is not convex.

The *minimal disturbance principle* [16] may provide an auxiliary view of the PMLR. That is, the *projection* onto a constraint set associated with a training sample is the set of connection weights for the net that is closest to the present weights while correctly classifying the new training sample[1]. It is interesting to note that the formula of the PMLR at the output layer is similar in form to the Adaline learning rule of Widrow and Hoff [15].

---

[1] Strictly speaking, the statement is true only for exact projection operations. With the approximation we made in the PMLR, this statement is only approximately true.

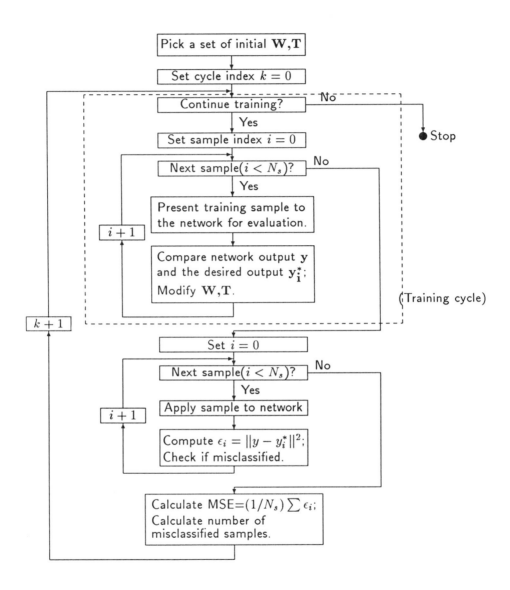

Figure 2: The generic procedure used for the simulation and experiment of neural network learning.

4 Experiments and Results

We simulate the PMLR and BPLR on the two-layer network and test them on the XOR problem and a classification problem. The simulation procedure, including the training and the monitoring portions, is drafted in Fig. 2.

4.1 XOR Problem

We started with a set of randomly assigned initial weights and biases, and applied the PMLR or BPLR using the four patterns repeatedly, i.e. each cycle of presentation of the learning samples consists of the successive presentation of the four patterns $00, 01, 10, 11$. The network has a certain number of hidden nodes whose biases are adjustable. The two output nodes are not allowed free bias. The nonlinear activation function of the hidden and output nodes is the function $1/(1 + exp(-x))$. The desired output values to be learned are set to 0.99 and 0.01, for the logic 1 and 0 respectively.

The results show that the PMLR learns faster than the BPLR for this problem, under every condition tested. The number of cycles of presentation needed for the mean square error to reach and stay less than 10^{-3}, averaged over 10 to 20 runs of experiment with different initial weights and biases, are listed in Table 1. The mean square error, whose computation is shown in Fig. 2, is computed after each training cycle to monitor the progress of the network's learning.

Several different learning parameters (i.e. the μ and η parameters) were tested. In general, for either BPLR or PMLR, learning is faster with larger value of the learning rate, as is the case that has been observed for BPLR by many others.

Another parameter that affects the speed of learning is the number of hidden nodes. It was reported that for the BPLR the number of presentations needed decreases in proportion to the log of the number of hidden nodes [13]. We tested three different numbers of hidden nodes and observed that the PMLR also learned faster as the number of hidden nodes increased. The PMLR outperforms the BPLR in all three cases.

	BPLR			PMLR			
number of hidden nodes	Learning parameter η			Learning parameter μ			
	0.25	0.50	0.75	0.10	0.15	0.20	0.25
3	6200	2935	1776	846	739	651	948
8	2791	1349	894	117	80	61	49
12	2584	1281	850	99	66	50	41

Table 1: Averaged number of learning cycles required to achieve a mean square error of 10^{-3} for the XOR problem. The numbers in the table are averaged results over 10 to 20 runs of experiment with different initial weightings and biases.

4.2 Distance-from-Origin Classification

In this example we are given two classes whose samples are represented by 2-tuples (x_1, x_2). For class 1 the samples satisfy $x_1^2 + x_2^2 < 1$; for class 2 the samples satisfy $x_1^2 + x_2^2 > 1$. Like the previous problem, this case is not amenable to solution by a linear discriminant function. The problem was used as an example in Ref. [9]. The training set we used consists of 100 randomly generated samples with approximately 50 samples per class. The samples are presently to the network one-by-one for learning and cycled iteratively, as in the manner shown in Fig. 2. The network we used has 2 input nodes, 8 hidden nodes with adjustable biases, and 2 output nodes. The activation function is $1/(1 + exp(-\alpha x))$; the parameter α can be used as a measure of the nonlinearity of the function, as the plot in Fig. 3 shows: the larger the α, the more nonlinear the function.

We used the same sets of initial weights and biases for comparing the performance of the BPLR and the PMLR. We chose the desired output vector to be $(0.01, 0.99)$ for class 1 and $(0.99, 0.01)$ for class 2. For neuron activation functions that exhibit strong nonlinear feature, e.g., $\alpha \geq 1$, we observed significantly different learning patterns for the PMLR and BPLR (Fig. 4 and 5).

The back-propagation learning is characterized by three stages: in the first few iterations it learns quickly; then it reaches a stagnation level where additional learning cycle has little effect on the misclassification rate, and the improvement on mean square error is

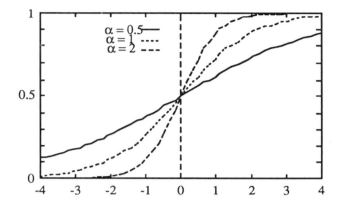

Figure 3: The sigmoid nonlinear function with three different parameter values.

extremely slow. This stagnation level can last for hundreds of cycles. Finally a critical point is reached beyond which the network learns rapidly again and corrects the errors in a few tens of cycles. In Fig. 5 is shown the learning history of the BPLR with various values of the learning parameter η, while $\alpha = 1$. It can be seen that the learning rate is strongly influenced by η. Generally the speed of learning improves with increasing η. Eventually, however, the learning becomes unstable and performs poorly when η is made too large.

The PMLR exhibits a very different learning pattern. The learning rate of the PMLR is, up to a point, much faster than in the BPLR, and is less dependent of the learning parameter. Figure 4 shows the behavior of the PMLR when $\alpha = 1$. However despite the fact that the PMLR achieves a high correct classification rate after a relatively few cycles of training, it continues to misclassify a few of the training samples (typically two or three out of 100) regardless of additional training, and the final MSE (not shown in the figure) is larger than that obtained by the BPLR. We may say that the PMLR captures the overall picture of the whole set of samples much faster than the BPLR, but finally it is not as accurate in detail as the BPLR can be. However we should recall that these classification rates apply to training samples, and this does not necessarily imply that the the

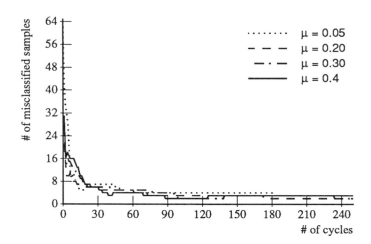

Figure 4: Learning history of the PMLR in terms of the number of samples still misclassified at the end of each cycle, with $\alpha = 1$.

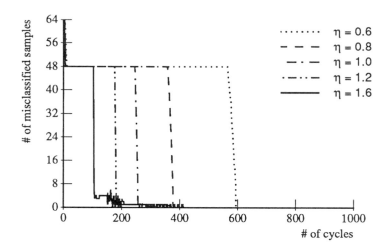

Figure 5: Learning history of the BPLR, with $\alpha = 1$.

nonl.	BPLR Learning parameter η						PMLR Learning parameter μ					
par. α	0.6	0.8	1.0	1.2	1.4	1.6	0.05	0.10	0.15	0.20	0.25	0.30
0.5	72	55	44	37	31	27	20	58	232	43	133	192
1.0	594	377	256	181	139	107	55	120	71	61	58	77
2.0	—	(>	4000	)			30	70	249	68	28	71

Table 2: Number of learning cycles required to reach and retain 96% correct classification of training samples, for the distance-from-origin classification problem.

network trained by the BPLR will outperform the network trained by the PMLR when a larger set of test data is applied.

For convenient comparison, the number of learning cycles required for the BPLR and PMLR to achieve and retain at least 96 percent correct classification of the training samples is listed in Table 2, with several values of the nonlinearity parameter α and learning parameters μ and η. These numbers show the relative ease with which the network can be trained using the different rules. For $\alpha = 1$, the PMLR never required more than 120 cycles of learning ($\mu = 0.1$) and as little as 55 cycles of learning ($\mu = 0.05$). The learning rate of the BPLR is critically dependent on the learning parameter η. For $\eta = 0.6$, it took nearly 600 cycles of learning; fastest learning occurred with $\eta = 1.6$ (107 cycles); increasing η beyond this value caused the BPLR to be unstable.

The significant advantage exhibited by the PMLR becomes less so when the neuron activation function becomes more linear (i.e. decreasing α), as can be seen from Table 2 and Figs. 6 and 7. This experimental observation is predictable from the theory. Comparing the PMLR as described in Eqs. (17) and (18) and the BPLR in Eqs. (19) and (20),we see that if the function $\rho(\cdot)$ is almost linear then the output error measures $e_k^{(0)}$ of PMLR and $\delta_k^{(BP)}$ of BPLR become essentially the same except for a scaling factor, therefore the two learning rules behave similarly.

The real benefit of using the PMLR over the BPLR is apparent when α is large, or the neurons operate mostly in the nonlinear

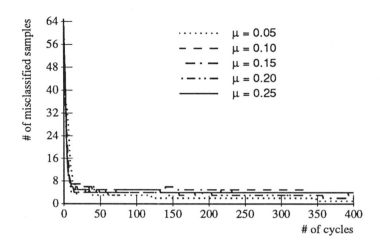

Figure 6: Learning history of the PMLR, with $\alpha = 0.5$.

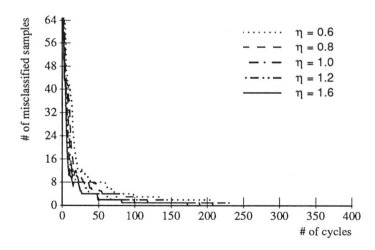

Figure 7: Learning history of the BPLR, with $\alpha = 0.5$.

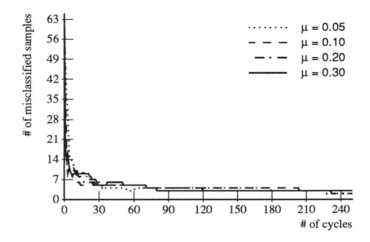

Figure 8: Learning history of the PMLR, with $\alpha = 2$.

region. The learning history for $\alpha = 2$ are shown in Fig 8 and 9. In Fig. 8 we see that with PMLR 96 percent correct classification of the training samples takes place in 100 or so iterations, which is similar to the case when $\alpha = 1$. On the other hand the BPLR, for every value of the learning parameter η we tried (from 0.1 to 3.0), is untrainable despite thousands of cycles of training (Fig. 9)!

In Tables 3 and 4 are shown how well the PMLR and BPLR classify a set of 1000 test samples as a function of the training time (the number of training cycles). As before the training involves only 100 training samples which are NOT subset of the test samples. If network adjustment on a single sample requires X seconds then a training cycle requires $100X$ seconds, and N training cycles will require $N \cdot 100X$ seconds; X is roughly the same for the PMLR and the BPLR in our simulation. The results in Tables 3 and 4 give the percentage of correct classification as a function of N for various values of the learning parameters μ (for the PMLR) and η (for the BPLR). In Table 3, the correct classification rates are shown for $\alpha = 1$. As before, the PMLR gives 90% or better classification rates after only 20 cycles of training while the BPLR becomes very sensitive to the learning parameter η. Best results are obtained for $\eta = 1.6$ in which

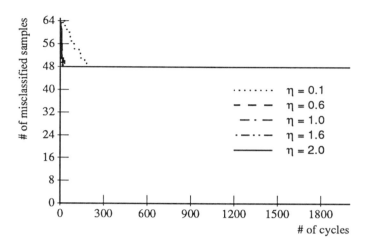

Figure 9: Learning history of the BPLR, with $\alpha = 2$.

case 90% or better classification occurs around 120 cycles. Thus under optimum conditions for the BPLR, the speed advantage of the PMLR is a factor of six. When $\eta = 1$, PMLR learns 10 times faster than the BPLR.

Table 4 shows the correct classification rate for $\alpha = 2$. Using one again a 90% or better classification rate as the criterion, the PMLR requires about 30 training cycles and this result, as always, is essentially independent of μ (in the range [0.05, 0.3]). The BPLR fails to meet the 90% criteria for any value of η even at 210 cycles. Further runs (not shown in the Table) show this to be true even after 10,000 training cycles.

Three conclusions can be drawn from the results shown in these Tables: 1) The PMLR typically learns faster than the BPLR, a fact that becomes more evident as α (the nonlinearity parameter) increases; 2) Learning by the PMLR is relatively insensitive to α, a result convincingly not true for the BPLR; and 3) Learning by the PMLR is relatively independent on the value of the learning parameter in the working range, while for the BPLR it can be critically dependent.

In Fig. 10 is a scatter diagram of the 100 random training samples

Projection Method Learning, $\alpha = 1.0$								
# cycles	10	20	30	60	90	120	150	180	210
$\mu = 0.05$	85	94	96	96	96	95	95	95	95
$\mu = 0.10$	92	92	91	93	93	94	94	94	94
$\mu = 0.15$	91	91	92	93	93	94	94	94	94
$\mu = 0.20$	90	91	92	93	93	93	93	93	93
$\mu = 0.25$	88	91	92	93	93	93	93	93	93
$\mu = 0.30$	86	91	92	93	93	93	93	93	93
Back-Propagation Learning, $\alpha = 1.0$								
# cycles	10	20	30	60	90	120	150	180	210
$\eta = 0.6$	45	51	51	51	51	51	51	51	51
$\eta = 0.8$	51	51	51	51	51	51	51	51	51
$\eta = 1.0$	51	51	51	51	51	51	51	51	51
$\eta = 1.2$	51	51	51	51	51	51	51	84	95
$\eta = 1.4$	51	51	51	51	51	51	96	94	95
$\eta = 1.6$	51	51	51	51	51	95	95	94	94

Table 3: Correct classification rate, in percent, out of 1000 test samples, as the function of the number of training cycles. The nonlinear activation function has $\alpha = 1.0$.

Projection Method Learning, $\alpha = 2.0$								
# cycles	10	20	30	60	90	120	150	180	210
$\mu = 0.05$	81	86	91	94	94	95	96	96	96
$\mu = 0.10$	87	92	92	95	95	96	96	96	96
$\mu = 0.15$	90	90	92	94	94	94	94	94	95
$\mu = 0.20$	86	90	91	95	95	95	96	96	96
$\mu = 0.25$	85	89	92	94	94	94	94	94	94
$\mu = 0.30$	88	90	92	94	94	94	93	93	93
Back-Propagation Learning, $\alpha = 2.0$								
# cycles	10	20	30	60	90	120	150	180	210
$\eta = 0.6$	44	48	51	51	51	51	51	51	51
$\eta = 0.8$	44	51	51	51	51	51	51	51	51
$\eta = 1.0$	40	51	51	51	51	51	51	51	51
$\eta = 1.2$	43	40	40	42	51	51	51	51	51
$\eta = 1.4$	45	51	51	51	51	51	51	51	51
$\eta = 1.6$	46	51	51	51	51	51	51	51	51

Table 4: Correct classification rate, in percent, out of 1000 test samples, as the function of the number of training cycles. The nonlinear activation function has $\alpha = 2.0$.

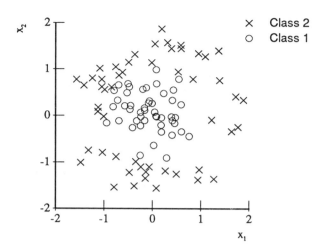

Figure 10: The training samples.

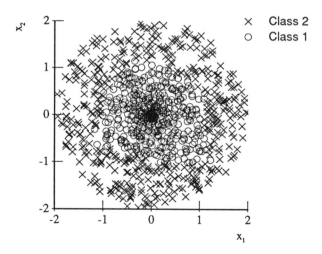

Figure 11: The 1000 test samples; symbols show the classification outcome by the network trained by the PMLR, with $\alpha = 2$.

that were used to train both the BPLR and the PMLR in obtaining the above results. The reader will notice that there is a dearth of training samples at 4 o'clock and 8 o'clock directions. Figure 11 shows the distribution of the test samples and the classification result by the network with $\alpha = 2$ trained by the PMLR. The correct classification rate in this case is 94%. The interesting observation to be made is that most of the misclassified samples occurs in regions where there was little or no training data, e.g. at 4 and 8 o'clock. Thus one may conclude that the PMLR works only as well as it is trained. This conclusion is true for pattern recognition algorithms in general as well as in humans.

5 Conclusion

We have found an efficient learning algorithm for the multilayer feed-forward neural network. This learning algorithm has its root in the projection-onto-convex-set concept but is ultimately based on the principle of generalized projections. The global strategy of moving toward the intersection of all sets in the projection method helps in explaining the greater efficiency of this learning rule over the back-propagation learning rule. In this paper we formulated the PMLR for the two-layer nets (i.e. with one hidden layer) and demonstrated, by simulation on the XOR problem and the distance-from-origin classification problem, that it outperforms the well-known BPLR. The PMLR learns much faster but finally gives less precise output values than the BPLR. Strong nonlinearity affects the BPLR severely while the PMLR is insensitive to it; this is a great advantage other than the speed of learning.

In applications where precision of the output values is required, it may be a good idea to use the PMLR to get a fast estimate, followed by the BPLR to "fine tune" the network weights.

The extension of the PMLR to more complicated networks, for example, networks with more layers, lateral connections, cross-layer connections or feedback connections, is subject to further research. However, understanding the capacity of networks of different constellation may be of more immediate importance than applying learning algorithms to complicated networks.

Acknowledgment

This research was partly supported by the National Science Foundation. Computing facility was provided by the Illinois Institute of Technology.

Bibliography

[1] L. M. BREGMAN, *Finding the common point of convex sets by the method of successive projections*, Doki. Akad. Nauk. USSR, 162 (1965), pp. 487–490.

[2] D. J. BURR, *Experiments on neural net recognition of spoken and written text*, IEEE Trans. Acoust., Speech, Signal Processing, 36 (1988), pp. 1162–1168.

[3] A. F. GMITRO, P. E. KELLER, AND G. R. GINDI, *Statistical performance of outer-product associative memory models*, Appl. Opt., 28 (1989), pp. 1940–1948.

[4] R. P. GORMAN AND T. J. SEJNOWSKI, *Learned calssification of sonar targets using a massively parallel network*, IEEE Trans. Acoust., Speech, Signal Processing, 36 (1988), pp. 1135–1140.

[5] L. G. GUBIN, B. T. POLYAK, AND E. V. RAIK, *The method of projections for finding the common point of convex sets*, USSR Comput. Math. Phys., 7 (1967), pp. 1–24.

[6] J. J. HOPFIELD, *Neural networks and physical systems with emergent collective computational abilities*, Proc. Natl. Acad. Sci. USA, 79 (1982), pp. 2554–2558.

[7] T. KOHONEN, *Self-organization and Associative Memory*, Springer-Verlag, Berlin, second ed., 1988.

[8] A. LEVI AND H. STARK, *Image restoration by the method of generalized projections with application to restoration from magnitude*, J. Opt. Soc. Am. A, 1 (1984), pp. 932–943.

[9] R. P. LIPPMANN, *An introduction to computing with neural nets*, IEEE ASSP Magazine, (1987), pp. 4–22.

[10] R. J. MARKS II, L. E. ATLAS, S. OH, AND J. A. RITCHY, *The performance of convex set projection based neural networks*, in Neural Information Processing Systems, D. Z. Anderson, ed., AIP, New York, 1988, pp. 534–543.

[11] Z. OPIAL, *Weak convergence of the sequence of successive approximation for nonexpansive mappings*, Bull. Am. Math. Soc., 73 (1967), pp. 591–597.

[12] F. ROSENBLATT, *Principles of Neurodynamics*, Spartan, New York, 1962.

[13] D. E. RUMELHART, G. E. HINTON, AND R. J. WILLIAMS, *Chapter 8: Learning internal representations*, in Parallel Distributed Processing, Volume 1, D. E. Rumelhart and J. L. McClelland, eds., MIT Press, Cambridge, MA, 1986, pp. 318–362.

[14] M. I. SEZAN AND H. STARK, *Application of convex projection theory to image recovery in tomography and related areas*, in Image Recovery: Theory and Applications, H. Stark, ed., Academic Press Inc., Orlando, FL, 1987, ch. 11, pp. 415–461.

[15] B. WIDROW AND M. E. H. JR., *Adaptive switching circuits*, in IRE WESCON Conv. Rec., 1966, pp. 96–104.

[16] B. WIDROW, R. G. WINTER, AND R. A. BAXTER, *Layered neural nets for pattern recognition*, IEEE Trans. Acoust., Speech, Signal Processing, 36 (1988), pp. 1109–1117.

[17] D. C. YOULA, *Mathematical theory of image restoration by the method of convex projections*, in Image Recovery: Theory and Applications, H. Stark, ed., Academic Press Inc., Orlando, FL, 1987, ch. 2, pp. 29–77.

[18] D. C. YOULA AND H. WEBB, *Image reconstruction by the method of projections onto convex sets–part i*, IEEE Trans. Med. Imaging, MI-1 (1982), pp. 95–101.

Index